Homer to Joyce

Homer to Joyce

WALLACE GRAY

Foreword by Steven Marcus

MACMILLAN PUBLISHING COMPANY · NEW YORK

COLLIER MACMILLAN PUBLISHERS · LONDON

Macmillan Publishing Company
866 Third Avenue, New York, N.Y. 10022
Collier Macmillan Canada, Inc.

Library of Congress Cataloging in Publication Data
Gray, Wallace.
Bibliography: p.
Includes index.
1. Literature—History and criticism.   I. Title.
PN524.G73   1985   809   85–8812
ISBN 0–02–545170–7

10 9 8 7 6 5 4 3 2

Designed by Jack Meserole

Printed in the United States of America

FOR MY STUDENTS

CONTENTS

FOREWORD

Professor Gray's book arises out of his many years of experience as an instructor in the Humanities course at Columbia College. This course was first instituted almost fifty years ago, and it is a well-known circumstance that it has had a widespread influence on undergraduate education in America. It continues to be taught today, with remarkable enthusiasm on the part of an interdepartmentally recruited staff, and responded to with equally surprising intensity by the freshmen and sophomores at Columbia, for whom this is one of a central array of courses required of all students. The course has changed surprisingly little over fifty years: some works have been dropped; others have been included; some dropped works put in regular or occasional reappearances—yet despite these fluctuations in emphasis the course has remained essentially stable. Professor Gray's academic home is in the Department of English and Comparative Literature, and he has with characteristic modesty limited his discussions to works commonly thought of as literature—epic, drama, romance, poetry, satire, prose fiction. He does, however, often refer to other works, and in the interests of clarity and fairness, I believe I should note that currently, in the first semester of the course, students also read selections from Herodotus, Thucydides, Plato, and Aristotle, while in the second semester several books from the Old and New Testaments are required, along with the *Confessions* of Saint Augustine, and selections from Rabelais and Descartes.

In subscribing to the assumptions and aims of the course, in teaching in it regularly, and even more in writing a book based on his experiences with the texts concerned, Professor Gray is affirming his allegiance to an idea that, during the last twenty-five years, has come to be questioned with increasing frequency and a certain degree of polemical asperity. This idea asserts that in any one of the great civilizations of the world there is a canon of books that has occupied, and should continue to occupy, a central place in shaping the minds—the tastes, thoughts, and imagination—of each successive generation of students and citizens. Socrates said that Homer was the teacher of the Greeks; by this he meant at least two things: first, that Homer in his epics set forth for those who ruled Greece certain models for what kind of men they should or might be; and second, that the Homeric epics present their audience with particular situations, crises, and conflicts that are paradigmatic in their significance, and in which the choices available are paradigmatic for an amplified sense of human life, and indeed for our humanity and its possibilities as a whole. This civilizing and educating work was carried forward, furthermore, by Dante for Italy, by Montaigne, Racine, and Molière for France, by Goethe for Germany, and by the Bible and Shakespeare for the peoples of the English-speaking world. In endorsing the notion that it was to be required of all undergraduates that they become acquainted with the central works of the artistic and intellectual traditions of their own civilization, the Columbia College course in the Humanities was at the same time subscribing both to this canon and to the ideas of education implicit in it.

This resolution has had to face a number of challenges in recent decades. On the one hand, it has become increasingly clear that contemporary undergraduates have not in general been prepared by their pre-collegiate education for induction into the canon: they come out of one set of cultural matrices— roughly circumscribed by the institutions of popular journalism, film, and television—and are thrust without adequate acknowledgment into another. On the other, the very idea of a canon has come in for critical scrutiny and has been made the object of a certain measure of negative discourse. The complex questions of canon formation, perpetuation, and transmission have been thrown open for review. Some of this discussion has been overtly political: the canon of the great works of Western civilization is on this argument largely an effort to perpetuate the hegemony—culturally, and hence socially and politically— of entrenched and established groups in our society. It is, in other words, a device both of exclusion and continued social control. Moreover, the canon is ethnocentric: it includes none of the great works of Indian, Chinese, Japanese, or Islamic culture. There is, no doubt, a certain cogency to a number of these charges, though this is not the place to discuss the matter. The continued success of the Columbia Humanities course, it seems to me, is to be found, at least in part, in the circumstance that it has not allowed itself to be detoured into the realm of ideological debate, that it has adhered to its rather simple—if not simple-minded—notion that these books are essential to a modern education, and that it has managed somehow, through the cooperative work of the instructional staff and a talented body of students, to sustain the spirit with which this venture was undertaken.

If, however, there is something like a canon of books that this course adheres to, there is nothing canonical about the way the course is taught. Each instructor has his own class of students, and if there is any truth to legend, no two classes have ever been the same. I think we can make out the general accuracy of these remarks from Professor Gray's book, which pursues its own trajectory and does so in its own way. Professor Gray has a general thematic, which he perceives as running through the works he addresses; he regards the conception of the search for the individual self, in its various forms and as they develop within different historical contexts, as the grand preoccupation of these classic works of Western civilization. And he does so through a specific means or device. He conceives of these books as "talking to one another." That is to say, he thinks of these books in one degree or another as being responses to one another in the sense that one has come before the others, and that the latter are in a variety of ways, and at least in part, a response to what has been written before them as well as a response to the pressures of experience in their own times. Thus he writes about the terrible harshness of the heroic code in the *Iliad*, a code that is inseparable from the exigencies of war, violence, brutality, and death, in which there are no good or bad men but only successful and less successful heroes. Yet the greatest of these heroes, Achilleus, is, he demonstrates, capable of choosing to transgress and break the heroic code of behavior, not once but twice. In the great climactic scene of that epic with both Achilleus and Priam shedding tears—for differing though similar reasons—of sadness and loss over the dead body of Hektor, Professor Gray sees Achilleus' agreement to return the body of Hektor, the slayer of his dearest friend and companion Patroklos, as "a heroic thrust *through* the heroic code," and sees as well that the grand song of the wrath of Achilleus ends in a "compassionate human rather than heroic gesture." He then follows this chapter with a discussion of the *Odyssey*, whose scene is not war but the journey home, the *nóstos*, or return. In this new world the hero's fate is largely determined by the choices he makes rather than by fate or accident. Thus Odysseus is both a counterpart of, and a development in, a different direction than Achilleus, although Achilleus' moments of significant choice already foreshadowed what was to follow. He then goes on to discuss a number of Greek tragedies and points out the evolution in them from one notion of justice (the idea of retribution) to another (the idea of fairness tempered with mercy) that corresponds at another level of structure with a development from primarily communal interests to concerns focusing upon the fate of the individual. And so the discussion goes. In each chapter, new forms, new characters, new stories and plots, and new topics coexist with recurrences, recursions, and reconsiderations in new contexts of themes that permanently assert themselves as central to human life—themes of choice, justice, suffering, reason, nature, and the irrational, themes that pose questions about what is involved in trying to discover the proper and satisfying ways in which men and women can hope to live. The book closes with a chapter on

Ulysses, an entirely conscious recursive work, in which the great masterpieces of the past are summoned up to speak once again, to one another, against one another, and with one another, all at the same time in a grand ending in affirmation of humanity's historical effort to make sense of its usually senseless existence.

If in Professor Gray's book the works that he discusses "talk to one another," then we may observe that this book "talks" as well. To read it is imaginatively to overhear an instructor talking to a class, listening to questions, and responding to them with information, interpretations, and explanations. Its tone is informal, its habitual address relaxed but not unbuttoned. It is written, to and for students, by a student who is a teacher of considerable experience. Professor Gray never loses sight of his pedagogical awareness of what is at stake in the works he examines; at the same time he never loses sight of the circumstances that these are all creations of the imagination, written down in language, and that they only come to us through our ability to read, and to respond to what we read, in the most intense and vivid ways. His calm, wry, conversational voice in prose forms a pleasant counterpoint to the grand, epic, tragic, comic, and heroic voices that speak out in his pages, talking to one another, talking across the ages, talking to us. That talk is still the talk of our civilization, and this book is a very good way of making acquaintance with it.

STEVEN MARCUS
Columbia University

INTRODUCTION

When I first taught humanities more than twenty years ago, the professor in charge of the offering tried to comfort uneasy newcomers by assuring them that all humanities teachers were charlatans, that no one person could possibly be a specialist on such a large number of great texts. I am not a specialist, but I'm not a charlatan either, and these essays are written neither for specialists nor for charlatans, but rather for students in literature humanities courses, and for those who want to read more about books they have found valuable.

There are a number of books written for this purpose, but they are collections of critical essays by various authors, and no connections are made among the texts discussed. The most important characteristic of the books I am writing about is that they talk to one another, and the dialogue is as exciting and interesting as any individual text—especially when the conversation is whispered, or composed of silent gestures in the direction of some other text. These books occupy a shared geographical territory of ideas and, as I do in my classes, I pay serious attention in these essays to the conversation—particularly in the later essays, where the "moderns" are talking to the "ancients."

The texts in a humanities course are not, as I have heard more than one teacher of humanities contend, just a "bunch of books." Rather, in chorus, the books ask one overwhelming question: "What must a person do to lead a complete and happy life?" In a course in literature, the texts are read for their own sake; in a course in humanities, they are read to enlighten the reader's own humanity.

Although I stand firmly behind the interpretations presented in these essays, and always base them on solid textual support, I must admit that some of the ideas are individualistic to the point of being idiosyncratic. This is intentional in my classes, as I find that, after I have paid my respects to traditional readings, such left-field interpretations cause students to look in unexpected directions that challenge and further expand their own ideas. It is more than intentional in these essays, as they were written to provide readers—particularly students—with ideas to supplement their own, or to contrast with those they received in the classroom or from other books.

The texts are not examined in isolation from the cultural and historical forces that produced them, as it is not my habit to separate a text from its environment. However, the emphasis in these essays is on the text rather than on the background.

When I began teaching, Mark Van Doren advised me that "teachers should be forgotten." As a beginning teacher, I found this disturbing, until I realized that he meant students should be led to develop their own ideas, and not be presented with dogma. I've forgotten where I originally received many of the ideas that fed my own teaching; in any case, much that I say in these essays is part of the canon we all possess regarding these texts, ideas that seem to float in the air we breathe.

As an aid to students, I have attempted in the bibliography to recapture the sources that fed some of my own teaching, and thus these essays; scholars will have recognized them long before they reach that point.

Except for the Robert Fitzgerald translation of the *Aeneid*, which has only recently become available in a paperback edition, all of the texts listed in the bibliography are those which have been used for many years in the Columbia College Humanities program. For line-number references I have used the Greek and Latin texts in the Loeb Classical Library, as these are more readily available than some of the other standard texts. Readers will find that the English translations of the Greek works seldom vary more than one line or so from the line numbers I have given; but there is sometimes a difference of more than a hundred lines between the Latin of Virgil and the translations, so I have given both the line numbers from the Latin text and those from the Fitzgerald translation.

As texts for *Ulysses* I have cited in the bibliography both the widely available Random House edition and the critical and synoptic edition issued by Garland Publishing in 1984. The quotations in the Joyce essay are from the Garland edition, and most of them differ from the Random House edition only in the matter of a few punctuation marks, which do not affect interpretation. However, three sentences I have quoted from the new edition do not appear in the Random House edition; I have indicated them in my essay.

Many years ago I had the pleasure of reading the *Odyssey* in Greek in the classes of Howard Porter (retired) of the Classics Department at Columbia. I have also benefited from studying Greek texts with other members of that department, primarily James Coulter and Seth Schein (now at the University of California, Santa Cruz). Discussions with the Humanities staff conducted by Laura Slatkin of the Classics Department and Helen Bacon of Barnard College continue to be of great value. The wisdom and scholarship of these teachers, along with those of my departed teachers and colleagues Mark Van Doren, William York Tindall, and Lionel Trilling, form the basis for my readings. None of them, of course, are to be held responsible for my interpretations.

Many of the translations of the texts listed in the bibliography are works of art in themselves and deserve attention from that viewpoint. However, because my essays deal with substantive issues in the texts, I have chosen to make my own literal prose translations.

In the transliteration of Greek names I have generally followed the spelling used by the translator of the edition listed in the bibliography. As strict consistency would have led to some unfamiliar spellings, such as Aineias for Aeneas, Akhilleus for Achilleus, and Dionysos for Dionysus, I have opted for the more familiar spellings.

Richard Sacks, of the Department of English and Comparative Literature, was kind enough to read this work for accuracy of textual representation. I am fortunate in having such a friend and colleague, who has taught—at Harvard and Columbia—Greek, Latin, Old Norse, Old Irish, and Medieval German texts.

Some very recent students have given me much encouragement and affection and I would like to thank them here: Peter Ansin, Roger Blumberg, Kevin Dalton, Rick Garvey, Eric Karp, Armin Kelly, Beth Knobel, Yu Jin Ko, Joseph Lease, Anne Mao, Geoffrey Mintz, Brice Moss, Kevin O'Connell, John Pagano, Tony Rudel, and Marta Torres. Special thanks are owed to Patrick West, a student of some years ago who is now a formidable friend.

I wish to express my appreciation to Joy Hayton for the advice she has given me in the years she has been Administrative Assistant of the Department of English and Comparative Literature, and especially for recommending Michael Neth, a fine young scholar, as my Graduate Research Assistant.

The Morningside Heights picture is not complete without Andrea Raab, my editor at Macmillan, who is a graduate of Barnard College. She is a young woman whose intelligence and taste have been a vital presence in this work since the writing of the very first essay. The words of Pericles to the Athenians can certainly be applied to Andrea: her love of beauty and of things of the mind has not made her soft.

W.G.
New York City, 1985

Homer to Joyce

Iliad

THE *Iliad* is not about the Trojan War; that war lasted ten years and the central actions of the poem occupy only a few weeks. War brutalizes men and women, wounds their bodies and minds, enslaves and kills them. This is Homer's message as he focuses on one hero, Achilleus, to demonstrate wrath's destruction of self and others. Achilleus' moral journey in the *Iliad* brings him face to face with his own humanity, leading him to a startling and essentially unheroic act of generosity toward his enemy. When he gives Priam the dead and mutilated body of Hektor, Achilleus stands for a few moments on the threshold of a different civilization, as Homer shows wrath dissolved through compassion, and human feeling overcoming the stringent heroic code of conformity.

A hero is one who willingly and eagerly confronts death, and three Greek words embody the heroic code: *áristos, areté,* and *aristeía. Áristos* is being the best at whatever is called for by the situation: in wartime, killing; in peacetime, husbandry; in seamanship, steering. To be known as the best requires *aristeía*— exploits which gain for the warrior the prestige of having comrades consider him possessed of *areté,* merit. *Areté* can only be bestowed by others, not by self. In the world of the *Iliad* what the world thinks of you is far more important than what you think of yourself. Indeed, it *is* what you think of yourself. Fame and glory, *kléos,* can only be achieved through action. This is why the withdrawal of Achilleus from the battle is such a devastating decision: without exploits he has no identity and can only sit in his shelter singing about fame and glory instead of achieving it. Achilleus is no longer *áristos,* the best of the Achaians, when Agamemnon succeeds in depriving him of Briseis. The girl, along with tripods, spears, and other paraphernalia of war, is war booty, a symbol of *aretê*. And so he has to sing of *kléos*: without exploits no poet is going to sing about him. In a pitiful and ultimately tragic attempt to regain *aretê*, he sends Patroklos into battle as his *therápōn*, a ritual substitute clad in the armor of Achilleus.

By permitting his beloved friend Patroklos, whom he knows to be a lesser warrior than himself, to reenter the battle, Achilleus is consequently responsible for the death of this gentle warrior.

However, according to a widely accepted theory, Achilleus feels no guilt, as this Homeric society is not a guilt-culture, but rather a shame-culture in which man does not consider himself responsible for his own behavior. Shame-cultures attribute human imperfection to external causes, such as failure to make proper sacrifices, or accidentally slighting the gods in some other way. These heroes do not yet understand that character is fate, and they project onto external forces whatever ills happen to them. Guilt and a sense of sin (a word not in the Homeric vocabulary) develop as societies grow older and men replace gods as the instruments of cause and effect.

But Achilleus is undoubtedly displaying all the signs of guilt in his behavior after the death of Patroklos, and he does feel responsible. Perhaps the most reasonable attitude to take is that shame-cultures and guilt-cultures are not mutually exclusive, and that it is possible for a Homeric hero, as well as for a contemporary person, to feel both shame and guilt in varying proportions.

Because these men are called heroes, the sensibility of the modern reader is often shocked and disturbed by behavior considered unheroic today. Achilleus stabs and kills Priam's naked and defenseless young son, who has taken off his armor and sword in weariness after escaping the river. On the nighttime spying expedition to the Trojan camp in Book 10, Odysseus and Diomedes capture Dolon, a Trojan sent to spy on the Achaians. After assuring him they will do him no harm if he gives them information, they lop off his head, which falls, still speaking, to the ground. Proceeding into the Trojan camp, they do not hesitate to slaughter the sleeping warriors. Victory, Paris says, goes first to one man and then to another: it's not how you play the game in the Homeric world, it's whether you win or lose.

Sarpedon's speech to Glaukos in Book 12 is the clearest expression of what it means to be a hero. He wonders aloud: Why are we given the best places at the banquet table, served the best meat and wine, given the choicest land, and why do men look upon us as being immortal? We deserve these benefits because we show our bravery by fighting in the forefront of the battle. If we were able to live forever, to be immortal, then there would be no need to fight in order to win glory. Now, however, the battle is upon us, we cannot escape it, so let us plunge in and win glory for ourselves or, by dying, give it to the enemy.

Glory, eternal fame, *kléos*, can only be achieved by killing or being killed in battle; either way one becomes a subject of epic poetry and lives forever in song. He is right, of course; Sarpedon dies, but lives forever in the *Iliad*.

This inflexible heroic code does not permit choice, and the fact that Achilleus chooses distinguishes him from the other warriors and makes him the hero of this epic. Knowing that he is endangering his status as *áristos*, the best, he chooses to disengage himself from the battle and retire to his shelter. Odysseus tells Achilleus of Agamemnon's offer of gifts if he will return to the battle. In response, Achilleus rejects the heroic code once again. We are all going to die, he says, both the brave and the weak, so it matters little whether you do a great deal or nothing. Look at me, how I've fought harder than anyone, and how I have nothing. And what was I fighting for, why are the Argives fighting the Trojans? For Helen? What is so special about Helen? (9.308–429. Arabic numerals are used for the Books of the *Iliad*, followed by the lines; the equivalent lines in the *Odyssey* would be indicated by ix.308–429.)

In a dramatic rejection of the heroic code, Achilleus questions the sexual cause of the war, finding it unworthy of dying for.

He has alienated himself from the war and has had time to question the standards of his society. Returning to the battle only after the death of Patroklos, Achilleus slays Hektor and then mutilates the body. That behavior is properly heroic. But then, in another brave defection from the heroic code, Achilleus takes a stance of compassion toward his enemy: he gives the body of Hektor to Priam for proper burial, a rite that will not only ensure the eternal peace of a spirit Achilleus has reason to condemn to a restless eternity, but will also give the body a continuing temporal fame in a burial marker. Achilleus ceases his erasure of the identity of Hektor.

In this first great work of Western literature, Homer shows war destroying not only cities and civilizations but the souls of men. War turns men into things, objects without pity. What difference does it make? Achilleus asks. We are all going to die. And he plunges his sword through the neck of the naked and defenseless young son of Priam.

Hektor, prince and defender of the city of Troy, becomes for the reader a more complete human being than does Achilleus. The latter deals primarily with other warriors, whereas Hektor is seen responding to his mother, Hekuba, his sister-in-law, Helen, and his wife, Andromache. Hektor is revealed through these three women, and they reveal themselves, especially by their positions when, in Book 6, Hektor returns to the city for respite from the fighting. These scenes gain for Hektor a sympathetic response from us that might otherwise have been reserved solely for Achilleus.

Hektor's first encounter is with his mother (the present Queen of Troy); this woman does not bury herself deep within the palace, but, herself a fierce warrior who can cry out that she would like to eat the liver of Achilleus raw, she comes rushing to greet her son. However, her first words to Hektor are not of comfort but of reprimand: she demands to know what he is doing behind the city walls, away from the fighting. No mother to coddle her children, she immediately commands

Hektor to offer a libation of wine to Zeus for victory in battle, and only then does she suggest that Hektor may drink some of the wine himself. But only to restore his energy for battle (6.254–62). This stern Queen of Troy is equal to the Spartan enemies besieging the walls of her city. How different she is from Thetis; Achilleus' mother treats him like a little baby before his final battle with Hektor (19.1–36).

Hektor continues on to the palace of his brother, where he finds Paris and Helen (the former Queen of Sparta) in a most appropriate place, her bedroom (6.312–68). Paris is polishing his battle gear rather than fighting with it, and Helen is berating him, projecting the blame for the war on the gods, and referring to herself as a vile bitch. When she suggests that future poets will, as they indeed have done, make songs about her and perpetuate her fame, one wonders whether she really does resent her "misfortune." The lady protests at great length, and she responds to Hektor with much more tenderness and regard than she does to Paris. And Hektor, for all the ten years of suffering Helen has caused, treats her with the respect due a former Queen of Sparta. (To be fair to Helen, it must be remembered that women of this period had no more control over their fate than did those in the male-dominated Athenian "Golden Age.")

When Hektor goes searching for his wife (whom destiny will prevent from becoming Queen of Troy in the future), he finds her in a place that reveals her character as the wife of a prince who is slated to be the future King of Troy: she is standing on the city wall, from which she can watch the battle (6.369–493). There she reminds Hektor that Achilleus had killed her father as well as her seven brothers, and was responsible for the death of her mother. Hektor, then, she tells him, is both father, brother, mother, and husband to her. Indeed, when she loses Hektor to the sword of Achilleus, she loses everything in the world. Both she and Hektor know Achilleus is the greater warrior; they realize Hektor is going to die. He knows the city of Troy will perish and that Andromache and his son will be lost. Although he may at times deny it, Hektor returns to the battle knowing that he will die; this is his heroic grandeur. But, before he goes, he reaches out for his baby son, who, not recognizing his father in plumed helmet and battle gear, cries out in fear and terror. Homer shows that war is not just glorious action bringing fame and honor to the participants; it is also a mechanism turning men into creatures from whom even their children draw back in fright. There are neither good men nor bad men in the *Iliad*; this is the humanity of Homer, who, Hellenic himself, doesn't favor Hellenes over Trojans.

Homer is given credit for anthropomorphism, for providing the gods and goddesses with human traits. He endowed them with richly human characteristics, turning Ares into the blood-thirsty young god of war, Aphrodite into the "flighty" goddess of love, Hera into a jealous and conniving wife, and Athena and Apollo into grandiose, superhuman beings. To Homer's listeners, as well as to many in the following generations, these divine gods and goddesses constituted their religious beliefs, and their participation in the two Homeric poems was real— the gods controlled and directed the events. The modern reader, however, can choose among a variety of ways of reading the poem: the gods and goddesses are actually real and present; they are external symbols for the internal emotions, desires, and drives of men and women, of their good and bad luck; or, they are both at the same time.

In the first instance the reader can suspend his disbelief in ancient Hellenic religion and enter into the spirit of the times. In the second—the symbolic reading—the reader can consider that everything that happens to the heroes in the *Iliad* could have happened *without* the actions of the gods, since they are personifications of the fears and aspirations of the heroes. If a hero is suddenly filled with courage, or overcomes his opponent, or has good luck, or lets out a war cry that terrifies the enemy, then a god or goddess is given the credit. Even Apollo's stunning of Patroklos, and Athena's return of a spear to Achilleus—two occurrences often cited as indisputable evidence of divine intervention—can be considered as symbols for human actions.

However, in reading imaginative literature it is possible to have the best of both worlds: the imaginative reader need not consider the two readings mutually exclusive, need not choose between the actually divine and the symbolically divine. Indeed, this dual function is expressed by Diomedes at 9.701–03 when he is speaking about Achilleus' rejection of the embassy: "He will fight when the heart in his breast urges him, and the god arouses him." The single combat between Menelaos and Paris and its aftermath (3.264–461) illustrate this dual role of the Olympians in Homer.

After ten years of battle it has been decided to resolve the conflict through single combat between Menelaos, Helen's first husband, and Paris, Helen's second husband. (This is one of a number of incidents in the poem which seem likely to have occurred earlier in the war.) In the first moments of the contest Menelaos throws his spear at Paris and misses the body. He then grabs Paris by the helmet, spins him around until Paris falls, and begins to drag him away by the helmet. Aphrodite, however, the protectress of Paris, breaks the chin strap holding the helmet, and Menelaos strides on, carrying only the helmet. Thus, what was accident, a worn chin strap breaking and saving Paris, is attributed to the intervention of a goddess. Paris escapes through a cloud of dust, carried off by Aphrodite and deposited gently in the bed of Helen. The goddess is given credit for spiriting Paris away from the battle, whereas it could also be read as an act of apparent cowardice on his part. Aphrodite leads Helen to the bedroom—or perhaps she is led by her own lust. What happens next in that bed is a startling precursor of the link between sex and death in succeeding literature. Paris, turning to Helen, tells her he has never before felt such passion for her. Although this may be a formulaic statement always uttered at each instance of lovemaking in epic poetry of this period, it appears Homer is suggesting that the exciting stimuli of danger and imminent death have served to increase Paris' sexual excitement.

The *Iliad* was the education of Greek youths in the fifth century B.C.; it was considered history, not literature. Children were expected to memorize large portions of the text, to model their behavior on that of the heroes, and to practice the ethical codes presented in the epic. They learned from the *Iliad* about bravery, courage, guest-friendship, the treatment of women as property or booty, ferocity toward enemies, the danger of arrogance, that gifts given should not be taken back, and that the gods listen to those who obey them. They also learned that only the gods have no sorrows and only they sleep well. As to their own afterlife, Achilleus' response to the spirit of Patroklos taught them that something in human beings lives on, but it is only a breath, an image without actual life in it.

The dates of the Iliadic society these Athenian youths were being taught to emulate have been as much argued about as the question whether or not the two Homeric epics were written by one and the same poet. Whereas in the nineteenth century there was a great deal of division in academic camps, most commentators today agree that one poet polished and refined traditional material into two epics, each unified by the genius of the poet. Speculations about the dates of the society reflected in the *Iliad* have ranged from the twelfth century B.C. to the eighth. Twentieth-century studies have fixed the date of the destruction of Troy at 1184 B.C., and have shown that the social structures in the poem are primarily those of the twelfth-century Late Bronze Age of the Minoan and Mycenean civilizations, even though some elements of the poem can be traced back to Hurrian and Hittite origins certainly as early as the eighteenth century B.C. (the time of the Jewish patriarchs). On the other hand, the *Odyssey* does reflect some of the aspects of the growing city-state society of the eighth century, the time at which the two epics received the form in which we have them, as well as the savage destruction of Aegean and Mediterranean cities by the fearsome Assyrian army.

At this early stage of Greek civilization, the concept of *díkē*, justice, is inconsistent and rudimentary. Although the *Iliad* has been read by some as a poem about divine justice—Zeus' punishment of Troy in retribution for Paris' abduction of Helen—the gods and goddesses themselves are all too humanly fickle, wrathful, inconsistent, and ambiguous in their behavior for a reading of the poem as one concerned primarily with divine justice; the poet, after all, opens by telling the listener that his poem is about the "wrath of Achilleus."

Díkē in the *Iliad* consists of getting one's own fair share of war booty, food, or land—the share due a hero who risks his life. And the wrath of Achilleus is first stirred when he is deprived of part of his "fair portion," the captive Briseis. Among men, brute force determines justice: Agamemnon has more warriors than Achilleus and can thus have his way, and Achilleus can only resort to withdrawing from the war and thus causing vital losses to Agamemnon.

Divine justice seems to be based on favoritism and whim, and Judeo-Christian concepts of an all-knowing God must be set aside for a Zeus who seems not always to know the future. In order to determine which of two battling warriors will die, Zeus places their death portions on the scale; the heavier one will die that day. In spite of teaching at one point that the gods listen to those who obey them, the *Iliad* shows Zeus granting some prayers and denying others. Zeus has two urns, one of evils and one of blessings, and he mingles gifts from the two urns to be distributed to an individual without regard for merit (22.208–13). The definition of human life seems to be that it is always a mixture of both good and bad experiences for every human being, that those experiences are not always merited, and that all must die. Heroes who forget their human nature and begin to act like deathless gods are soon reminded of their mortality.

In the Homeric poems two kinds of *díkē* exist side by side;

one for wartime and another for peacetime. In wartime a hero's experiences are usually the result of force or chance; in the city at peace on the shield of Achilleus, the poet presents a different concept of justice. When two men disagree, they go to arbitrators, elders of the city who listen to the men's cases as well as to the voice of the people; two talents of gold are given to the judge who speaks the best opinion (18.497–508). Homer portrays justice and love and dancing in the city at peace, but only destruction and death in the city at war. There is no arbitration in war, no peaceful solution, no restitution through the payment of a blood price, but only desecration by dogs and vultures. Deliberation and arbitration result in recompense for the killing of a man in the city at peace, whereas the victorious warrior on the battlefield always rejects the payment promised by the defeated warrior for his proper burial. In the *Odyssey*, Odysseus conquers the suitors through cunning rather than brute force, and his victory over them, as we shall see, is one that rights a civic injustice. In the two Homeric poems it appears that war is a time when justice is subject to irrational, arbitrary, and hasty determinations, and peace a time for reflection and rational deliberation.

The *Iliad* and the *Odyssey* are oral epics to which many poets contributed, and not literary epics composed by an individual poet, such as Virgil's *Aeneid* or Milton's *Paradise Lost*. Many unknown poets over a long period of time, perhaps hundreds of years in the case of the *Iliad*, sang an epic and passed on to other poets revisions, inventions, and polishing of poetic devices, until a version was reached that everyone considered the best. This particular rendition survived and came to be attributed to a particular poet who at least had a name, Homer. Little is known about him except that he was born in the eighth century B.C., probably on an island off the coast of Asia Minor, and he may have been blind.

The fact that an epic poet could recite more than fifteen thousand lines of verse is truly astonishing. What must be realized is that he was not performing totally from memory, but rather composing the lines (not the story) as he delivered them. The singer had been immersed for years in traditional epic language, and he had at his fingertips building blocks of phrases, lines, and even entire episodes that facilitated his ability to weave them all together in effective ways. Thus we see extensive repetition of epithets: strong-greaved Achaians, brilliant Odysseus, Diomedes of the great war cry, wide-ruling Agamemnon, swift-running horses, laughing Aphrodite. Not only does the poet repeat phrases to fill out the metrical line but he also repeats entire passages: Zeus recites a speech to Dream; a few lines later Dream relays the identical speech to Agamemnon; this is followed by Agamemnon's delivery of the message to the assembled warriors (2.1–75). Such extensive repetition not only aided the poet in his oral composition of the song but, while chanting such repetitions, he could think well ahead to remind himself of the next stage of the poem.

Similar episodes must have abounded in a number of epics: battle scenes, catalogues of ships and forces, funeral games, seductions, descriptions of shields. Arriving at such a situation in the story he is telling, the poet need merely pull out the appropriate piece from his storehouse of episodes and plug in appropriate names.

As singers of tales made their way from palace to palace, they earned food, drink, and lodging for the evenings of entertainment they provided. By inserting names of forefathers of the kings and nobles in the after-dinner audience, the poet was able to flatter his hosts by providing them with heroic kin. Not only kin but guest-friends: two enemies who meet in battle and discover that one of their forebears once entertained the other's and who then embrace rather than fight. Thus, Diomedes and Glaukos discover they are guest-friends because the grandfather of Diomedes was once host to the grandfather of Glaukos (6.119–236). Given kinship and guest-friendship, Hellenic heroes had many close relations.

Homer seldom relents in showing the brutality of war. Within a hundred lines at the beginning of Book 5, various fighters are struck in the back by a spear that drives on through the chest; pierced by a spear through the right shoulder; struck in the right buttock by a spear that plunges in under the bone and through the bladder; struck in the back of the head by a spear that drives on through the teeth and under the tongue until the spearhead sticks out through the warrior's mouth and he falls, gripping the spear between his teeth; struck by a spear that severs the arm, which then drops bleeding to the ground.

By using similes from experiences common to everyone at that time, Homer succeeds in making battle vivid to those in his audience who may never have been to war. He likens combat to lions attacking sheep, to the fury of thunderstorms, to lightning and raging forest fires: the comparisons are always to destructive elements or to violent animals. Heroes may achieve glory and fame on the battlefield, but war itself is brutal and degrading. On the point of death, a warrior pleads pitifully for mercy he knows is not forthcoming, while the hero stands crowing and vaunting over him, spearhead pointed at the sprawled warrior's chest.

Striking illustrations of Homer's technique of using familiar comparisons occur in lines 455–83 of Book 2. He first shows the visual aspects of war: the battle is like a raging forest fire running across mountaintops whose glorious bronze light dazzles all the way up to the heavens. He next compares the sounds of battle to flying geese and cranes, to the throated sound of swans and their wings as, when they are settling, meadows echo with their clashing swarms. The sound is also like horses' hooves thundering. Next he presents the kinetic movement, the impetus of thrusting armies, comparing them to swarming insects frantically buzzing around the milk pails in a sheepfold. The leaders of the armies are compared to goatherds separating and organizing goats, to the strongest ox of the herd, to a chief bull who stands out among the cattle. A touching comparison occurs when Apollo leads the Trojans in their destruction of the ramparts of the Achaians; Homer sings that they do this as easily as a little boy at the seashore amuses himself by trampling his carefully built sand towers with his feet (15.360–66)

Homer frequently employs what we would call a cinematic approach in dealing with large battles, photographing from a distance, then moving to the foreground, and only at the last showing a close-up of two specific warriors. At the beginning of the battle, at line 422 of Book 4, he gives an overview of two armies surging toward each other, and the comparison is to sea surf pounding in toward the shore, driven by the wind. The cries of the oncoming army sound from a distance, and the cries are compared to those of sheep waiting to be milked and yearning for their lambs. At line 445 the camera moves in closer to show still-unidentified men killing and being killed, and, Homer sings, blood running along the ground like rivers rushing down from mountain streams. The sound of armies clashing is like thunder. Having provided a long view followed by a move to the foreground, the poet is now ready for a close-up of a distinct individual: "Antilochos was first to kill a chief man of the Trojans."

One of the chief men of the Achaians is Patroklos, the dearly beloved friend of Achilleus. Patroklos is so youthful, so guileless, so saddened by the sufferings of others, that, given Achilleus' protective attitude toward him, it is necessary to remind ourselves that Patroklos is the older of the two: *he* has been sent along to protect *Achilleus*.

Patroklos initiates the final climactic scenes of the story. Moved by the sight of his wounded comrades, Patroklos—his name means glory to the fathers—pleads with Achilleus to allow him to reenter the fighting. Thus, clad in the armor of Achilleus, he goes forth only to be killed by Hektor. In an ironic foreshadowing of the final battle between Hektor and Achilleus, Patroklos, wearing the armor of Achilleus, is surrogate for that greater warrior. In larger terms, Achilleus experiences his own death, as well as that of his dear friend. "Die all," Achilleus shouts at a later point. And they *will* die all, including Achilleus, as he symbolically dies in the *Iliad* when he kills Hektor, a warrior clad in the armor of Achilleus that he stripped from Patroklos. Achilleus knows the prophecy that he is to die shortly after the death of Hektor; he thus embraces his own death when he kills Hektor, especially so since the armor makes that warrior another surrogate Achilleus. Like Patroklos, Achilleus also requires three instruments of death—in his case, Patroklos, Hektor, and finally, Paris—the actual killer.

Odysseus is a different breed of Iliadic warrior. The skill of the hero of Homer's second epic is not in brute force but in crafty strategies. Odysseus is intelligent and resourceful, descriptions not applied to other warriors. From the very beginning, in Book 2, he seems to take charge through speech and persuasion when decisions are to be made. And when Agamemnon finally gives in to the fact that he needs Achilleus, it is Odysseus who is put in charge of the embassy to persuade Achilleus to return. This embassy in Book 9 consists of the wily Odysseus, the older and respected Phoinix, and Ajax, that plainspoken, tough, honest warrior. Each has his own approach to the unyielding Achilleus.

Odysseus speaks first, repeating the speech Agamemnon has delivered to him, promising numerous gifts to Achilleus if he will come to their aid (9.225–306). Odysseus cleverly omits the one part of Agamemnon's speech that would have much offended Achilleus: Achilleus should yield to him because he is the kinglier of the two. Achilleus is unpersuaded; there is a standoff between the *mêtis*, cunning, of Odysseus and the *bíē*, might, of Achilleus. Both *mêtis* and *bíē* are needed to win the Trojan War. In the *Iliad* they are represented by the characters of Odysseus and Achilleus, whereas in the *Odyssey*, melded as they are into one hero, Hellenic awareness takes a sophisticated step forward in the realization that man needs to have both *mêtis* and *bíē* to be *áristos*, the best.

Phoinix next recounts a somewhat lengthy but pointed story (9.430–605) about a warrior, Meleagros, who also withdrew from battle and, in spite of the failure of the army without him, refused the entreaties of mother, sisters, and friends to return to the fight. He succumbed only to the pleas of his wife, Kleopatra. Phoinix is being even more subtle than he perhaps realizes. He knows Patroklos is Achilleus' dearest friend, that only Patroklos could possibly persuade him, and he has chosen this particular story because the name Kleopatra is Patroklos in reverse, and he hopes the echo will set up some kind of emotional response in Achilleus. Kleopatra is the only one who is successful in persuading her husband, Meleagros, to put on his armor and return to the battle: Homer is here brilliantly foreshadowing Achilleus' return to the war because of Patroklos: the dead body of Patroklos becomes the ultimate persuasive force.

Finally, at 9.624–42 the blunt Ajax speaks, and doesn't try to be psychologically clever or wily; he is incapable of either. He speaks directly: We're not getting anywhere with this stubborn and proud man, he is so hard that he doesn't even listen to his friends, and he is being selfish. This short, direct appeal succeeds more than the others—at least enough for Achilleus to promise to return to the battle should the Trojans fight their way up to the ships.

Achilleus is a new and different epic hero; he breaks rules, forswears sacred oaths, is moved by compassion for the enemy. The partially successful embassy to Achilleus is a stage in his development which reaches a climax in Priam's own embassy to Achilleus to plead for the mutilated body of his son.

The war and the world have come to a halt with the death of Hektor. Following the funeral games for Patroklos, Achilleus spends twelve days without sleep, alternately rolling in the dirt, weeping over the death of Patroklos, and tossing and throwing the body of Hektor in the dust as though it were some despoiled rag doll. Even the gods are upset by his behavior: Apollo complains that Achilleus doesn't even feel helpful shame about what he is doing, and that he has destroyed pity by tying Hektor's body to horses and dragging it around the tomb of Patroklos (24.33–54). Thetis, Achilleus' immortal mother, descends and urges him to return the body (24.120–37). Although this external appearance can be interpreted as the internal promptings of Achilleus' spirit to give up his wrath, he does say that he will, for ransom, turn over the body. The emotional scene in which he offers Hektor's corpse to Priam shows that this action is for reasons other than ransom.

Within the walls of Troy, Priam prepares for his journey to Achilleus, much against the fears of Hekuba, who argues at 24.194–227 that Achilleus cannot be trusted, will show no pity, and is an "eater of raw meat." Despite her warnings, Priam sets out on a strange, eerie, frightening journey past the great tomb of Ilos, alongside a river, and into the darkness. Zeus sends Hermes down to guide him, and even though Hermes appears to him as a young man, Priam is so frightened that his hair stands on end. Hermes questions him, asking why he is traveling through the immortal black night. Conducting him to the barricades protecting Achilleus' dwelling, Hermes casts sleep on the sentries (24.322–467).

All of the components of a fearful journey to Hades are here, as Priam travels past tombs and rivers through an immortal black night in which Hermes, who guides souls to Hades, casts sleep on watchdogs. This can only be a symbolic journey to Hades to visit Achilleus, who has truly become King of the Dead. And his dwelling is no ordinary battlefield shelter, but an imposing structure worthy of this symbolic King of Hades.

Priam enters alone, falls to the ground, clasps the knees and kisses the hands of Achilleus. Moved by the tears of the groaning father, the hero of the *Iliad* weeps at the thought of his own father's devastation had the body of Achilleus lain on a battlefield to be ravaged by wild dogs and vultures. As Priam and Achilleus shed tears of sadness and loss in recognition of their common human condition, Achilleus, in a heroic thrust *through* the heroic code, agrees to return the body of Hektor, slayer of his dear friend and companion Patroklos. The days of wrath thus end with a compassionate human rather than heroic gesture.

Odyssey

THE *Odyssey* presents a man who goes out and gets what he wants, the first total man in Western literature. Unlike Achilleus, who sulks in his shelter waiting for the world to come to him, Odysseus confronts the world in all its possibilities, both the magical world and the real world of Ithaka. This Homeric hero deliberately throws himself into battle—not only against Trojan warriors but against one-eyed monsters, cannibals, witches, and any other dangers he can find. Indeed, the name of Odysseus means trouble and pain; he is a man eager to kill every boar and get every scar. In the *Odyssey* man is born to trouble; to remain eternally in the womblike cave of Kalypso is to avoid the pains of rebirth. Odysseus' renewal in this poem can only come from experiencing and transcending trouble and pain.

To achieve what he most desires, his homecoming, Odysseus invents and manipulates experience through every wily stratagem he can imagine. In the world of the *Odyssey*, guile is needed to survive, and Odysseus is so committed to the necessity of mendacity he will lie even when he doesn't need to. Survival requires a single-minded devotion to one's self and one's own desires. The war is over; the world is changing; and the *Odyssey* is a rejection of outworn laws and codes, leading to the creation of a new society. The old society, that exclusive club of gentlemen suitors to Penelope who follow the rituals of the past, is defeated by the combined forces of Odysseus, his son, Telemachos, and his wife, Penelope, a family equal to Odysseus in cunning and contrivance.

Odysseus' world is a new world, a world in which you get what you deserve, and the Greek word for it is *tísis*. Hektor doesn't get what he deserves; he was not responsible for the

Trojan War, his playboy brother Paris was. There is no justice in the *Iliad*. Where is justice in the single combat between Menelaos and Paris when the accidental breaking of a chin strap, not the bravery of the more courageous man, determines the outcome? Odysseus, however, obeys the new law of *tísis*: recompense, vengeance, punishment to evil-doing suitors who have taken over his palace and are competing for his wife.

One of Homer's greatest techniques comes to the fore here, as questions of choice become more important than accident or fate. Warriors don't ponder alternatives in their hearts in the *Iliad*; they have no alternatives but to kill or be killed. A hero doesn't learn by experience. He doesn't live long enough to profit by it. But Odysseus is always pondering in his heart, determining the best course of action. The man has learned to be patient. To be still. To wait. To watch. Lessons that King Lear must learn. Lessons Leopold Bloom, the twentieth-century Odysseus in Joyce's *Ulysses*, will learn very well.

What Odysseus learns is the necessity for disguise, for not laying one's cards on the table. Iliadic heroes are all too eager to play before the deck has even been shuffled—a deck already stacked against them. Throughout most of the poem Odysseus is in disguise, never revealing his true identity until he has had an opportunity to survey the situation. He is often disguised as a beggar—the least threatening member of society, the most helpless, the most dependent upon others for food and clothing. But Homer has a darker purpose in view here. Odysseus *is* a beggar; he is in disguise even from himself. "I am Nobody," he shouts to the Cyclops. And his words are truer than he realizes. Ten years fighting the Trojan War have turned him into an object of war, a man who no longer knows who he is. The quest in the *Odyssey* is that of a man searching for self. Just as it is necessary for Achilleus to be purged, cleansed of the destructiveness of his wrath, the war instinct must be washed from Odysseus. He is no longer the prewar husband Penelope describes as never having been violent against any man (iv.687–91). When he sets sail from Troy, the wind blows him to the shore of the Kikonians, where he sacks the city and kills people who have not offended him (ix.39–42). After this, Odysseus does not kill again on his voyage home. Once he has arrived there, the destruction of the offending suitors is not only a requirement of civic justice but is also, according to the text, a requirement of the gods.

The travails of Odysseus are a journey through the interior geography of the soul. The monsters he encounters, the lustful and seductive women, the wrath of Poseidon, the sea are not just external threats; they are at the same time internal psychological aspects of Odysseus: the bloody monsters within him that he must meet and master, lusts with which he must come to terms, and his own suppressed wrath which he must tame. He accomplishes these things, as witness the final episode in the book when Athena, perhaps an aspect of his own spirit, turns him away from the final slaughter of the relatives of the suitors. For these relatives are not responsible, and the new code is not the Iliadic one of "Die all!" but rather a code of justice.

Odysseus journeys through a geography of fantastic imagination peopled by such strange creatures as Polyphemos, Circe, Kalypso, and Nausikaa. It is not only a magical world, but a landscape where the human soul must confront and control itself, its own eternal monsters of blood lust, the seductiveness of the goddesses of lust, and the aggressive wrath of human nature. That these can be controlled and manipulated is the lesson of the *Odyssey*. Tiresias, in Hades, predicts a future for Odysseus that will involve a long inland journey, carrying an oar—that supreme Homeric symbol of the sea-god Poseidon and of war—until he reaches a people who have never known oars or ships rowing to war, and who thus will mistake the oar for that most peaceful of symbols, a winnowing fan for separating wheat from chaff. Odysseus, at peace with himself at last, achieves redemption among people who make bread, not war.

Time and narrative in the *Iliad* unfold in a straightforward process. In the *Odyssey* time and the narrative fold, unfold, and

fold back upon themselves in a narrative structure more complicated than that of the earlier epic. Time here is both Augus-
tinian time, in which the future determines the present, and
Bergsonian time, in which the past is directing and influencing
the present. Homer plays against the pattern of linear expectations. All art speaks to expectations, either pleasing by satisfying those expectations or shocking by snatching them away.
The artistic process is one of jolting, shocking, or reassuring:
great literature not only communicates the truth of experience,
but acts to vivify and revivify experience.

Upon opening the *Odyssey*, one expects to find, as in the
Iliad, a central hero. But the poem confounds us, as, instead of
plunging into the adventures promised by the title, it first
presents Telemachos. Initial expectations have been jolted, but
the reader is still left with anticipation and suspense, awaiting
the appearance of Odysseus.

To open with Telemachos is to show the power of the father-
son theme, as both father and son are homeless and in search
of identity. Telemachos, like his father, has been dispossessed.
The suitors have taken over his home, they are in control, are
eating his cattle and his provisions, and are trying to take
possession of his mother. Telemachos is locked in childhood, a
condition so poignantly presented at the end of the first book
when Eurykleia, his nurse, accompanies him to his bedroom,
helps him undress, hangs up his clothes, and then gently locks
the door after she exits. Telemachos, like Stephen Dedalus, his
counterpart and modern-day representation in *Ulysses*, is ex-
iled—although not self-exiled like Stephen. He is locked in by
the adult world, not, like Stephen, locked in by his own ego.
Telemachos does not yet have an ego; its development has been
stunted by the society of suitors. Like Stephen, who is stunted
by the society of Dublin, Telemachos is in need of a father.
They both need to grow up.

Homer employs a single plot thrust in the *Iliad*, but begins
the *Odyssey* with the subplot, Telemachos' need for identity, and
follows this with the plot, the search by Odysseus for identity.

The singer of the *Odyssey* has abandoned the sequential structure of his earlier poem for one that is more freewheeling, one in which he can weave and unweave his story in rhapsodic fashion. Rhapsody means a stitching together, and a story is thus a number of threads of different colors which the storyteller weaves to make his pattern, a pattern not complete until the final thread is woven in. Homer begins with a thread of one color, Telemachos and the present, and slowly weaves in other colors of the past, present, and future of Odysseus.

The narrative present of the subplot, the adventures of Telemachos, begins in the first book and continues with the journey of Telemachos to the palace of Nestor and then to Menelaos. In Book 4, at the palace of Menelaos, Menelaos first weaves in the thread of time past with the story of his journey homeward to Sparta. Only in Book 5 does the narrative present of the main plot begin when Odysseus is encountered on the island of Kalypso. From there the story of Odysseus continues in linear fashion through Books 6, 7, and 8 as he arrives at the island of the Phaiakians. In Book 9, on that island, he begins the longest trip back into the past as he tells the stories familiar to children: his encounters with the Lotus-Eaters, Polyphemos, Circe, Hades (in which Odysseus is telling a story in the present about a past in which he learned of the future), Sirens, Skylla and Charybdis, and then Kalypso.

Circles within circles are being woven. Book 5 is the present, with Odysseus leaving Kalypso for the the island of the Phaiakians. Then, on that island the story moves into the past, ten years to be exact, to the departure of Odysseus from Troy, followed by all the episodes of monsters and witches of that ten-year period, until Odysseus concludes the story in Book 12 with his arrival on the island of Kalypso. Returning to linear time, he leaves the Phaiakians in Book 13, and arrives, finally, back home in Ithaka. In Book 15, Telemachos arrives; and in Book 16, with the meeting of father and son, Homer firmly positions the reader in present linear narrative time until the end of the story, Book 24.

This complicated structure achieves a number of objectives, known or unknown to Homer. His audience is constantly jolted by juxtapositions that make them see the world anew. They are kept in suspense, never knowing where they will be at the next moment—past, present, or future—or whether with Odysseus or Telemachos. The book satisfies symmetry in that the first twelve books primarily concern the past, whereas the final twelve books take place in the present. Moreover, the first twelve books, with all their interweaving of past, present, and future, have a leisurely, fairy-tale quality that strongly buttresses the magical nature of the episodes. Beginning with Book 13, this gives way abruptly to the swift, sustained present-time realistic adventures of the homecoming and the slaying of the suitors. There are no accidents in the storytelling: Homer is always in complete control of his story and his audience. Telemachos grows to manhood; Odysseus journeys to home and identity. Telemachos is a surrogate Odysseus; they are both lost, homeless. Homer underscores this in the first vision he gives of each of them. They are both grieving: Telemachos for his father and a home that has been taken over by suitors, Odysseus for his wife and son and home.

The poem is thus a poem of rebirth based on both physical and metaphysical journeys, journeys that lead Telemachos from childhood to self-assertion, and Odysseus from wanton killer to protective husband and father.

The *Odyssey* is a story about *nóstos*, the Greek word for homecoming but primarily for the journey home, and there were many such *nóstoi* about the heroes of the Trojan War. The *Odyssey* even provides an additional one when Menelaos tells the young Telemachos about his own *nóstos*, his shipwreck and his struggles with Proteus—the Old Man of the Sea, that creature who, as one wrestles with him to pin him down to the truth about the future, slips from his opponent's grasp as he changes from lion to serpent, from leopard to boar, and from water into tree (iv.306–569). For Proteus represents changing identity, the illusionary quality of truth, the slippery nature of reality and time; it is Proteus who knows what will happen on the journey home. Stephen Dedalus, in the third episode of *Ulysses*, the one Joyce called "Proteus," will also wrestle with that creature in his struggle for future identity.

In their first conversation with Telemachos, Menelaos and Helen unwittingly reveal much about the nature of their *nóstos* (iv.60–295). One suspects that Helen, having spent ten years watching the slaughter of her husband's comrades and her would-be rescuers, would feel some guilt when confronted with the son of Odysseus; she is, after all, the ostensible cause of everyone's troubles. And that Menelaos, having suffered the wounds of battle to rescue a woman who may have been willingly abducted and who spent years weaving a tapestry depicting what was to her the eternal glory of a fought-over beautiful woman, would feel some resentment. Homer does indeed reveal both guilt and resentment. At the beginning of the dinner Helen secretly, as is apparently her custom, pours nepenthe ("no-sorrow") into the wine they are drinking, a drug which causes one to forget sorrow to such an extent that no tear would fall even if the drinker's mother and father died, or if a son or brother were murdered. Apparently, Helen and Menelaos are leading a drugged existence in order to forget their guilt and resentment. But no drug can blur the Trojan War, though it may keep back tears. In an effort to show Telemachos how she aided Odysseus, and that she was really against the Trojans, Helen tells how Odysseus, disguised as a beggar, slipped inside the Trojan walls on a spying expedition and that, recognizing him, she provided him with all the information he needed. Not only a marvelous story of Helen of Troy as counterspy, as double agent, but an ingenious foreshadowing by Homer of the later episode when Odysseus—again disguised as a beggar—spies on the enemies in his own palace.

Menelaos, of course, aware of Helen's ploy for Telemachos' sympathetic understanding, checks her magnificently by reminding Helen how, in an attempt to discover whether or not there were Greeks inside the Trojan Horse, she walked three times around the horse, scratching its sides and calling out the warriors by name, even that of her husband, Menelaos, and it was only Odysseus who kept them from eagerly answering her. As if to show conclusively that Helen was totally on the side of the Trojans, Menelaos points out that she was accompanied by Deiphobos, the brother of her dead lover, Paris. At least he has the good taste not to say aloud what they both know: that after the death of Paris she took Deiphobos, his brother, as her husband. What a grisly *nóstos* for Helen and Menelaos, one made even more so when the reader is told that they will spend eternity together in the Elysian Fields, where seasons never change—a true Sartrean hell of eternal bickering, without even nepenthe (iv.561–69).

Recognition and reversal are primary characteristics of those homecoming stories. In the only recognition scene in the *Iliad*, Glaukos and Diomedes meet on the battlefield and recognize they are guest-friends. The *Odyssey*, on the other hand, is crowded with scenes of this sort, from the recognition by Helen and Menelaos that the physical features of Telemachos prove him to be the son of Odysseus, to the many scenes in which strangers and enemies come to recognize the identity of Odysseus, to the moving scene in the hut of the faithful swineherd Eumaios when Odysseus and Telemachos recognize each other as father and son. The great recognition scenes are, of course, the nurse Eurykleia's identification of Odysseus by the scar on his thigh and Penelope's acceptance of her husband when he reveals his knowledge of the secret of their marriage bed; he is the only one who knows both the secret foundation of the bed and the secret of Penelope.

Recognition scenes involve the world's knowing who you are and thus are scenes on the way to knowing yourself, your own identity. And recognition usually brings a reversal of fortune; in the episodes in this text, a reversal for the enemy when he knows the identity of Odysseus. Actually, the entire epic is about

Odysseus' reversal from being "Nobody" to becoming King of Ithaka again when he is "recognized" by Penelope. The ironic humor here is that Penelope certainly knew this was Odysseus from the moment he first appeared outside the palace. A true consort of Odysseus, she has every intention of testing him to discover whether or not he has been reborn a true husband—a man who has shed his war skin—before she will accept him as *her* consort.

The *Iliad* and the *Odyssey*, two such different yet complementary works, were most likely composed by the same poet. Linguistic evidence in the *Iliad* suggests that it was sung earlier than the *Odyssey*. The first work was perhaps composed by a man of middle age, whereas the *Odyssey*, with its sad atmosphere of longing, memory, and nostalgia, was composed by a man in his later years.

Both poems are epics and there are certainly similarities. The basic nature of the conflict, fighting over besieged women, is identical; real husbands, Menelaos and Odysseus, fight against surrogate husbands, Paris and Eurymachos, at times in single combat. Both poems are crowded with oaths, feasts, and contests. Thetis, the immortal mother of Achilleus, watches over her son, as Athena watches over her adopted son, Odysseus, a man like her in disposition. Aphrodite protects Helen and Paris.

But the two texts are markedly different in attitudes. The *Iliad* is an Oriental work, facing the East; it even takes place on the eastern coast of Asia Minor (present-day Turkey). It is a poem about the destruction of a city and the disruption of the foundations of the past. The *Odyssey*, on the other hand, is a movement toward the West, even in the geographical direction in which Odysseus is returning from Troy. Rather than being a text about destruction, it is a text about re-creation, about Odysseus' refounding and reestablishment of his city, his civilization. The *Iliad* is a realistic work, and by subsequent Greek civilization it was considered history, whereas the *Odyssey* is a work imbued with illusion and imagination. The earlier epic is fact, the later one fiction. The *Iliad* takes place in an eternal present, whereas the *Odyssey* is so much concerned with memory. In modern terms, we can consider that the first is Realistic, the second Romantic.

The *Odyssey* is about purification and rebirth, symbolized significantly by the pervasive imagery of the sea and water. Indeed, the tale of Odysseus begins on an island described as the *omphalós*, the "navel," of the sea; he is at the sea's center and must journey long distances over water to achieve his destination. Most of all, there are baths. The heroes are constantly being bathed, refreshed, renewed. The nurse Eurykleia recognizes Odysseus as she is bathing him, thus indicating that he has, upon his return to Ithaka, been reborn. Homer is intent upon showing the reader of the *Odyssey* his purpose in using water as a symbol. There is a rare and striking use of this symbol in the *Iliad* when Hektor is running away in terror from the final confrontation with Achilleus. Homer takes the risk of losing the impetus of the chase by interrupting Hektor's flight to tell us about a nearby river where the wives and beautiful daughters of the Trojans used to wash their clothes in the time before the coming of the Achaians, when there was peace (22.147–56). In a chilling juxtaposition, Homer seems to be emphasizing the horrors of war by wresting the attention of the audience from images of violent death and focusing it on visions of peace.

Sleeping is another distinctive feature of the *Odyssey*. The heroes, Telemachos and Odysseus, are always entering the day refreshed from sleep, and the scholiasts who originally separated the poem into twenty-four parts highlighted these natural divisions by ending many of the books at a point where one of the heroes is falling asleep. In the *Iliad* sleep is fitful—usually broken by dreams, nightmares, visions—and there is no renewal. Only the gods have restful sleep.

Homer also uses dogs in strikingly different ways. In the *Iliad* they are not friends to man, but rather enemies always ready to tear apart the mutilated and dead bodies of warriors. In the *Odyssey* they are protective, faithful. They fawn over

Telemachos, recognize him, welcome him when he arrives at the hut of Eumaios. Even Odysseus' dog, Argos, expires in happiness when Odysseus arrives at the palace.

In the two epics, even the gods and goddesses play somewhat different roles. In the *Iliad* they seem to be only spasmodically interested in what occurs on the battlefield; occasionally something happens to catch their interest and they swoop down in a rush to make things go their way. They are usually otherwise occupied with their own affairs, and their affection for the heroes seems fickle, all too human. They are not interested in justice. But in the *Odyssey* the Athena who is absent from Odysseus' fantastic voyages returns as disguised protectress when he arrives at the island of the Phaiakians, and as visible participant upon his arrival in Ithaka. He has accomplished the transition from the battlefield to home, and justice, the goddess Athena, has consequently returned to his side; she will not desert him from this point on.

The *Iliad* is concerned with group interest, with the action of heroes, with the plural, with the community of warriors, whereas the *Odyssey* focuses primarily on the action of one man, one hero. Moreover, the *Iliad* consists of a more abstract social structure; most of the men are kings and leaders, aristocrats, and all are, with the exception of garrulous old Nestor and a few others, close in age. There are virtually no ordinary or common men in that book. The *Odyssey*, however, is a detailed story of particular societies, and of a more complex social structure. That epic presents all ages and classes: kings, queens, nobles, faithful and unfaithful maids, farmers, mysterious strangers, sailors, duplicitous friends, monsters and young men, temptresses and faithful and devoted wives. The *Odyssey*, situated as it is in complex societies, is a richer *story* than the *Iliad*. This world and its people are knowable, familiar, closer to home than the bloody world of the *Iliad*. Indeed, that world seems primarily one of boasting and of vaunting pridefully over dying opponents, as, for example, Hektor over Patroklos. But such display is not the world of the later epic. In that world there is no stripping of armor from dead bodies, no mutilation of the dead. Above all, no vaunting. In one of the major differences between the moral codes of the two texts, Odysseus says to Eurykleia after the slaying of the suitors in Book 22: Don't cry out with pleasure, keep your joy hidden in your heart. It is not pious, he says, to glory over these dead men. He contends that he didn't slay them, the gods destroyed them because of their own rude behavior, destroyed them because they did not pay enough attention to their fellow men, either those who were base and common or those who were noble. He concludes that the suitors died in shame because of their own recklessness (xxii.411–18).

This is certainly a transition phase between the Iliadic world, where men died because of external forces, and the coming world of fourth-century Athens, when Plato and Aristotle teach that men are responsible for their own fate. There is the further implication that men are *agents* of the gods; they are not gods, but they do not act alone. Much of this is contradictory, but it befits an epic where old codes are being destroyed and new ones constructed.

Some of these differences in moral outlook are caused by the fact that Iliadic heroes are so turned inward upon themselves, so much concerned with valor and reputation, that they have little awareness and true understanding of others. Their vision is so clouded by their own overwhelming need for glory and reputation (not a concern of the hero of the *Odyssey*) that they are not aware of the nature of the world surrounding them. It is truly a matter of *noticing*, as, again and again in the *Iliad*, heroes suffer because they "didn't notice." Zeus has so stolen away the wits of Glaukos that the man doesn't notice he is exchanging his own gold armor for the bronze armor of Diomedes. Zeus is always confusing the crafty perceptions of the warriors; they do not notice the enemy stealing up behind them until it is too late. They seem to notice only those things which are *forced* upon their field of vision; they do not take in the horizon, but the horizon succeeds in taking *them* in.

The world of the *Odyssey* is a world of observing, of noticing, of being alert to all angles. In the opening of Book 1 a disguised Athena enters the palace of the absent Odysseus and the only one to notice this stranger is the grieving Telemachos; he is, the poet tells us, "by far" the first to see her, even though he is turned inward in grief. The fact that the suitors do not notice her foreshadows their doom: he who does not notice, he who is unaware of the world around him, will be destroyed. Polyphemos, literally and symbolically, has only one eye, and even that indication of his one-sided vision is destroyed. Ultimately, he is unable to notice anything, any more than the suitors, who should be suspicious of a strange new beggar at the palace, do not notice that he might be Odysseus. Homer never tires of pointing out those who notice and those who don't. Penelope, in her bedroom, hears someone sneeze in another part of the palace and recognizes that it is Telemachos who sneezes (xvii.541–50). Certainly, that is the height of noticing and recognition. But then, the entire family of Odysseus is a family of noticers: father, wife, son, maid, and dog.

The importance of noticing, of being aware, indicates a world different from that of the *Iliad*, one with distinctive characteristics.

First, there is no necessity to notice, to be aware of multiple possibilities, unless one is in the position of being able to choose. Pondering in the heart, as Odysseus is constantly doing, is useless when there is no possibility of choice. The Iliadic warriors don't have choices. Only Achilleus does, which makes him the hero of that epic. One must ponder, be thoughtful—a frequent epithet in the *Odyssey*—ask questions, be curious.

The very first words Telemachos utters are reassurances to the disguised Athena that, after he has provided her with dinner, he will find out why this stranger is here, what her needs are. And after Athena has eaten, Telemachos, at i.170–77, is full of questions: Who are you? Where do you come from? What city? Who are your parents? What kind of ship did you come here on? How did the sailors get you here? What kind of men are they? Is this your first time here? Are you a friend of my father? This young man is going to be a survivor; indeed, his name means far-off fighter. Children were frequently named for the attributes of their fathers, and Telemachos is indeed his father's son, that father who plugs the ears of his sailors with wax but has himself tied to the mast so that he can hear the song of the Sirens without being drawn into destruction by it. This man, like his son, wants to *know everything*—and wants to *survive*.

Odysseus and Telemachos survive because they learn from their experiences, whereas Iliadic heroes usually die from theirs. In the opening lines of the *Odyssey* the hero is described as having seen many cities. Homer specifically states that Odysseus suffered many pains and learned "the minds" of the men of those cities. Aeschylus will show again and again that knowledge comes through suffering. Odysseus knows this because he sees the world, and experiences the pain of the world. Throughout the poem he is also frequently a shipwrecked stranger in disguise. Telemachos' growth to manhood begins when he leaves home for the first time and journeys to Pylos, the city of Nestor, and to Sparta, the city of Menelaos. The overweening Agamemnon doesn't suffer and doesn't learn the minds of other cities; consequently, when he returns home to Mycenae, the only city he knows, he is murdered.

Because of his experiences, Odysseus has learned to conceal his intentions. The *Iliad* is a world of unthinking reflexive thrust and counterthrust where everyone has an accepted identity dictated to him by his comrades and the social position of his ancestors. Odysseus knows that to reveal your identity too soon is the quickest way to die. He is a loner, a hero of a Wild West movie, and he probably learned self-reliance from his grandfather, Autolykos, whose name in Greek probably means lone wolf. Achilleus may have retired to his shelter to sing about fame in the company of his friend Patroklos and their two women companions, but he does have them, and he can watch the battle. Odysseus, on the other hand, is the first alienated hero. He is truly alienated from society and foreshadows so many twentieth-century heroes. Alienation allows one to see from a distance, usually creates difficulty, and thus knowledge, through crisis. The Greek word *krísis* carries within it the meaning of separation and judgment. In order to judge, one must separate, make distinctions, make choices. Odysseus is a man of choices.

This hero undergoes three rites of passage in the *Odyssey*: a rite of separation from his warrior past at Troy; a rite of transition and change as he journeys through the unreal world of monsters, witches, and cannibals; and, finally, a rite of reincorporation upon his return to Ithaka. Literally, as well as figuratively, Odysseus is frequently seen standing at thresholds. The rite of passage through the magic world of the first part of the book is a necessary stage in his disengagement from war and his preparation for peace. It is appropriate that his final stop before reaching Ithaka is the island of the Phaiakians, for this island partakes of the unreality of the previous journeys and is, at the same time, real in ways the sites of the preceding adventures are not. Phaiakia is peopled with such identifiable personages as Nausikaa and King Alkinoos. They provide the bridge between the past and the future. They are truly fantastic creatures who live on a fantasy island where the orchards continually bear fruit, yet they behave as human beings: Nausikaa apparently wishes for Odysseus to be her husband. The purification of Odysseus requires that he come to this island, far apart from all others, a place where, as Nausikaa says, no enemies can come bringing war because the Phaiakians are loved by the gods. This is truly a community of love and perpetual peace.

Further purification takes place at the banquet given by King Alkinoos when Demodokos sings about the Trojan War. In an amazing piece of self-referential writing, anticipating Cervantes and Borges, Homer incorporates himself into his own text as Demodokos, the blind singer: Homer portrays himself as an excellent singer loved by the muse. And the song Demodokos/Homer sings (viii.62–82) is a song about a quarrel between Achilleus and Odysseus, a miniature version of the *Iliad*. One can imagine Achilleus or Diomedes reacting with enormous pride to this recounting. But Odysseus is a transformed man, and the song which gives such joy to the rest of the audience only causes him to cover his head with a mantle to hide his tears of sorrow as he groans over his past existence. There is no vaunting here, no pleasure in the glory the song is supposed to give, but rather immense sorrow. The Trojan War is finally over for Odysseus and he is now prepared to return home.

Homer concludes his poem by showing that learned behavior becomes instinctive. After Odysseus has regained complete control of Ithaka, he goes outside the city to visit his aged father, Laertes, a man who has retired from the world to tend his own garden (xxiv.205–355). When Odysseus arrives, he has no reason not to reveal himself and have an immediate happy reunion with his father, but ten years of wily, protective, and crafty behavior, learned in order to get home, cannot be abandoned. First, he tells his father he is a stranger to this land, but that once he had entertained Odysseus in his own country. Laertes breaks into tears and wants further news of his son. But Odysseus continues the cruel—but now instinctive—lying in detail, saying that his name is Eperitos, that he is from another country, that it has been five years since he entertained Odysseus, and he has no knowledge of what happened to him. This so saddens Laertes that, in sorrow, he kneels, grasps dust in his hands, pours it over his face and his gray hair, and begins to groan. His howl of desperate grief so moves Odysseus that he embraces his father, kisses him, and reveals himself as the son of Laertes.

The reader of the *Iliad* and the *Odyssey* is also struck with recognition, as the final scenes involving the heroes of both epics end with tears of fathers for sons and sons for fathers: Achilleus weeps in common humanity with Priam, the father of the dead Hektor, whose body Achilleus is restoring to the father, and Odysseus holds his weeping father. These moving moments of reconciliation dominate the final passages of both epics, highlighting fathers and sons, a central theme of much Western literature. Both epics end with forbearance as Achilleus tells Priam he will not attack the city during the days when Troy is mourning Hektor and Odysseus refrains from killing the kin of the suitors.

Nevertheless, Achilleus will again put on his armor and the Trojan War will continue; but that is not part of the *Iliad*. At the conclusion of the *Iliad* and the *Odyssey*, Achilleus and Odysseus, those two great heroes who have given and received so much pain, discard the armor of killing for the nakedness of the human condition.

Oresteia

THE *Iliad* shows the destructive wrath of Achilleus purged through compassion for the enemy. In the *Odyssey* the wrath of Odysseus is dispelled by the desire for peace. Wrath is the moving force of the *Oresteia*, and it gives way, in the hands of Aeschylus, to a civilized form of justice.

Each of the three plays that make up the *Oresteia* contains a trial. In the first play Agamemnon is executed and then tried by Klytemnestra; in the second, Klytemnestra is tried and then executed by Orestes; in the final play wrath is tried and then transformed by Athena and the citizens of Athens. All three plays are concerned with the wrath of Klytemnestra.

She is mentioned briefly in Book 1 of the *Iliad* when Agamemnon, unaware of her future plans for him, speaks admiringly of her as a woman superior in body, form, and accomplishments (1.111–15). Unfortunately for him, the point of Agamemnon's praise is that he prefers the captive girl Chryseis to Klytemnestra and would like to take her home with him. The seed of Agamemnon's future at the hands of Klytemnestra is in these arrogant words, for, although it was acceptable to return with war slaves, what is foreshadowed here is Klytemnestra's reaction: Agamemnon's return with the Trojan princess Kassandra is one of the reasons she gives for slaughtering him (*Ag.*1438–47). The contrast with the gentlemanly Laertes, Odysseus' father, is implied in the first book of the *Odyssey*: when Laertes brings home to Ithaka the young slave Eurykleia, future nurse to Telemachos, he treats her with as much consideration as he does his wife and does not sleep with her for fear of his wife's anger (i.430–35).

Further background on Klytemnestra is provided by the ghost of Agamemnon in Hades. He thought he would be welcomed home by his wife, but Klytemnestra's thoughts were of bloody murder, and, in killing him, she brought shame not only on herself but, he says, on all women to come (xi.405–34). In the final book of the *Odyssey*, Agamemnon's conversation with Achilleus in Hades is interrupted when the recently slaughtered suitors come streaming in; Agamemnon, shocked by so many sudden deaths, demands to know whether a storm at sea drowned them, or if a battle on land caused their deaths. When told they died because of the craft of Penelope and Odysseus, Agamemnon responds with praise for the intelligent and virtuous Penelope, who, he says, will be the subject of pleasing songs by the poets, in contrast to his wife, who, having awaited him with evil in mind, will be the subject of hateful songs (xxiv.106–202).

In *Agamemnon* Klytemnestra gives three reasons for murdering her husband: he slaughtered their child Iphigenia, he slept with Kassandra and brought her home, and he was cursed by the gods (*Ag*.1415–18; 1438–47; 1500–04). These justifications need to be investigated.

Gathering the army to rescue Helen from Troy was not an easy task; no one really wanted to go, even though all Helen's former suitors had vowed at the wedding of Helen and Menelaos to assist her should she need help. Various stratagems were employed by the future warriors to avoid conscription by Agamemnon, the older brother of Menelaos. Methodically plowing up and down the furrows of his field, pretending he had no volition, Odysseus feigned madness to avoid service. Agamemnon placed the infant Telemachos in his path; Odysseus stopped, proving himself sane, and was off to war. Achilleus fled to another palace, where he disguised himself as one of the daughters of the king; Agamemnon and Menelaos, suspecting the ploy, arrived with gifts for the princesses; the daughters rushed for the jewels and fine dresses while Achilleus gave himself away by lifting and admiring the heavy sword the brothers had cleverly placed among the gifts.

After ten years of such voluntary and involuntary enlistment, the ships were ready to sail; but there was no wind. The high priest assured Agamemnon the winds would blow if he sacrificed his daughter Iphigenia. She was sent for on the pretext that she was to be married to Achilleus; her father, the war-lover Agamemnon, performed the bloody sacrifice.

The slaughter of Iphigenia is Klytemnestra's most powerful justification for murdering Agamemnon. The Furies, ancient defenders of order, can now use her as their instrument of revenge. These hideous women with writhing snakes for hair are the servants of Zeus who descend in righteous wrath whenever someone steps over established bounds. According to Heraclitus, if the sun goes out of orbit the Furies will force it back. They avenge those who cannot protect themselves, in this case the innocent and defenseless Iphigenia.

The Furies are primitive and barbaric, not part of later civilized codes and laws. They protect the four sacred and unwritten ancient laws: do not shed the blood of kin, do not break oaths, do not offend a host, and do not attack one who is supplicating to a god. Agamemnon has shed the blood of his daughter, and Klytemnestra is charged by the Furies with wrathful vengeance.

Agamemnon's flaunting of his mistress Kassandra is the next justification Klytemnestra presents to the townspeople. This is a weaker point than the first, as the cultural codes of the time allowed heroes to return with captive women as war booty, and even to have sons and daughters by them. Furthermore, Klytemnestra had planned the murder long before she knew he was returning with Kassandra.

Her final contention, that she is continuing the curse on the House of Atreus, is her weakest point. Certainly, for generations Agamemnon's family has been involved in the murder of kin; but the slaughter and revenge were always committed by male relatives. Klytemnestra is a member of the House of Atreus only by marriage.

Klytemnestra murders Agamemnon because her love has

turned to hate: he killed their daughter and spent ten years away fighting for the glory of Helen, Klytemnestra's beautiful half-sister, rumored to have been fathered by Zeus, whereas Klytemnestra was the child of a mere man. But Klytemnestra carefully avoids expressing that motive.

Agamemnon is a vain, pompous, arrogant, selfish husband whose disdainful treatment of the proud Klytemnestra has turned her into an emotionally battered wife. Aeschylus shows this quickly and deftly in the first minutes of Agamemnon's arrival: he responds to Klytemnestra's speech of welcome by saying it was as lengthy as his ten-year stay in Troy. After thus haughtily telling her she talks too much, he contends that praise of him really belongs to others, apparently meaning males, not females. Berating her for treating him like an Oriental potentate or a god, he piously utters what by the time of this play was a trite platitude that was first uttered by Solon in Herodotus: Don't call any man happy until he has reached the end of his life without misfortune. As she continues to plead with him to step down from the carriage onto the welcoming carpet, he charges that her desire for controversy is not womanlike; but he relents and, in one of the most arrogant actions in drama, takes the first step down to his death.

Aeschylus is not presenting a characterization of Agamemnon that an audience would find unrecognizable or unbelievable. They knew him from the *Iliad*: he boasts of his possession of Chryseis, he bullies his little brother Menelaos as well as others, lies about his intentions, and he is an inept strategist who cannot win battles without Achilleus. Klytemnestra does not deprive the world of a great human being, but her hatred does not justify murder.

Klytemnestra gives three reasons for murdering Agamemnon, but one of her strongest motives is the unspoken one— her desire for sexual dominance, and in this Aeschylus is a bold precursor of twentieth-century theories of sexuality. Klytemnestra has a "strong male heart," and she dominates the weak and "womanly" Aegisthus. Living in a society of male supremacy, she can only assert herself by assuming a male role rather than by becoming a strong woman. She is fond of the metaphor of a spear as phallus: Kassandra, she says, was the captive of Agamemnon's spear. Taking up that spear, the sword and phallus of her husband, she strikes him three times because of the conflict between men and women born of "ancient bitterness." As he dies spurting his "bitter" blood on her, Klytemnestra compares the blood to rain giving birth to flowers. Her murder of Agamemnon is a powerful sexual act; she stands over his naked body, phallic sword in hand, bathed in his symbolic semen. After murdering Kassandra, she places her in the arms of naked Agamemnon, saying that the memory of the two of them lying naked together in death will enhance her future orgasms (*Ag.*1438–47).

Klytemnestra is a monstrously complicated woman and we feel sympathy for her because of her treatment at the hands of Agamemnon and the society in which she lives. We marvel at her single-minded determination and strategy, admire her keen intelligence and powers of persuasion in a male world, and finally are overwhelmed by her bristling sexuality.

Homeric imagery makes the experiences of the heroes vivid to the listeners or reader; Aeschylean imagery *is* the meaning of the work.

Aeschylus uses image clusters in *Agamemnon* to reveal the society he is portraying as primitive and barbaric. The people are animals: they are described as dogs, wolves, oxen, captive animals, lions, savage beasts; they are trapped, yoked, curbed, netted, caught in spider webs, and restrained by bits. They are not in control: they are beasts. Their life in darkness is portrayed by repeated images of night, gloom, blackness, darkness. They are in need of the light of a new civilization, a new concept of justice, represented by images of light—shining, blaze, flare, beacon, torchlight, sunlight, glowing, and dawn. Images of dark and light are frequently paired to show an emerging consciousness of justice. This society is a nightmare world where people are asleep and dreaming about blood. Another image cluster, perhaps the most telling, is that of medicine: this diseased society is in need of a healer.

Aeschylus assails the spectators with these image clusters of animals, night, and illness; they occur more than one hundred times in the first six hundred lines of *Agamemnon*. The *Oresteia* charts the progression of the Hellenic world from an irrational, dark, animalistic society of never-ending revenge, where retribution is in the hands of blood kin, to a fifth-century Athenian world, where justice is the prerogative and responsibility of a rational and enlightened city-state capable of liberating man from his animalistic condition.

In the *Libation Bearers* Aeschylus presents the second trial, but this is a trial with a difference. Whereas Klytemnestra tries herself *after* the murder of Agamemnon, Orestes and Electra painfully try their mother *before* the murder of Aegisthus and Klytemnestra. Aeschylus shows pity for this primitive world where there are no courts of law and individuals must put themselves on inconclusive trial.

Electra, a fatherless girl with a domineering mother, is perhaps undeserving of the Freudian complex attaching her name to morbid or excessive love of daughter for father. Not only does she have a dead father and a deadly mother, but she has been bereft of a brother. Years without retribution have turned her into a young woman of bitterness and irony who even questions the libations she offers at their father's tomb, comparing her pouring of wine on the grave of Agamemnon to the emptying of Klytemnestra's garbage pails (*L.B.*96–99). Nevertheless, she daily prays for the return of Orestes and vengeance for her father's murder. On this day of libation-bearing she finds a lock of hair and a footprint that matches hers and must, therefore, belong to Orestes. This is a far flimsier recognition scene than Eurykleia's discovery of the scar of Odysseus. Euripides, in his *Electra*, has her scoff at the messenger who reports the similarities. Her foot, she insists, is not as large as that of Orestes. Indeed, the *Electra* of Euripides combines with the works of Aeschylus and Sophocles to provide the only three extant plays treating the same event. Whereas Aeschylus' play is patriotic and religious, Sophocles shows the years of imprisonment by Klytemnestra turning Electra into a rebellious, bitter woman; Euripides, with a sense of heightened theatricality bordering on melodrama, has Klytemnestra marry Electra to a peasant farmer to prevent noble offspring. He first shows her returning from a spring carrying a heavy jar of water on her shoulder.

Electra and Orestes are going to commit the most heinous crime known to man, and they must conduct their own trial beforehand to assure themselves they are just. Aeschylus engages the audience's sympathy by extensive use of imagery demonstrating their helpless position: they are orphaned children attacked by a viper; both father and children are lost; they are defenseless eaglets in a nest. These two "children," with encouragement from the Chorus of captive women, work themselves up to commit an act they abhor; when they weaken, the Chorus urges them to leave the darkness and come into the light, and Orestes realizes the awful paradox of the situation: Right against Right (*L.B.*461). Klytemnestra was Right to kill Agamemnon for the murder of their daughter, and he is Right to kill Klytemnestra for the murder of Agamemnon. Resolution cannot be achieved in a barbaric world where there is no Right or Wrong, and Orestes must become, as he says, a snake to kill his mother (*L.B.*549–50).

Following the murder of Aegisthus and Klytemnestra, the Chorus exults upon thinking that light has returned to the house and the bit has been taken away: this is as hopeful and hopeless as Klytemnestra's assurance to Aegisthus, after she has killed Agamemnon, that they can now bring good order to their house. For darkness descends again. As Orestes is leaving— confident that Apollo, who condoned the murder, will cleanse him, and after the Chorus has assured him he set the city free when he chopped off the snake heads of Klytemnestra and

Aegisthus—the Furies dramatically swarm onto the stage to confront and torment him. They appear to the soul of Orestes: the Chorus does not see them, but they are visible to the audience. Never before, and never again in Greek drama, was such a shocking event presented on the stage. The Athenian audience believed in the Furies; but they had never actually seen these fierce women with writhing snakes for hair and blood dripping from their eyes.

These Furies, because they hunt and capture murderers of kin, carry torches, nets, and whips, and wear hunting dress. They are associated with avenging eagles, with snakes, with dogs tracking down the murderer by sniffing bloody footprints. They have been present in the imagery of the *Oresteia* from the beginning of the first play when the Watchman crouches on his knees and elbows like a dog waiting for a beacon, a flare. It continues throughout the trilogy as Klytemnestra dreams of snakes, calls Orestes a viper, and tells him her curse will drag him down like a dog. Aegisthus speaks of the house as having been bitten and poisoned. Orestes and Electra are eaglets who will avenge the slain eagle, Agamemnon.

These Furies have now descended on Orestes, and he will be tormented until they find a killer for him. And then a killer for that killer. And then . . . There is no end to this. But Aeschylus, in the *Eumenides*, shows gods and men cooperating to find an end.

By the time the performance of the *Eumenides* begins, the Athenian sun, at its zenith, blazes down on the Theater of Dionysus—built into the slope of the Acropolis just beneath the Parthenon—lighting up the giant figures of Athena and Apollo. The play has come to the spectators, and the action is taking place not just in front of them but above and behind them at the Temple of Athena, the patroness of Athens. Many of the spectators have journeyed for days from the far countryside to attend the Greater City Dionysia, and the Priest of Dionysus is himself seated on a throne in the center of the first row. They have been there since before daybreak, and Aeschylus brilliantly uses natural light to illuminate the progress of his trilogy. He begins at dawn with the Watchman on the lookout for beacon lights just as light breaks onto the stage of the theater. The play progresses from the darkness of the barbaric world to the high noon of fifth-century Athenian clarity.

Sophocles and Euripides will make further innovations in drama, but the one this audience is watching consists of only three actors and a Chorus of twelve—all of them male. The Chorus comments on the action, engenders suspense, and dances while singing the choruses to musical accompaniment. These lyrical choruses also provide interludes during which the actors retire and put on different masks to become the characters in the next scene. Not only did the actors wear masks more than a foot high, they also wore thick-soled boots to increase their height. They were imposing figures whose powerful voices were amplified by the shape of the masks as well as by the brilliant acoustical design of these massive outdoor theaters; they were clearly understood by audiences of more than fifteen thousand spectators. The complicated masks and boots help explain why violence had to take place offstage. These were grandiose productions, with the acting, singing, dancing, and music making them more like opera than plays.

The *Eumenides* pits the Furies, older goddesses of irrational blood-vengeance, against Apollo, a younger, rational god. The jury is composed of Athena and twelve citizens of her city. Justice will henceforth be determined by impartial voters.

The Furies—"old children," Apollo calls them (*Eum*.69)— protest the attack on their power, demanding their right to punish Orestes, declaring Klytemnestra innocent of the stain, as she did not shed kindred blood when she killed her husband. Apollo, in a spirited defense of the marriage bond, argues that the matter is larger than oaths and that the sweetest things in life proceed from married love (*Eum*.213–24). Aeschylus is in a difficult situation, as the Furies and Apollo both have Right on their side. Klytemnestra and Orestes are equally stained. Aeschylus needs to show the argument at an impasse because, a patriotic Athenian, he wants to bestow upon Athens the invention of courts of law and trial by a jury of citizens. And so Athena arrives, haughtily pretending not to recognize the Furies, who identify themselves as the "gloomy children of the night." The argument between them goes nowhere, and Athena realizes the Furies can't remain and can't be driven off (*Eum*.397–489).

Orestes takes the witness stand, is interrogated by the Furies, Athena, and Apollo, and in spite of Athena's earlier opinion that persuasion should not win by technicalities, Apollo triumphs. Whether or not audiences actually believed the sophistry of his genetics argument that male seed is an embryo transplanted into the merely nurturing mother, these Athenians spent much of their time attending trials and appreciated clever arguments. There can be a father without a mother, Apollo asserts, pointing to Athena, who sprang from Zeus' head and never knew a woman's womb, as living proof (*Eum*.657–73).

The outcome is decided by the vote of Athena and twelve citizens of Athens. Athena, casting the final ballot, announces it to be a vote for Orestes since, having had no mother herself, she always supports the male. The ballots of the citizens are even, Athena casts the tie-breaking vote, and Orestes escapes the charge of murder (*Eum*.734–53). Justice has become the prerogative of Athena and the citizens of her city-state, not of the individual or the family.

The Furies remain to be appeased; they claim that anarchy will be let loose in the land if people do not fear their power of retribution (*Eum*.778–92). At last Aeschylus is ready to reveal what he has been designing from the beginning.

The *Iliad*, the *Odyssey*, and now the *Oresteia* all demonstrate that the threat most disturbing to the Athenian desire for clarity, rationality, and order—both in the individual and in the state— must have been uncontrolled fury and wrath. Wrath must be contained, somehow absorbed. Athena does not know what to do with the Furies, whether to let wrath remain or to banish it. Aeschylus knows that this is the quandary of every individual and state controlled by wrath, and that both alternatives are impossible. Wrath won't go away, but it will destroy. Only one solution remains: transform and incorporate wrath, channel its enormous power into a new, beneficent direction.

This is precisely what Aeschylus has Athena do when she wisely relinquishes some of her own power and offers the Furies a place of their own alongside her on the Acropolis, next to the Erechtheum. There they will sit in shining chairs of eminence, accepting devotions from the citizens of Athens. "Your citizens," she tempts them. Athena assures the Furies they will come to love Athens, will increase the dignity of the city-state, and will lead Athenians away from the war spirit that "directs their fury for battle inward on themselves." She admonishes them to do good so they will be honored with good and share in a country loved by the gods. She promises no household will prosper without their assistance. The power of good overcomes the wrath of the Furies and they feel hate melting away as they are transformed from the Erinyes, seekers of vengeance, to the Eumenides, favorable and gracious goddesses (*Eum.*848–926). And in fifth-century Athens their representation changed from gorgonlike monsters to the image of beautiful young girls.

In what must have been an exalting experience for the audience, Athena invites them to join her and the Eumenides in processional. Calling first on the women in the audience, whose noble honor it was to guard and protect the image of Athena, she beckons this grave company of "maidens, wives, elder women" to form in parade behind her. Followed by the entire assembly of citizens, Athena, with the Eumenides singing blessings of peace, leads them through the streets of Athens and up to the Acropolis to assist in the final absorption and transformation of wrath as it is incorporated into a city of eternal benevolence (*Eum.*1021–47).

This gloriously optimistic, patriotic, and religious play from Athens' Golden Age becomes, in retrospect, chilling and infinitely sad. Aeschylus had fought in the triumphant defense against the Persian invasion of Greece, and is warning the Athenians not to transform victory into arrogance and pride, into a hunger for expansion and power. Just when wrath had been changed into benevolent and vigilant love for country, Aeschylus saw the possibility of the Eumenides again becoming the Furies and leading the Athenians into a self-destructive war. Twenty-seven years after the *Oresteia* was produced, the Peloponnesian War exploded and the arrogant Athenian empire was demolished.

Oedipus the King

M ANY READERS OF *Oedipus the King* erroneously think the actions within the play are predetermined. This "everything-is-fated" theory of the play destroys its significance and renders it unworkable as tragedy. The tragic hero must have free will, must work out his destiny without divine command. The only action Oedipus cannot avoid is killing his father and marrying his mother: Apollo has so decreed. But that happens long before the events in *Oedipus the King*; every action taken by Oedipus in the play is initiated by him. Apollo sends the plague, but he does not know what Oedipus' response will be; he informs Creon that the plague will end when the murderer of the king is sent into exile, but he does not know whether or not this will happen. Oedipus can, at any moment, even when he is questioning the Herdsman, who provides the conclusive proof of his identity, go back into the palace, lock the doors, and choose not to blind himself.

Gods can either predetermine the end result or they can simply attempt to influence the final action: such as by sending a plague, as Apollo does, that will start a search for the murderer. Being divine, they know the future, but do not necessarily direct it. In the classic example of this, Christ informs Peter that before the cock crows he will deny Him three times. Christ knows what is going to happen, but He doesn't force Peter into the denial; Christ knows Peter and He also knows, as did Sophocles, that character is fate. The character of Oedipus, not the will of the gods, brings about the recognition and reversal in the play. He is a remarkable man whose strength of character is unappreciated by readers who would deny his freedom of will. He is kind, generous, tender with those he loves, firm against threats, confident, courageous in accepting his own decree, and, most of all, determined to be intellectually honest.

Unfortunately, generations of readers have allowed Aristotle to "read the play for them" rather than read it for themselves. The speculations about *hamartía* and *húbris* in Aristotle's *Poetics* have caused the most damage: *hamartía* is usually translated as "tragic flaw," and *húbris* as "pride." Aristotle is a descriptive rather than prescriptive thinker; however, readers since his time have gone through Greek, Elizabethan, and modern tragedies looking for tragic flaws. Weaknesses can always be found: characters in plays are capable of being wrathful, mean-spirited, cowardly, avaricious, cruel, ambitious. Even if these be considered tragic flaws, none of them describe Oedipus. At the end of the play he is a man despised and avoided, but the reader should not despise or avoid him, as Oedipus is a man who acts out of love for his family and his city, and ultimately out of deep respect for himself. He acts neither out of pride nor wrath: the two culprits one might suspect to be his *hamartía*. One can hardly call Oedipus' quick temper in his eagerness to heal the ills of Thebes a tragic flaw; if temper led to tragedy, few of us would escape whipping. There is no tragic flaw in the character of Oedipus unless intellectual honesty be labeled such.

The play, then, is about man's insatiable quest for knowledge of himself and his universe, even when that knowledge leads to certain destruction. Further, the play is about acting: acting in ignorance and acting in knowledge. Finally, and most tragic of all, the play shows the incalculable power of accident and chance.

Oedipus bears the wound of his identity, just as other heroes before and after him have done: the scar of Odysseus, Jacob's limp from wrestling with the angel, Captain Ahab's whalebone leg. The name *Oidípous* is his identity; it means swollen-foot, and it derives from the wounded ankles he suffered when, as an infant, he was abandoned on Mount Cithaeron. But the first element of his name, *oidí-*, "swollen," resembles forms of the verb "to know," and Sophocles ironically echoes the verb in close proximity to the name *Oidípous* throughout the play.

Oedipus is a man who doesn't know the most important

thing in his life: his identity. Certainly, one of the reasons
Oedipus is now King of Thebes is that he saved the city by
solving the riddle of the Sphinx, the monster with the body of
a winged lion and the face of a beautiful young woman, who
took one Theban life for each failure to answer her riddle.
When confronted by the Sphinx with the question "What walks
on four feet in the morning, two at noon, and three in the
evening, and is weakest when it has the most feet?" Oedipus
answers correctly, "Man." The play is about both man the doer
and man the knower.

The play abounds in images of knowledge, action, and
chance: the first speech of the Priest foreshadows these motifs.
The words associated with knowledge are "speaking," "teaching," "hearing," and "learning." Throughout, the Chorus admonishes Oedipus to listen: knowledge comes not from self but
from the external world, from the spoken word. The play, like
the *Eumenides*, is in the form of an investigation, a trial: and the
Furies have returned. Oedipus is the prosecuting lawyer and
the guilty defendant, as well as the presiding judge. His are the
crime, the verdict, and the punishment; and Sophocles makes
subtle use of legal terminology familiar to Athenians, words
associated with testimony, prosecution, evidence, eyewitness
accounts, character assassination, even torture—as in the twisting
of the arms of the Herdsman, an accepted method of evidence-
gathering in the Athens of Sophocles' day.

Knowledge and action can be ineffectual unless they accom-
pany each other. In the next century Aristotle will put the
emphasis on action and Plato on thought, but throughout this
play Oedipus grasps the importance of both: even before the
play begins, he has sent Creon to Delphi to discover by what
"act or word" he could save the city. Athenians of the fifth
century would have found the twentieth-century preoccupation
with dissociation of sensibility incomprehensible; to them, as to
the characters in the plays they watched, thought, feeling, and
action were all one. Oedipus responds to each new piece of
knowledge with swift action: he learns of the plague and sends

Creon to Delphi (69–70); he learns from Creon of the murder of Laius and sends for Tiresias (287–89); he discovers specifics of the murder from Jocasta and sends for the Herdsman (765); he learns from the Messenger from Corinth that he is not the son of the king of that city and demands to see the Herdsman (1069); he learns from the Herdsman the words conclusively proving he killed his father and married his mother (1171–81) and he swiftly takes his final steps. This pattern of learning and acting constitutes *Oedipus the King*.

The other truly haunting theme of the play is that not only is man's fate subject to chance and accident, but some of his most important acts are based on ignorance. In the opening speech to Oedipus (14–57), the Priest speaks of knowledge and learning, of acting and saving the city, and of Oedipus as "the first of men in the chances of life." The word "chance" echoes throughout the remainder of the play.

Such concern with the power of chance is new to Athenian citizens. Although the idea occurs now and then in the *Iliad*, and Paris can speak of victory in battle passing back and forth between men, destiny in that poem is attributed primarily to the gods. Herodotus, a fifth-century Athenian and a close friend of Sophocles, tells many stories of men attempting unsuccessfully to avoid their own fates. He is careful, however, to illustrate an important difference between the Asiatics and the Athenians: Eastern rulers immediately and unquestioningly act on the advice of the Delphic oracle. Croesus, when told he would destroy a mighty nation in a forthcoming battle, never stopped to consider that the nation destroyed might be his own. Athenians, however, sent to Delphi again and again for clarification, and then argued in the Assembly about whether or not they should accept the oracle's prophecy. They felt destiny was in their hands, that they ultimately had control of every situation.

Such self-confidence, very like that of Oedipus, drove the Athenians to the construction of a far-flung empire that controlled the seas and most of the country outside of Sparta's Peloponnese. The growth of these two powers, Athens and

Sparta, led to the inevitable Peloponnesian War, a war that lasted for almost thirty years. In the funeral oration in the first year of the war (Thucydides), Pericles, the leader of the empire, could still speak of the victory over the Persians in the preceding war as the triumph of intelligence over chance, and tell the people that in this war the soldiers and the citizenry should ignore hope and trust only "their own selves."

Sophocles himself fought in the war, particularly at Samos, where he saw chance in operation; a year after Pericles' stunningly confident funeral oration, the Athenians were twice defeated by the Spartan army, retreated inside the city walls, and were there struck by the unanticipated and devastating plague. Chance, they discovered, was the equal of intelligence in power. The Athenians turned violently against Pericles, who still insisted intelligence would allow them to evaluate the facts and obtain a clear vision of what was going to happen next. But even he admitted that the plague had been "something which we did not expect." And a few moments later he told an angry audience that even if Athens went down to defeat, they would be remembered by posterity (Thucydides).

Sophocles' experience both of battle and of the plague may have prompted his use of the Oedipus story to show the devastating power of chance, a power no intelligence can anticipate.

Sophocles is expanding a story referred to briefly in the *Iliad* (4.376–80). The singer of that epic knows of Polyneices, the son of Oedipus, and his war against Thebes, and a father of one of the warriors attended the funeral games in Thebes after the death of Oedipus (23.676–80). (The word used to refer to his death is one employed in situations of violent death.) The story is expanded in the *Odyssey* (xi.271–80) when Odysseus encounters Epikaste (Jocasta) among the dead and is told that Oedipus killed his father and married his mother, that this fact was shortly discovered, and that Epikaste hanged herself and Oedipus continued to rule. No curse. No children. No plague. No investigation by Oedipus. No blinding and exile. The story is blunt, without elaboration; it does not have the psychological reverberations that Sophocles provides. Lost epics, as well as lost poems of Hesiod, apparently also told the story, but these usually provided a second wife for Oedipus as the mother of Polyneices, Eteocles, Antigone, and Ismene, probably in order not to visit incestuous stain on noble houses that proudly claimed descent from the children of Oedipus. There were also other plays based on the story, including ones by Aeschylus and Euripides, but none of these have survived. The final Greek version is that of Sophocles, and he not only made it his own, but defined it for all time.

A comparison of Aeschylus' and Sophocles' titles illustrates the former's concern with the community and the latter's concern with the individual. By Aeschylus: *Suppliant Maidens, Persians, Eumenides, Seven Against Thebes.* By Sophocles: *Philoctetes, Ajax, Antigone, Electra, Oedipus the King,* and *Oedipus at Colonus.*

The change of emphasis from community to individual is also evident earlier in the presentation of the community of warriors in the *Iliad* as opposed to the focus on a central hero in the *Odyssey.* Because Odysseus and Oedipus encounter many different kinds of adversaries, they can be more completely understood than Achilleus and Klytemnestra.

Aristotle, in his *Poetics,* praises *Oedipus the King* because the recognition scene and the reversal scene are not separate, one following the other, but occur at the same moment: as soon as Oedipus recognizes who he is, he falls. This is certainly far more powerful than the sequential recognition and reversal scenes in the *Odyssey.* But then, epics tend to be episodic works, and thus extensive, whereas tragedy is climactic and intensive: every scene is a climax leading to the ultimately blinded Oedipus, the slaughtered Agamemnon, the triumphant Klytemnestra, the slaughtered Klytemnestra, the redeemed Orestes.

Jocasta matches Oedipus in intelligence, strength, and courage; indeed, they rule equally in Thebes. Her first words to

Oedipus in the play are the chastising remarks of a mother: accusing Oedipus and Creon of "foolish squabbling" and brawling, she orders them both into the house as a mother would call in rambunctious children (634–38). Later this mother of Oedipus turns into a wife as she pleads desperately with the husband she loves when she realizes, long before he does, that he is both son and husband and attempts to stop further investigation. But this is her son, he equals her in determination, and Jocasta goes into the house to kill herself. Oedipus blinds himself so that he will not have to look upon his mother and father in Hades; Jocasta chooses not to continue a life of stain and shame, and she is willing to see everything in Hades: her murdered husband and, later, her blind son-husband.

After calmly entering the palace, Jocasta abandons her composure, tears her hair, rolls on her double marriage bed in rage and grief, groaning over her double bond. But Oedipus appears to have gone mad (1237–84). He bursts into the palace, ranges frantically through the corridors, begging the servants for a sword with which to kill Jocasta, "the wife no wife," by plunging the sword into her "teeming womb." Sword in hand and bellowing like an animal, he tears the bolts out of the door sockets (foreshadowing his own blinding) and charges into the bedroom, where he sees his "wife" hanging from a roof beam. Cutting the noose, Oedipus takes down her body and then, "dreadful to see," says the Messenger, he tears away the golden brooches that "upheld" her robe, lifts them high, and dashes out his own eyeballs. The Athenian audience, knowing the nature of robes and brooches, is stunned by this report: the robe would have fallen from Jocasta's body, so that Oedipus' last vision on earth was of his naked mother-wife.

Oedipus has acted out man's life span: he himself is the answer to the Sphinx's riddle. The tragedy itself opened with a vivid presentation of the answer, as the spectators saw very young children, the middle-aged Oedipus, and the ancient Priest; it closes with the same picture, but with a horrifying change: the young children are now the miserable daughters of Oedipus, Creon is the man of middle age, and Oedipus, with his cane, is the three-legged, helpless—but still heroic—man.

Oedipus is *pharmakós*, the Greek word that can mean poison, medicine, and scapegoat. He has polluted and poisoned both Thebes and himself; he heals the city twice, first when he answers the riddle of the Sphinx, and then when he discovers the murderer and exiles himself. He is the scapegoat who must be punished in expiation of the sins of all the citizens.

By the time of Sophocles, *díkē* had more than the uncomplicated Homeric meaning of fair portion; now the word signified trial, judgment, penalty. Oedipus puts his unidentified self on trial, acts as the prosecutor and the defense attorney, judges himself, and determines his penalty. In Homeric times there was a grandeur and a nobility to man's tragic fate as the heroic Achilleus faced Hektor, knowing the prophecy that he himself was to die shortly after Hektor. The Homeric heroes accepted without question the "fair" dictates of the gods and fate. Sophocles, in *Oedipus the King*, shows man living in a mysterious and incomprehensible world where suffering is not always justified, and where man, in spite of the powers of accident, fate, and sometimes frivolous gods, acts out and accepts his own tragic destiny.

Oedipus at Colonus

I N *Oedipus at Colonus* the tragic hero challenges other men, the gods, and his own judgment of himself; he becomes a blessing for the city of Athens, and he does not experience physical death when the gods translate him from life to afterlife. The play is a moving examination of redemptive grace, the treachery of power, and the mystery of atonement and love.

To the Greeks, *krátos*, power, almost always connoted power achieved through violence, through usurpation by a *túrannos* (tyrant). Here is *húbris*, that awesome force so often weakly translated as "pride"; the word means wanton violence, insolence, lewdness, outrage, assault and battery—the latter having specific Athenian legal usage in charges of rape. The root is employed in verbal form to describe the neighing, snorting, and prancing of overfed horses, and to vegetation run wild, grown overrank. None of these descriptions fit Oedipus in either play; they are, however, appropriate to the power-mad Creon and Polyneices of *Oedipus at Colonus* in their struggle for the possession of the body of Oedipus, whose burial place will be a source of victory and power for the "host" city. Oedipus has become for Thebes a repository of past evil and future good; they will deal with this mixture by burying him on their border, hoping, by this cautious act, to secure the good and avoid the evil. The Athenians react with initial horror and loathing to the polluted Oedipus, but progress to the point where they recognize only the grace in this suffering hero.

Oedipus embodies both the Furies and the Eumenides. At the beginning of the play he recognizes he has come to his place of death when he discovers the grove is sacred to the Eumenides. The Stranger informs him (42–43) that "we call them the Eumenides, others call them the Furies," and the Chorus warns

54

Oedipus that it is dangerous to step onto the sacred ground (148–69). Through his actions as a Fury—and there *were* male Furies—Oedipus avenges his past and becomes a "kindly one" himself; a holy communicant with the Eumenides, Oedipus safely enters the sacred grove to be translated to the afterlife.

"Athens," Oedipus says at line 260, "has power." And Theseus reveals the humanity of that power when, as King of Athens, he consents to visit the grove at the request of Oedipus. His first reaction is one of compassion, and he offers Oedipus any favor that he or the city can give (551–68).

But this is not the Athens of Sophocles' youth. The Athenians who are watching this play, produced posthumously in 401, had lived to see Athens, that democracy praised by Pericles at the beginning of the Peloponnesian War as a model for the world to admire and emulate, turn into an insolent, snorting horse, violating allies who tried to withdraw peacefully from their league by murdering all the men, selling the women and children into slavery, and wantonly destroying conquered cities. The year 405 saw Sparta's victory over Athens at the battle of Aegospotami; the coming year would see Athens itself under siege: like Oedipus, without friends, money, or armor. Athens accepted the terms for peace and became subject to Sparta. Oedipus refuses the peace terms offered by his son and his uncle/brother-in-law and turns to Theseus and Athens for atonement. In Theseus, Sophocles presents the audience with a memory of Pericles and what Athenian democratic power once was; in Oedipus he leaves his final testimony on the simultaneously blessed and cursed state of humanity.

The awesome and mysterious power of Oedipus is that he has become a sacred instrument of grace, *kháris*, a gift. Unlike *Oedipus the King*, this is not a play of discovery for Oedipus; before the opening of the action, he knows that he "didn't do anything." (The translation "did not sin" at line 539 is widespread; there was no Greek word for sin, and Sophocles wrote "didn't do anything.") He was a man without freedom of choice, he asserts, the gods having forced him to kill his father—an act, moreover, committed in self-defense—and marry his mother (540–48). As these were involuntary acts, he should not have been punished. Athenians knew their laws, and the Athenian Assembly would have found Oedipus legally not guilty. But morally, of course, Oedipus is guilty: knowingly or unknowingly, he did do these things. A son who accidentally shoots and kills his father on a hunting trip is found legally not guilty; nonetheless, the son considers himself morally guilty. Couldn't I have been more careful? he asks himself repeatedly. But what might have been is no longer the case; nor should readers of *Oedipus the King* wonder why, given the prophecy, Oedipus would kill any man old enough to be his father and marry any woman old enough to be his mother. Ideas that are not in the play are not part of the play: counterfactual speculations are no longer commonly accepted in contemporary historical theory, and they never should have been in literary criticism.

Oedipus has learned and the gods have learned; Apollo, having caused Oedipus so much suffering, rewards him with sacred gifts as belated recompense; Oedipus accepts them in the kindly way befitting a man who has himself become a gift of grace. In a remarkable anticipation of Christian doctrine, Oedipus directs Antigone to perform the libation to the Eumenides of which he is physically incapable: It does not need to be performed by me, he says, anyone can go for me as one soul can pay in full for countless others, if it is kindly (495–502). The role of Oedipus himself has been to become an offering in payment for the sufferings of others: through his own unfathomable suffering he has cleansed the stains of pollution from Antigone, Ismene, Jocasta, and Laius. And through this suffering have come not only wisdom and the transfiguring beauty of redemptive grace and love, but the strength to bring down curses on threatening enemies, even if they be an uncle and a son. Love is the concluding message of *Oedipus at Colonus*; love has the greatest *krátos*, power, of all.

Since at least the time of Homer there have been three Greek words relating to love: *érōs, agápē,* and *philía. Érōs* is the word associated with sexual desire. *Agápē* refers to brotherly love, charity, and the love for a beloved son or man. *Philía* extends this love for kin out into the world of friends, dear ones, those to whom one is loving and kindly. Homer frequently used the word to express feelings about one's own body, as he does in expressing Achilleus' love for the strength of his own arm or for his own heart.

Érōs is not a part of *Oedipus at Colonus*, but *agápē* and *philía* are. When the daughters of Oedipus are returned to him by Theseus, he exclaims at line 1110: "I have what is dearest to me in the world." Shortly thereafter, thunder and lightning herald his imminent departure from life; suffering and time have taught him *philía*, love for his own heart, and *agápē*, to receive lovingly those who love him; he can now leave in *shantih*, the Sanskrit word for "the peace which passeth understanding." In a final message to his children and the world, Oedipus reveals his transcendent knowledge: "One word frees us of all the weight and pain of life: love." And the word for love Sophocles uses in this speech is not *érōs* or *agápē*, but one of the forms of *philía* (1611–19).

The gods, impatient in their longing for Oedipus, call out: "You delay too long; you delay too long." The Messenger reports that the blind Oedipus says farewell to his children, and when the Messenger and the children have gone on a little way, they turn back and see that Oedipus has vanished. There was no bolt from the sky or whirlwind from the sea, the Messenger continues, "but he was taken."

Only Theseus, King of Athens, is allowed to see Oedipus' leave-taking, for the Messenger himself is momentarily blinded by the sight and knows only that an attendant from the heavens came for him and lifted him up, or that the doors of earth opened in benevolent welcome. Oedipus is now both Hero-god of the Sky and Hero-god of the Earth: like earlier hero-gods such as Achilleus, Oedipus will have worshipers who will offer libations at his sacred shrine.

He has become *pharmakós* for Athens as he was *pharmakós*

for Thebes, but this time he is a healing medicine, not a poison, and he has been offered up for the purification of others. The Chorus admonishes those assembled to cease weeping and mourning, as everything is in the hands of *kûros*. This last word of the play, the last written word of Sophocles we have, signifies not only supreme power and authority, but also validity, security. The verb from which it is derived illuminates this apocalyptic moment: everything has been accomplished, satisfied, validated. Settled.

Antigone

T HE ACTUAL CHRONOLOGY of events in the three Theban plays is not the sequence in which they were written. *Antigone*, the first play, was written when Sophocles was in his mid-fifties, *Oedipus the King* when he was around seventy, and *Oedipus at Colonus* when he was ninety. At the heart of all three plays is Sophocles' concern with the relationship between the individual and the state during a time when the Athenian empire was growing in power over its own citizens as well as its allies. The Peloponnesian War began ten years after *Antigone* was produced, the war was in its early stages when *Oedipus the King* was written, and the Athenian empire was on the eve of final collapse when Sophocles wrote *Oedipus at Colonus*. Although all three plays are concerned with the same family, they do not form a trilogy: unlike the *Oresteia*, they were written and produced separately.

Antigone is the first heroine of Western drama, and the play bears her name rather than Creon's, even though she disappears halfway through the action; indeed, some commentators have suggested the play should be named after Creon, but the specter of Antigone hovers over the play after her entombment, and it is she who has the determination, strength of character, and willingness to accept her fate—characteristics heretofore reserved for heroes. Klytemnestra has determination and strength, but she cries out against her fate. Moreover, Antigone is a strong *woman* with no desire to play a masculine role; she is marrying death rather than Haemon. No gods protect her, any more than they did her father in *Oedipus the King*. Like Oedipus, she stands alone.

This lone individual, isolated from the gods and from other people, is the representative Sophoclean hero or heroine. Ajax,

Philoctetes, Oedipus, Electra, Antigone: the heroes and heroines who give their names to these plays are all truly alienated from the world around them; they are angry people, and they fight fiercely for their rights. Ajax can be overcome only when he is driven mad by Athena, Philoctetes refuses to bend to the will of Odysseus, Oedipus is transformed into a hero-god, and Electra conquers Klytemnestra. But Antigone dies the death of a tragic heroine: after her farewell to the world in the long and beautiful extended lyrical processional, she kills herself rather than allow Creon to slowly starve her to death. Antigone, like her mother, Jocasta, hangs herself.

Sophoclean characters are possessed by *thumós*, vehement passions of spirited wrath and courageous anger; Achilleus in the *Iliad* foreshadows Sophoclean tragic figures. But *thumós* can also mean life, breath, soul, heart, and Antigone rages against the world with all her heart and soul.

The Sophoclean character chooses death: Ajax, Jocasta, Antigone, and, before them, Achilleus. These characters are truly independent. Because they refuse to compromise, they are impossible people to deal with. Totally lacking in moderation, unable, as Haemon says of Creon, to bend with the wind or take in their sails, they break apart like trees in hurricanes or ships in storms. But they are neither trees nor ships: Sophoclean men and women *are* the hurricanes, the tornadoes. These tempestuous souls are full of irate temper, sure of their rightness, and unyieldingly stubborn. The Chorus says of Antigone that she is stubborn and does not know how to give in to misfortune (471–72). They are wrong: she doesn't know how to give in to Creon's refusal to bury her brother, but she does know how to give in to death. Sophoclean men and women are *autónomos*; they are laws unto themselves.

The traditional interpretations of *Antigone* focus on individual versus state, religion versus state, natural law versus man-made law, and man versus woman. Because these unchallenged interpretations usually come along with the play as part of the package, they need to be examined.

The *Oresteia* is about justice, and in each of the three plays a case is argued: that Klytemnestra is just, that Orestes and Electra are just, and, finally, the older justice of the Furies contends with that of the new, younger gods Athena and Apollo. But nowhere in *Antigone* is there such sustained argument about the rights of the individual versus the rights of the state. Rather, the play presents an unyielding *túrannos* against an unyielding young woman in a contest of wills in which neither person wins. Like the brothers Eteocles and Polyneices, both are devastated by the battle. Had one been victorious, it might then have been said Sophocles' *primary* concern was the individual versus the state; however, if anything, the play is concerned with wrong against wrong, as two stubborn people absolutely refuse to compromise.

Closely related to the above is another theme most often cited as the "meaning" of the play: religion versus the state. According to this interpretation, Antigone's religious conscience commands that she bury her brother and this comes into conflict with Creon's civic decree that he not be buried. The play is far more complicated than this conflict, or the one between natural law and man-made law: that natural obligation everywhere to bury the dead as opposed to an edict decreed by one man prohibiting burial. Antigone herself argues against these interpretations when she states that if she were married and had children, she would not defy the decree of the state, but rather let her husband or child lie rotting in the field, as there would still be the possibility of acquiring another husband or child; but since her parents are dead, she can never have another brother. With this outrageous sophistic reasoning Antigone denies religious motivation, devotion to natural law, and the old order—the traditional readings of her character.

One of the most important factors in the interpretation of literature is the determination of a critical *position*. A text can be regarded from three viewpoints: that of readers at the time the work first appeared, that of readers at any time since, and—the most crucial—that of the author of the text. For what

Sophocles thinks about Antigone is the one central factor that does not change throughout time or from reader to reader: it *is* the text, it *is* the meaning of the play.

Certainly, the battlefield of critical interpretation is strewn with the bodies of victims of the intentional fallacy, those readers who think they know why an author wrote a text when there is no evidence the author even knew. Did Shakespeare write *Hamlet* because of the recent deaths of his son and of his father? And, if so, what light does it throw upon the meaning of the play? None, other than satisfying the natural hunger for extraliterary information.

But great writers don't shout out their position in the text; rather they demonstrate their position through action. The most significant evidence is not what the characters say about themselves, but, more often, what the author has them do.

Antigone is a play about doing, about action, rather than about thinking. It is thus closer to epic than most Athenian dramas, and Antigone is comrade-in-arms to Achilleus. Even when Haemon indulges in such Aeschylean thoughts as "moderation is best," he presents them in terms of trees bending in the wind and ships taking in their sails rather than in an ethical epigram. Antigone and Creon are Aristotelian actors rather than Platonic thinkers.

Sophocles constantly employs words of action rather than Aeschylean noun patterns such as net, snare, trap, light, dark, sick, and medicine. Noun images work well for picturing stasis, for creating moods, but Sophocles is more interested in men and women in action in *Antigone* than in Aeschylean philosophical speculations; the *Eumenides* is talk, not action; telling, not showing. Before *Oedipus the King* begins, Oedipus steps into the snare Apollo sets, and he spends the play in pursuit of information about the trap, whereas Creon, one suspects, knowingly sets a trap for Antigone that will snap on her *during* the action of the play.

Antigone is a tough, strong-willed individual, and she is proud. How dare Creon, she exclaims to Ismene (31–32), give orders *"to me!"* [emphasis mine]. Creon is *túrannos*, and she will have none of him. He has been King of Thebes only a few days, assuming that role after Eteocles and Polyneices, the two sons of Oedipus, died stabbing each other to death. As Eteocles was defending the city against the attempted usurpation of Polyneices, he is buried, but the body of Polyneices is tossed away like garbage and left to be scavenged by dogs and vultures; unburied, he will spend a restless eternity, unclaimed by the gods of the underworld. Creon's edict against burial is the outrageous action of a tyrant: anyone who attempts to bury Polyneices will be stoned to death. Unlike Aegisthus, the lover of Klytemnestra, Creon assures Antigone at line 524 that "no woman will rule me while I live." This tyrant disdains the advice of everyone. He turns away Tiresias, ignores the pleading of his son, and he is especially disdainful of women, casually responding to Ismene's plea that Antigone should be spared as she is Haemon's betrothed with the lewd suggestion that Haemon will find "other fields" in which to plant his seed. Sending the two sisters into the house as prisoners, he assures the Chorus (578–79) that he has succeeded in forcing the two sisters to "live as women and not run free."

Antigone, contrary to the usual interpretation, is not really fanatically committed to the laws of religion and the gods: she buries her brother only because he cannot be replaced. Commentators since Aristotle have recoiled from her argument, deciding that it weakens her character. They miss the point. The Greek syntax of her speech is confusing, aberrant, mangled: apparently Sophocles is showing that Antigone is at her wits' end, that even she doesn't know why she buried her brother (891–905). Antigone only knows that she has been figuratively dead for many years, and that she wants to die. This death wish of Antigone is her most powerful motivation in the play: "My life died long ago," she says to Ismene, using a word that means life, heart, *and* soul (559–60). Antigone is—not without reason— an obsessed and frantic young woman.

The reasons for her hysterical obsession with death are

obvious: her mother killed herself, her father was also her brother, and she spent her adolescent years wandering with him as exile, as beggar. Exiles are effigies of human nature; they must be *autónomos*, laws unto themselves, because they are the outlaws of civilization: they live outside the world of law and have no defenses. Now Antigone has returned to Thebes, her brothers are dead by each other's hands, her uncle, Creon, has become *túrannos*, and he is desecrating the body of her brother. She knows only how to be *autónomos*, and she wants to join her mother, her father, and her two brothers in death; but Polyneices will be absent from the family portrait in Hades unless he is buried.

And buried he is. But not by Creon in expiation, as he claims. No, Sophocles is careful to point out that Polyneices has been buried by Antigone the first time, before she was caught. Sophocles has the Guard tell Creon that the "burial is accomplished," that the dust on the flesh makes the "ritual complete." To drive home his point, Sophocles continues with the Guard saying that the dust Antigone hastily sprinkled on the body was "enough to turn the curse," as no wild beast or dog had been near and the body had thus been buried untorn (245–77).

And so Creon gives the desperate order that the dust be removed from the body and that it remain in the open to be mutilated by wild animals. Does this mean the body is returned to an unburied state? Do the gods of the underworld wait around for Creon's permission before they accept the soul, or do they claim what is theirs the moment Antigone "accomplishes" the burial? Sophocles certainly believes the latter to be the case. The "ritual is complete," he writes. Then what is Creon doing? At this point the outrageous *túrannos* is insulting the body of Polyneices; he can no longer touch the soul. It is for this reason that the Iliadic heroes not only deny the vanquished entrance to Hades but, by stripping their armor and leaving their bodies to vultures and dogs, they attempt to erase bodily identity as well by preventing a memorial marker at a grave site.

If the burial is now complete, then why does Antigone make

her dangerous return when the body is even more closely guarded? It cannot be to protect the body from wild beasts: no specks of dust or drops of wine are going to accomplish that. Antigone returns to be apprehended. To be tried. To be stoned to death. She grasps at straws when she says, in the syntactically mangled speech that betrays her inner turmoil, that she buried him only because he was a brother and thus irreplaceable. No, Antigone buries her brother so that she can join him and Eteocles and Oedipus and Jocasta in death. Truly, for Antigone, her life ended long ago when she was a child and discovered that her father was also her dishonored brother.

The dead are killing the living (871). This is Sophocles' point in the play, and although he makes certain it will not be overlooked, readers since Aristotle have somehow managed to do so by accepting the received interpretations of the play without question. "In my beginning is my end," Eliot writes in the *Four Quartets*. The text is clearly concerned with the past devouring the future. In the antistrophe that begins at line 582, the Chorus sings, after the arrests of Antigone and Ismene, that woe generates woe and "sorrows never end" but are handed on from generation to generation. At line 1064 Tiresias warns Creon that he will suffer just as Antigone and Haemon have suffered. During the emotional processional to her tomb, Antigone responds to the suggestion of the Chorus that she is perhaps paying for her "father's pain" (856) with the words that she goes to join her family in death. Antigone addresses her dead brother in tones that certainly indicate she believes him to be at rest in Hades, for, as she has paid her "due rights" (902–03), she does not bemoan a task unaccomplished.

All the characters in the play are confused about who is living and who is dead. Antigone, sent to be buried alive, takes her own life; Haemon rushes at his father to kill him, and then turns the sword upon himself; and the dead kill the living when Eurydice, upon hearing of the death of her son, takes her own life. Tiresias tells Creon (1064–90) that before the day is out Creon will give up his son for Antigone—"corpse for these corpses," he warns. He admonishes Creon that he has confused the "upper" and the "lower" worlds by sending a living person, Antigone, to a tomb, and that Creon keeps up here on earth what belongs below. Apparently sharing Creon's belief that the body of Polyneices remains unburied, the precautious Tiresias warns Creon of the dangers of robbing the underworld gods of the soul that is rightfully theirs.

Tiresias is a character in a play, not the voice of Sophocles any more than Hamlet is the voice of Shakespeare. The error in interpreting the play is to assume Sophocles agrees with Tiresias' and Creon's belief that the soul has been somehow snatched from the arms of the underworld gods when the dust was removed from the body. Either Antigone and the Guard are right and the burial is accomplished for all time, or Tiresias is right in assuming that Creon has become more powerful than the gods. Thebes has been physically shattered by the Seven Against Thebes, and moral and spiritual decay has swiftly followed.

Sophocles believes that man cannot make himself the center of the universe. Antigone, *autónomos*, does put herself at the center of the universe. The Chorus, in one of the most ironic moments in all Greek theater, sings the great hymn to the glory of man immediately preceding the entrance of the captured Antigone. Praising the wonders of man, the Chorus extols his accomplishments as helmsman who conquers the seas, plowman who makes the soil fertile, hunter who snares birds and beasts and fish, clever trainer who tames wild animals, and, finally, through mastering "language," "thought," and "feeling," the builder of civilization. The hymn has been a constant source of puzzlement to commentators, as it seems to be out of place at this point and even in this play. But this is not the case if Sophocles, a deeply religious and patriotic man, is presenting a secular view of man as the center of the universe to which Sophocles himself is not committed.

But death will claim everyone, and pride and stubbornness

will show their destructive power in this play about a man and a woman who refuse to honor both god and state. Antigone dies; Creon becomes a "living corpse." One must, Sophocles is saying, accept the human condition and not try to become a god. Antigone is wrong; Creon is wrong. The action of the play pits wrong against wrong.

Bacchae

I N HIS *Poetics* Aristotle quotes Sophocles as saying that he presented men as they ought to be, whereas Euripides painted men as they are. It is certainly true that Euripides' earthy view of women gained him a reputation as a misogynist; he is, however, neither misanthrope nor misogynist; he simply paints men and women as he finds them. To Sophocles, Electra is a resolute, rebellious heroine; to Euripides, she is a self-punishing, mocking, ironic, and, at times, vicious young woman.

Euripides is also quite capable of seeing the comic in the tragic, of turning Menelaos into a buffoon and Klytemnestra into an eagerly expectant grandmother. He is a dualist who tricks us into switching our sympathies from Medea to Jason when Medea slaughters their two children, or changing our dislike of the wrathful, prideful, petulant young Pentheus into pity for his wretched end at the hands of his mother. Audiences at the performances of these plays in Euripides' time were as shocked as modern readers and audiences; this is reflected in antiquity in the paltry number of prizes (four) awarded Euripides in Athens during his lifetime. Although he became immensely popular only after his death, he has always been loved by intellectuals for his paradoxical views and his ironic humor.

Sophocles and Euripides died in the same year, 406 B.C.. They lived long lives that saw the victory over the Persian invaders, the rapid rise of the Athenian empire, Athens' descent from benevolent democracy into one hungry for power, and her imminent defeat at the hands of the darker and even more tyrannous force of Sparta. Their final plays, *Oedipus at Colonus* and the *Bacchae*, present opposing world-viewpoints: Sophocles finds the gods forgiving, merciful, generous, whereas Euripides finds them wrathful, jealous of their power, vain, and untrustworthy.

The *Bacchae* is a highly problematic play and there may well never be a definitive interpretation to satisfy every reader. Perhaps there could not and should not be such certainty, particularly as the play itself is about the unpredictability of fate and the disorder of existence. Humans may be, as Nietzsche claims they are, more humane than the gods, and life may not be fair, as it is not when Dionysus punishes *everyone* in the play, including his eager early believers, the harmless Cadmus and the well-meaning Tiresias.

The play is to be *apprehended*, grasped by the senses, rather than *comprehended* by the mind, for Euripides is concerned in the *Bacchae*, as he is in so many of his plays, with the strength of natural forces—with love and revenge in *Medea*, with honor and jealousy in *Hippolytus*, and with the nonrational, ruthless natural force of Dionysian instinctive ecstasy in the *Bacchae*. The world of morality is one of conscious choice, of will and the intellect. Nature, instinct, and necessity do not partake of that world; instead, they disrupt and destroy man's cherished notion that he is in control of a rational and ordered universe. The Dionysian force is not concerned with ethics; it is "beyond good and evil," and it makes human beings who deny elemental human instincts strangers in their own strange land, alienated from world and self. Euripidean heroes and heroines suffer total degradation, not only of their physical but also of their spiritual natures; Euripides anticipates Flaubert, who said of his characters, "I will dip them all in *merde*."

The meaning of the Dionysiac experience can best be understood by examining the myths associated with the god.

When Diomedes and Glaukos first encounter each other on the battlefield at 6.119 of the *Iliad*, before they realize they are guest-friends, Diomedes asks first if Glaukos is a god, explaining that he would never fight a god. (Although he actually does this—wounding both Aphrodite and Ares—it is only with Athena's explicit permission.) As an example of why he would not, he briefly recounts the story of Lykourgos, who once chased the female followers of the "raving" Dionysus through sacred woods, slaying them as they dropped their "sacred implements" to the ground; the "terrified" boy-god Dionysus dived into the waves of the sea, where Thetis comforted him at her bosom. The older gods on Olympus, enraged at the behavior of Lykourgos toward the newest of the gods, blinded him and shortly afterward took away his life.

The basic elements of the story are present from the beginning: Dionysus is both immortal god and "terrified" man, he has women followers who carry sacred implements (the thyrsus), and Dionysus and his women are attacked by a warrior who, like Pentheus, is possessed by arrogance. Although no reason is given for Lykourgos' attack on the women, Homer's listeners would well imagine it to be an attack on their "orgies"—a word that means religious ecstasy rather than sexual frenzy. Lykourgos and Pentheus, to their peril, cannot distinguish between the two.

Dionysus is a god born of a mortal woman, and he may well be a god only because Hera, jealous of Zeus' infatuation with Semele, convinces him that he should "visit" her as a god—rather than in the human form he usually assumes for his seductions of mortal women—knowing that the lightning blast of the sexual union will destroy Semele at the moment of penetration and conception. Zeus snatches Dionysus from Semele's flaming womb and conceals the embryo within his own body; upon giving birth to Dionysus, he provides Hera with a dummy for her to destroy and gives Dionysus to the infant's aunt to be brought up; she is driven mad and slaughters her own child.

Dionysus is thus part man and part god, and he plays both roles in the *Bacchae*, being god in the beginning and the end, and "stranger," man, in the middle section. He is also symbolically killed twice, once when he is entombed in the dungeon prison and again in the person of his surrogate, Pentheus, who, in the investiture scene in which he is dressed as a woman, becomes *therápōn* for Dionysus, as Patroklos became *therápōn* for Achilleus when he put on his friend's armor.

Dismemberment and subsequent resurrection of the body of Dionysus are essential elements of the story of his origin, as are the intricate involvements of the family of Cadmus.

Demeter and Zeus were children of Cronus; through union with his sister Demeter—the goddess earth-mother who taught man agriculture—Persephone was born. This young woman, so beloved that she was carried off by Hades to become Queen of the Underworld, obviously represented the agricultural seasons, as she spent six months underground and six months above. In one of the mythical stories of the origin of Dionysus, the union of Zeus and Persephone, his daughter by his sister, resulted in the birth of Dionysus. The Titans, encouraged by the apparently perpetually jealous Hera—who certainly had reason to be so—destroyed and devoured the infant Dionysus. But Athena, born full-grown from Zeus' head, rescued her brother's heart and brought it to Zeus, who swallowed it. Zeus destroyed the Titans with lightning; from the ashes sprang up the race of men, who were thus both human and divine. Zeus, in his fiery sexual union with Semele, miraculously implanted in her the heart of Dionysus; Semele went up in smoke, Dionysus was again rescued, implanted in Zeus' "male womb," his thigh, and he was finally born. Another name for Dionysus is Zagreus, which might be Thracian and certainly means "torn in pieces."

One must erase from the mind the cherubic, jolly, drunken, dissolute Roman Dionysus (Bacchus), and replace him with the terribly insecure, wrathful, and jealous young god we find in Euripides. Associated with him in the stories are multiple human and divine mothers, a father who creates a womb within himself, a nature both human and divine, the bringing of intoxication in the form of wine to humanity, and female followers who, in religious frenzy, slaughter their own children. A youth with the form and grace of a young woman, Dionysus is grandson to the goddess of earth and grain, son to a father who was also his mother, and is himself the powerful, androgynous nature-god.

The final feature of the Dionysiac ritual is *sparagmós* and *ōmophagía*. Part of the ceremony in honor of the god Dionysus is *sparagmós*, the tearing apart of the live body of an animal or a human being who has become *therápōn*, the ritual substitute for the body of Dionysus, and *ōmophagía*, the eating of the live flesh and drinking of the warm blood. By eating the god and drinking his blood, one becomes *éntheos*: imbued with the power of the god.

The plague that struck Athens in the first years of the Peloponnesian War, the unnecessary butchery of both friends and enemies, and the total loss of self-control led many Athenians to return to the earlier and more primitive Dionysiac celebrations. The religion, complete with rituals of animal or human sacrifice, lasted well into the second century of the Christian era.

Dionysus is also the god of theater, for the origin of drama lies in the choral odes, dithyrambs, sung in his honor, odes that became drama when Thespis, traditionally the first actor, stepped out from the Chorus and engaged in dialogue with it. The Theater of Dionysus, on the slope of the Acropolis, where the *Bacchae* was first performed after the death of Euripides, contained, like all Greek theaters, a throne constructed in the center of the first tier to be occupied by the High Priest of Dionysus at all theatrical productions. And this Priest was at the performance of the *Bacchae*, watching, along with fifteen thousand spectators, the god he served act out the cruel and terrible ritual of *sparagmós* and *ōmophagía* on the body of Pentheus, whose name means grief and mourning.

The *Bacchae*, then, is a play about the Dionysian irrational force, not only in the world but in all human beings, a force one must accept and learn to live with or die; about an adolescent, Pentheus, who decides too soon who he is, and who would deny his own sexuality and suppress that of others; about the punishment of mankind when a new god, a new religion, a new ideational force is accepted too soon, too casually, or not at all;

and, finally, it is a tragedy about tragedy, a construct of theater about theater. From beginning to end the play explores all these ideas as Euripides dramatically illustrates two responses to Dionysian force: his Bacchants, the onstage Chorus of women followers, have gratefully accepted the life-enhancing spirit, whereas the offstage women of Thebes—and women and men are separated throughout most of the play—have had it rudely forced upon them. If accepted, as it is by the Bacchants, then the Dionysian force is absorbed and controlled: it becomes a source of wisdom and joy in a *measured* intoxication with life. But the women of Thebes have mocked and rejected the power of Dionysus, and when that power is denied and suppressed, it explodes into a totally uncontrolled irrational frenzy, into the extremes of their behavior on Mount Cithaeron.

Euripides is not as guilty as some readers charge in his use of the *deus ex machina*, the "god from the machine" who appeared suspended from a crane to resolve an otherwise unsatisfactory ending. He does, however, frequently begin or end a play by presenting a god or goddess, using one in the opening to relate the background of the action, stress the ways in which the divinity has been wronged by a human being, and outline what is going to be done about it. There is no contest; the human beings have no chance. At the opening of *Hippolytus* Aphrodite casually announces her deadly plans for Hippolytus, a young man, blood brother to Pentheus, who also suppresses his sexual nature. Dionysus appears at the opening of the *Bacchae*: he is an effeminate youth with long blond curls, and he wears a smiling mask that will continue to smile even when he is at his most cruel. He announces to the audience his previous conquests, the reluctance of many people to accept him as a god, especially here in Thebes, the place where he was conceived by Semele and Zeus—and that, having driven the women of the city mad, he is now going to prove himself a god, especially to Pentheus. The audience knows Pentheus and Dionysus are cousins: of the three children of three sisters, Actaeon is hunted down and killed by his own dogs when he *accidentally*—but even then impiously—spies the naked Artemis bathing in a pool, and Pentheus is destroyed for impiously rejecting the godhood of his cousin Dionysus. To this end Dionysus has taken on mortal form; he has changed his "shape" to that of a man. The Bacchants, his followers, respond to his speech with celebration of Dionysus in one of his names, Bromius, the clangor-god, the boisterous dancing-god.

These choruses are charged with nervous energy, as is the entire play, an effect made even more powerful by the startling contrast between the Aeschylean archaic formality of the verse and the wild frenzy of the content; the meter, rhythm—and at times the vocabulary—are traditional and stately as the chorus sings of Dionysus savagely hunting down wild goats and killing them, and his delight in eating their raw flesh.

There is further contrast in the ridiculous appearance of Tiresias and Cadmus, two distinguished elderly men dressed in the wild-fawn skins of the Bacchants. Their incongruous appearance is heightened by the image of *sophía*, wisdom, which occurs over and over in their dialogue, for theirs is the false wisdom—to Euripides—of conformity. They perhaps represent the power politics of Athenian rulers toward the end of the war.

The most striking aspect of Pentheus is his youth: he is a beardless young man (1185–88), a phrase used in Athens to describe a boy of fourteen or fifteen, that awkward age between puberty and young manhood; indeed, his grandfather Cadmus refers to him as a "boy." This, of course, is the great tragedy of Pentheus: an unformed youth, just past puberty, who should be in the process of *becoming*, has too soon settled down into *being*. Dionysus himself is also in the process of becoming, of establishing himself as a god, and Euripides pits god-becoming against man-becoming. God wins.

Pentheus has a prurient and lewd interest in sex, not a boyish curiosity; sex both attracts and repels him, and the first response of this youthful king is to lock up women he suspects of performing "deeds of shame" with men in secret hideaways

(221–25). This is all so terribly sad; to him, his mother and his aunts are animals to be hunted down and captured by armed horsemen (778–86): Pentheus has not yet learned that no bowmen can restrain the Dionysian force. He intends to cut off the head of the god who leads them (239–41); were it not for their age, he would send Tiresias and his own grandfather Cadmus to prison also (258–62).

Pentheus confuses political power with sexual power; to him, to submit to sexual drives is to give up control of both his masculine self-image and his political image. He thus represses his own sexuality and would suppress that of others.

Tiresias delivers to Pentheus a lengthy speech on the good that Dionysus brings to mankind by entering the body through wine; but Pentheus, he warns, has gone mad, and there is no medicine to save him (266–327). Unfortunately for Tiresias and for Cadmus, expediency is their prime reason for accepting Dionysus—that and family pride on the part of Cadmus: even if Dionysus is a "fraudulent" god, he insists (330–42), Pentheus should persuade himself that he isn't; after all, he continues, it brings distinction to have a god in the family!

Pentheus, of course, makes a deadly mistake in ordering force employed against Dionysus. Like Creon, Pentheus is a tyrant and will come to a bad end: both of them threaten to have those who disagree with them stoned to death.

The choral ode that follows the order to imprison Dionysus is apparently close to the heart of Euripides (370–433). Scorned by Athens as an atheist and an independent-minded trouble-maker, he had retreated into self-exile to spend his last years in the court of a Macedonian king. There he found himself close to the Thracian origins of the Dionysian religion, and discovered more of a kinship with this god of nature than with the sophisticated urban society of Athens. Euripides has the Chorus sing of his own renewal, of the happiness the good things of nature bring, of the wisdom of embracing simplicity. Wisdom, the Chorus asserts, is bought not with knowledge but with an uncomplicated pastoral existence. One should beware of arrogant attitudes, and by this Euripides must mean Athenian society and the festering Athenian empire, where men's spirits attempt to soar "too high for mortal men": they "shall see few days." Happiness is to be found among common people and simple things. "For me shall suffice," he concludes this great choral ode, again—it seems to me—speaking for himself, "the faith of the heart of simple people." He wrote this shortly before his death in 406; a few years later, in 404, the Athens that soared "too high for mortal men" would collapse in defeat. Euripides is perhaps suggesting that Pentheus is the Athenian empire, a world that has lost self-control, moderation, and human decency, and is barbaric to friends and enemies alike.

It is rash and dangerous to treat brutally a god who is capable of working miracles, as Pentheus does when he has the Bacchants chained, and the captured and bound Dionysus brought before him, guarded by soldiers.

In this first *agṓn* with Dionysus (451–518), Pentheus, against his will, finds his beautiful young cousin attractive; but, quickly correcting this statement, he modifies it: "to women, that is." Pentheus mocks the fair skin and long curls of Dionysus, but shows a vulgar materialistic curiosity about the benefits to be enjoyed from the Dionysian experience. And he is obsessed with sex. When Dionysus speaks of the nightly devotions to him, Pentheus asserts that they must be "lewd"; Dionysus, referring to Pentheus' obscene interest in sex, suggests that lewdness can occur in the daytime also.

Pentheus cannot accept the androgynous nature of human sexuality, and so he threatens to cut off the "dainty tresses" of Dionysus. Pentheus fears the spirit of woman in man, fears the woman in himself, and attempts to transform Dionysus' male-female nature into one that is solely masculine.

The order of Pentheus to have Dionysus chained is answered in the most revealing lines to Pentheus in the play: "You don't know anything about your life," Dionysus charges, "or what you are doing, or *what you are*" [emphasis mine]. The androgynous sexuality of the religion of Dionysus becomes pointed when the

Chorus of Bacchants sings (526–30) that Zeus, addressing Dionysus as Dithyrambus—theater itself—calls the wombless unborn infant to enter the "womb of the father."

The chained Dionysus—Bromius, the "clangor-god"—performs his second miracle when, amid thunder, lightning, and an earthquake that destroys the palace of Pentheus, he resurrects himself, after Pentheus has wrestled vainly with a bull—one of the manifestations of Dionysus—that he thought was the actual Dionysus; but then, throughout the action of the play, Pentheus confuses illusion and symbol with reality.

The report of the Messenger to Pentheus (677–774) concerning the behavior of the women of Thebes who have been transformed into a maddened and extreme form of Bacchants on Mount Cithaeron—that place where Oedipus was left to die when he was an infant—displays the closest connection yet between the Dionysian religion and nature: the women are overcome by nature. They sleep with oak leaves as pillows, modestly, not drunkenly. Euripides makes an important point here: had they accepted Dionysian "wine," they would not shortly have burst forth from this extreme lethargy into wild and uncontrolled murderous frenzy.

Dressed in fawn skins, they wear around their shoulders writhing snakes that lick their cheeks. Breasts swollen with milk, new mothers who have left their children at home nurse fawns and wolf cubs in their arms. Wearing ivy and oak leaves in their hair, they commune with nature. When one of them strikes her thyrsus against a rock, cool water comes springing out; another touches the earth, and wine pours forth; when they scratch the "breast" of the earth with their fingertips, milk begins to flow; honey streams from their wands.

This exaggerated version of a gentle and bountiful nature that has been forced upon the women of Thebes can also suddenly turn cruel and terrible. When the Messenger and his companions attempt to seize Agave, the women turn upon the men, who barely escape the rending grasps. The women, frenzied, swoop down upon the pasturing cattle, and with their

hands they rend the bellowing cows, tear the calves to bloody
shreds, hurl ribs and cloven hooves among the trees as they
gobble raw meat, flakes of flesh hanging from their lips and
blood dribbling beneath the pines. They hurl bulls to the earth,
drag them off, and then strip the raw flesh from the bones.
Most horrible of all, and certainly recalling the origins of
Dionysiac ritual when, instead of a goat or a bull as sacrificial
therápōn, the worshipers of Dionysus slaughtered human beings,
the Bacchants swoop down on a village, where they slaughter
men, women, babes in arms, and then return to the forest,
where the snakes lick the blood from their limbs.

The Messenger pleads with Pentheus to receive Dionysus
into the city so that the slaughter will end: "Dionysus gave men
wine that assuages grief; when no more wine is allowed, then
Love is not, and there is no more joy."

The Leader of the Chorus assures Pentheus that Dionysus
is no less than any other god (775–77). No reason is given, but
it is obvious that Euripides thinks Dionysus is great because he
does not live on Mount Olympus among the other gods and
goddesses, but rather in the physical and spiritual world of
mankind itself. But, of course, Pentheus immediately calls out
the troops; he knows no other response to necessity: he will not
endure this behavior from women. Again he behaves toward
women and the instincts of women as does that other tyrant
who also little knows himself, Creon.

Then follow two scenes that are among the most pitiful and
terrifying in all drama: Dionysus tempts the Peeping Tom in
Pentheus to dress as a Bacchant in order to spy on the women
and then—following a choral ode in which Euripides praises
ancient religions, calls for glory and honor to that which time
has sanctioned, and urges that long tradition turns human laws
into the laws of nature—Dionysus appears with the transformed
Pentheus.

The important point here is that Pentheus is totally mad
now: he sees two suns, and Dionysus has become a bull with
horns. Euripides, in a brave and daring theatrical stroke, pro-

vides a last vision of Pentheus that is both stingingly comic and devastatingly sad: with petulant vanity—he is going to his death—this King of Thebes worries about whether or not his curls are in place, his girdle straight, his dress hanging in proper folds, and in which hand he should carry his wand. Pentheus has become so insane he thinks he can not only lift onto his shoulders the glens and valleys of Mount Cithaeron, but the Bacchants as well. In his imagination he can already see the women mating in the bushes "like birds."

As he is tempted further, Pentheus complains that Dionysus will make him soft and delicate and effeminate. In chilling response, Dionysus assures him that he intends to do just that, meaning that he will transform and destroy the real Pentheus. (A fairly free translation of these lines—but one that communicates the message—has Pentheus saying: "You will spoil me," followed by Dionysus: "I mean to spoil you.") While Pentheus is off meeting his death, the Chorus sings the great ode to humility, a quality totally lacking in both Pentheus and the Athenian empire.

One should perhaps resist an interpretation of the destruction of Pentheus (1043–1152) that reads sexual symbolism into the images. But then, after all, Dionysus does bend a tall fir tree to the ground, Pentheus does climb astride it, the trunk does rise gently at first before it "soars" up to the heavens with Pentheus "throned upon its crest." When the women spot him, they try to pry the tree at the base of the trunk; failing in this, with myriad hands they tear the phallus tree up by the roots and bring down the shrieking Pentheus. Thousands of Greek vases attest to a fifth-century Athenian ironic humor in phallic symbols, and, given Euripides' duality in mixing the sensual and the sublime, the sexual symbolism may well be intended. But what follows is sheer horror as Agave, the aunts of Pentheus, and the other women tear his body apart, play ball games with the feet and the arms, and toss the pieces around the mountainside.

Horror follows horror as Agave enters triumphantly with

the head of Pentheus (1168), thinking that she has killed a lion, and invites the Chorus to join in the Dionysiac ritual feast of *ōmophagía* on the body. Made insane by Dionysus, as was her son, Agave is slowly led back to sanity by her father, and faces the utmost anguish and grief when she looks at what she holds in her hand. Dionysus has destroyed them all for denying his godhood, for mocking him, for imprisoning him, for blaspheming against him. This is *krátos*, the power of nature and *érōs*—not the love reflected in *philía* or *agápē*, but *érōs*: if denied, it will destroy. The Dionysian force is beyond good and evil; it is instinctive and amoral and sweeps away, without distinction, the entire House of Cadmus.

There is complete Euripidean irony in the fact that these "children," Pentheus and Actaeon and Dionysus, are sons of the daughters of Cadmus and Harmonia. Harmonia herself, the grandmother of these children, is the daughter of Aphrodite and Ares, the goddess of love and the god of war. Euripides, like so many other participants in the Greek genius, inherited from myths the powerful relationships between love and war, sex and aggression, and sexuality and power.

Frogs

IN HIS COMIC MASTERPIECE *Frogs* Aristophanes attacks two of his favorite targets—politicians and intellectuals—with his usual mixture of brilliant wit, verbal antics, crude slapstick, and deadly seriousness. He demonstrates in his comedies the ability of fifth-century Athenians to maintain seemingly contradictory philosophical, tragical, comical, and sexual attitudes toward life. Indeed, the Athenians considered those four attitudes to be simply different ways of looking at the same event. Aristophanes himself is one of the major characters in Plato's philosophical dialogue, *Symposium*, a work in which that philosopher explores the relationships among philosophy, tragedy, comedy, and sexuality to show that sexual attraction toward another person is merely the first step in the long climb upward to the love of beauty and wisdom.

A symposium in ancient Greece was an all-male dinner party during which a philosophical topic was sometimes discussed. Among the notable Athenians debating the subject of *érōs* in Plato's imaginary but extremely realistic party are Agathon, the tragic poet who has just won the prize at the City Dionysia and who is giving the party in his own honor; Socrates, the elderly philosopher; Alcibiades, the clever and handsome warrior and politician; and, of course, Aristophanes, the comic poet, who delivers the comically outrageous speech on lovers as literally divided bodies searching for their original other halves. Plato, as we discover in his *Republic*, fears poetry, wants to censor it and finally cast it out entirely from his contemplated state as a corrupting influence, in that men are inclined to imitate the sometimes immoral behavior of heroes and gods in epic or tragedy. Plato is, ironically, a great poet himself, not only in the sharpness of his characterizations and dialogue, but also in his brilliantly created myths. In the *Symposium* he makes clever use of dramatic devices to score philosophical points, especially in the conclusion of the dialogue.

Following the all-night discussion of *érōs*, only three people present have the stamina to remain awake: Agathon, the tragic poet; Aristophanes, the comic poet; and Socrates, the philosopher. Plato is establishing a point through character and situation—that tragedy, comedy, and philosophy are the most essential and durable aspects of man's experience. At daybreak, however, Agathon and Aristophanes finally fall asleep on their couches, whereas Socrates—philosophy being stronger than either tragedy or comedy—spends his usual day at the baths and in the marketplace conversing and philosophizing. What is of utmost importance here is the final topic of conversation among the three men. Socrates is attempting to get the two writers to agree that the comic writer should also be capable of writing tragedy, and the skillful tragic writer capable of writing comedy. At this point Agathon and Aristophanes, on the verge of giving in to the arguments of Socrates, begin to nod and fall asleep.

These few moments brilliantly illustrate the three ways Athenian intellectuals looked at life in the latter part of the fifth and the first part of the fourth centuries B.C. Plato suggests that all three viewpoints are necessary for the healthy citizen and the healthy state, but that the comic sense and the tragic sense should defer to the life of the mind, the philosophic sense. On the other hand, Aristophanes, a man of the upper class but not the aristocracy, a person who occupies the middle ground between the nobility and the common man, shares the average Athenian's distrust of abstract reasoning, refined intellectuality, and hair-splitting argumentation. This is why, in *Frogs*, Aristophanes prefers the patriotically religious Aeschylus over the intellectually witty Euripides.

Aristophanes was fifteen at the outbreak of the Peloponnesian War, his great comedies were written during the progress of that war, and most of them are attacks on politicians who failed either to win the war or to sue for peace when peace was still possible. Indeed, his first extant play, *Acharnians*, as well as *Knights, Peace, Lysistrata,* and *Frogs,* is critical of the failure of the Athenian leadership to win either the war or the peace. Aristophanes writes both tragedy and comedy, in that these comic plays are concerned with the tragic behavior of the Athenian empire. Comedy, for Aristophanes, is truly the opposite side of the coin to tragedy. Both serve the same end: to save the individual and the state from ruin. They do this through the purgation of the emotions of pity and fear.

Tragedy's function as the purgation (catharsis) of pity and fear is, of course, part of Aristotle's famous definition of tragedy in his *Poetics*. The *Poetics*, like many of his other works, may actually be the lecture notes of a student, with perhaps some emendations by Aristotle himself; like all lecture notes, they omit a great deal of explanatory and illustrative material that was surely part of the original lecture. Thus the lack of elaboration of the definition has caused many misinterpretations and arguments over the centuries.

Simply put, it comes down to the following. Aristotle apparently believed that we feel pity at the sight of undeserved suffering in others (Oedipus), knowing that we and those we love are also possible victims of unmerited suffering; consequently, we live in "fear" (the word is sometimes translated "terror") for our own safety in a mysterious world of unanticipated and unwarranted fate. Living daily with such emotions is not a healthy condition; however, through experiencing tragic plays where we empathize with a good but not perfect person who suffers a reversal of fortune through *hamartía*, an error in character *or* in moral judgment, Aristotle believes our own feelings of pity and fear are purged and we are, for a little while, cleansed and at harmony with ourselves. That this is true is shown by the experience of anyone who has had the good fortune to see a first-rate performance of a great tragedy. One does not leave the theater depressed but, rather, strangely exhilarated, purged of pity and fear.

Comedy, by engaging our laughter rather than our tears in response to a character who is experiencing pain and terror, also serves as a purgation of pity and fear when that character comes to a happy ending.

Comedy, like tragedy, was a fifth-century Athenian development, and both had their roots in ancient celebrations: tragedy in dithyrambs sung in honor of Dionysus, rituals that may, as we have seen, sometimes have contained *sparagmós* and *ōmophagía*, and comedy in the *kômos*, processional revels in which the participants costumed themselves as animals and other creatures of nature (note Aristophanes' titles: *Birds*, *Wasps*, *Frogs*), costumes that were also ithyphallic (*ithús*, Gr., straightforward). The leader of the *kômos* engaged in banter with the spectators and insulted prominent citizens, activities that took their formal part in comedy as the *parábasis*, the traditional address to the audience (the requirement being that as much of it as possible be delivered in one breath) that is so powerful in *Frogs*. Aristotle, in the *Poetics*, points to the ludicrous, the ugly, and the ridiculous as being essential elements of comedy, and they must have been so from the ritualistic beginnings.

Although there is a substantial body of theoretical work on tragedy, explanations of comedy are insubstantial and the ones we have tend to be ludicrous. However, comedies do have certain basic elements in common, particularly those of Aristophanes, and these can be examined.

INCONGRUITY. This element is based upon our expectations that certain objects or ideas are congruous, belong together in a fitting and suitable way. The incongruous world is one of disorder; it is ridiculous and absurd: the great god Dionysus in ill-fitting clothes, a mangy lion skin—in imitation of Herakles—thrown over his shoulders, being spanked by the chief janitor of Hades. Lords of Misrule are comic, especially when the mighty are brought low by banana skins, and Chaplinesque self-effacing characters win. In *Peace*, a comedy written by Aristophanes when he was twenty-four years old and the war was less than ten, a simple young farmer flies to heaven, challenges Zeus, who has buried Peace, and escapes the two monsters of War and Turmoil that Zeus has placed over the Greeks. With the help of a Chorus of other farmers, he digs up Peace—lifting her out with block and tackle—and walks down the air with Peace and her two attendants, Harvest and Sacred Embassies. At home again, he stages a carnival in which warmongers and profiteers are driven into exile as well as into further insanity, and he marries Harvest.

FANTASY. Through the heroes and heroines of comedy we live in dream worlds where everything is possible, from descending to Hades with Dionysus in *Frogs*, to flying to heaven with Trygaeus in *Peace*, to bringing war to an end through the weapon of sexual denial in *Lysistrata*. In *Acharnians* Dicaeopolis makes a private peace treaty with Sparta; in *Knights* a sausage-seller overcomes Aristophanes' favorite target, the Athenian ruler Cleon; and in *Birds*, generally considered Aristophanes' masterpiece, Peithetaerus, tired of Athenian and Spartan turmoil, is helped by birds in building a heavenly ideal city which cuts off the sacrificial smoke from earth, causing the gods to submit. Peithetaerus then becomes Lord of the Universe and marries Basileia—"Princess" or "Empire."

DISGUISE. Along with role-switching—Dionysus and Xanthias in *Frogs*—disguise and mistaken identity are frequent sources of comedy in Greek Old Comedy, Elizabethan, Restoration, and Wildean plays, as well as in early or late Hollywood films, and supremely so in Cervantes. The pleasure is in watching the underdog assume an ill-fitting role of authority and the authority figure placed in an uncomfortable subservient role. *Lysistrata*, misunderstood by twentieth-century audiences as a play praising the cleverness of women, was rather—to Athenians—a comedy based on the humorous, ridiculous notion that women could possibly be strong, clever, witty, intelligent, and—most absurd of all—sexually chaste. Although both Greek and Elizabethan female roles were played by male actors, the masks and robes of the Greek theater prohibited its playwrights from suggesting

Elizabethan multiple levels of sexual ambiguity when a male actor played a female character who—disguised as a boy—was subjected to the unwanted attentions of a female character played by a man.

RECOGNITION AND REVERSAL. These are sources of triumph or despair in both epic and tragedy, as in the reunion of Odysseus with Telemachos and then with Penelope in the *Odyssey*, and the recognition scene between Electra and Orestes in the *Libation Bearers*, or the fearful reversal in *Oedipus the King*. In comedy, recognition is both surprising and shocking, and is usually accomplished by the revelation of the true identity of the disguised personage—especially in the plays of Shakespeare.

Another type of recognition takes place in the audience rather than in the onstage characters—the pleasure of recognizing parody and satire in the representation of politicians, philosophers, and playwrights. *Frogs* was one of the few plays so popular that it received a second production—and there is evidence that the audience attended the play with copies in hand and increased delight in the recognition of the lines of Aeschylus and Euripides being parodied or satirized.

SEXUALITY. Many of the sexual jokes are homosexual in nature; these are in no sense always derogatory, as traditionally the first experience for a young man just past puberty was courtship by a mature man. The ensuing relationship, which could last several years but sometimes considerably longer, involved material gifts, sex, and introduction to society, literature, and philosophy by the *erastēs*, the older male lover. When the *erómenos*, the young man who was loved, began to grow a beard, he was no longer attractive to the *erastēs*. These phases were totally accepted by Athenian society, as love between man and woman had to be rare in a society where upper-class women were usually uneducated and certainly not part of the cultural and intellectual life of the city. (Aspasia, the celebrated courtesan from Miletus, who was the lifelong companion of Pericles—his *hetaíra*—was a notable exception.) Women could enter the theater, for example, but were prohibited from staying unless there were empty seats after all the men were seated, or a place to stand without blocking the view of a man.

The comedies of Aristophanes and his generation, called the Old Comedy, were not of the romantic "boy gets girl, boy loses girl, boy regains girl" type, nor were they the domestic situational comedies of the New Comedy of Menander and others of the generations after Aristophanes. Although Aristophanes' comedies sometimes end in marriage, as does *Peace*, the search for love is not the point of the action. These are plays about men without women. Homosexual relations were on a par with heterosexual—indeed, considered superior by many because of the element of love—and the jokes and situations were primarily homosexual.

Dionysus, in *Frogs*, participates in this humor, and in particular the Athenian credo that distinctions are not to be made among sources of sexual pleasure. When he confesses to Herakles that he has a craving—although he means for the works of Euripides—Herakles immediately assumes the craving is sexual and asks if it is a woman that Dionysus desires. When Dionysus responds with a "no," Herakles immediately assumes it must be for a boy. When the answer is again negative, Herakles is shocked that it might be for the only other alternative—a grown man (52–57). Homosexual affairs were accepted between a man and a boy before the boy had taken on manly features. His role was passive; relations between two men were frowned upon, as one of them was assuming the disgraceful—to the Greeks—passive, feminine role. Just before this exchange Dionysus speaks of having been served aboard a lovely boat (rowing was a standard metaphor for sexual intercourse) named Kleisthenes. He refers, of course, to a well-known Athenian man with a preference for young men. Dionysus apparently enjoyed the encounter, as his "extended" metaphor suggests at least twelve further "engagements" with Kleisthenes. This is the same man referred to later in the play, when, having lost his latest young man—again an actual, named person—he sits in a cemetery engaged in the womanly behavior of tearing out his hair—

not, however, the hair on his head but the hair on his anus—
because he has lost his "dear little rear-end friend," Sebinos of
Anaphystos (422–27).

LANGUAGE. Much of Aristophanes' wit, consisting as it does
of puns, word games, double entendres, tongue-twisters, on-
omatopoeia, alliteration and assonance, ridiculous rhymes, and
quirky rhythms, is impossible to translate: the exhilarating joy
of the speech itself is gone, and all that remains are bawdy jokes
and slapstick, the words that first come to mind when Aristophanes is mentioned. As a corrective, we need to be reminded
of the epitaph for Aristophanes attributed to Plato: "The Graces,
seeking an appropriate shrine,/ Found it in the soul of Aristophanes." The translations convey the grace of his imagination,
but cannot do so for the poetic grace of his language.

The comedies of no other playwright survive from this
period of Old Comedy. Aristophanes' generation considered
him the best, and his plays are typical of the comedies of the
time in being extravagant variety or vaudeville shows in which
the plot was not as important as wildly inventive sketches
elaborating a theme, fantastic fun with dialogue and lyrics, lively
music, dances of birds and wasps and other improbable chorus
figures, obscenity, exuberant sexuality, political satire, parody,
and—above all—seemingly meaningless nonsense dealing seriously with important matters of man's life in a political state.
Aristotle considers man to be an animal who lives in the city,
and Aristophanes excels in his portrayal of that man as he treats
not the superficial mores of fashionable trends that quickly
make obsolete so many comedies, but rather the timeless subjects
of war, peace, sex, education, and—a curiously persistent theme
that is over twenty-five hundred years old—the upward ambi-
tions of the middle class.

Comedies were presented, along with tragedies, at the City
Dionysia in Athens, probably during the month of March. The
festival, which lasted for three days, began with a procession
through the streets of Athens in honor of Dionysus in which a

huge phallus was carried to symbolize the god and his power. At each of the three days of the festival, three dramas and a satyr play by one tragedian were presented, followed by a single play by a comic writer. Thus, each City Dionysia saw competition among three tragic writers and three comic writers. The plays were chosen six months beforehand, but rewriting could continue until the last minute; this was especially important with comedies, as the more recent the topical reference the better. As with tragedies, each comedy was produced—and most expenses paid—by a wealthy citizen of Athens who considered this both a civic duty and an honor; in time of war such citizens were expected to provide and outfit warships by the same token. There were prizes, but there has always been a mystifying quality about the judgments, as the judges were chosen by lot and did not necessarily possess any literary expertise.

Comedies were limited to four male actors, but there could be as many nonspeaking actors in a scene as needed. One lively feature of the comedies was the caricature portrait masks of contemporary leaders worn by actors in those roles. And, although women never took part in tragedy, the dancing girls in comedies—when they were called for—were actually played by women. The physicality of the humor, the mock-cruelty, especially the beating of important characters, as in the whipping of the god Dionysus in *Frogs*, may have served as an outlet for the enormous self-control necessary to Athenian citizens: the law against *húbris*, arrogant violence, could and did result in death penalties for citizens who so much as struck another citizen. Other outlets for physical violence were the beating of slaves (an act not punishable by anything), the brutality of Olympian boxing matches, where spiked metal studs were allowed on the fist coverings, and the *pancratium*, a combined boxing and wrestling event that permitted everything from kicking and choking to arm-twisting.

The High Priest of Dionysus sat in his first-tier throne watching the god he served being defecated upon by a donkey, beaten by a janitor, boasting of his homosexual one-night stands, and at one point calling on the Priest as a fellow member of the same club. And the Priest, as well as many in the audience, had, sometime during the past twenty-four hours, participated in myteries in which they offered up prayers and poured sacred libations to this powerful nature-god Dionysus. The Athenians were able to live simultaneously in a comic world, a tragic world, and a philosophic world—recall the conclusion of Plato's *Symposium*—without allowing one of those worlds to disrupt or profane the others. Similar relations between art and religion since the classic age of Greece are unimaginable: Moses and Christ cannot easily be made figures of levity, except in the novels of Joyce, and many readers even there find the result sacrilegious rather than comic.

But *Frogs* is about Dionysus only in that it is a comedy about tragedy. It is divided into two halves. The first half is a parody of the dangerous trips to Hades made by such heroes as Herakles, and Odysseus' sword-in-hand encounter with the dead; the second half is a more than serious selection of the tragic poet who is best able to help in bringing an end to the disastrous Peloponnesian War.

The play was produced and received first prize in 405—apparently the judges shared Aristophanes' opinion that Athens should negotiate peace terms with Sparta. The years between 411 and 405 had seen two revolutions in Athens, one a successful antidemocratic coup and the second a countercoup. Further, a recent sea battle had proved to be a Pyrrhic victory in that for the first time Athens had used slaves and noncitizens to man the ships and a storm following the victory had caused the generals—some of whom were later executed—to abandon twelve foundering ships, which sank and drowned thousands of Athenian warriors. In the year 404 the Athenians, all of their ships lost (and that had been their strength), were starving under the siege of Sparta; they capitulated, not to negotiated terms, but to Spartan dictates.

These were also tumultuous years in the theater: Sophocles and Euripides died in 406, the *Bacchae* and *Frogs* were produced in 405, and *Oedipus at Colonus* in 401. *Frogs* pleads for peace, the *Bacchae* for acceptance of necessity, and *Oedipus at Colonus* for humility and reconciliation with the gods.

In *Frogs* the Leader of the Chorus speaks out to the audience—and the politicians seated there—against bribery, warmongering, and war profiteering, the debasement of currency, and the importance of freedom and rule by aristocratic Athenians rather than by immigrants; the Chorus ridicules politicians and lovers with one breath, and then flirts with any female members of the audience in the next.

Aiakos, the janitor of Hades, provides the necessary explanation for the exclusion of Sophocles from the competition (786–94). The permissibility of last-minute rewriting came as savior to Aristophanes, as, Sophocles having died in between the acceptance of *Frogs* for production and the actual performance six months later, Aristophanes was left in a difficult situation: given the esteem in which Sophocles was held, there would be no competition—Sophocles would hold the Chair of Poetry and he would naturally be the one selected over either Euripides or Aeschylus to return to earth. But the playwright cleverly allows Sophocles to stand above such petty rivalry, reluctantly agreeing to occupy the Chair only while Aeschylus is away.

Theater—both tragedy and comedy—was a vital part of Athenian life, and Athenians would recognize the bombast, the metaphors, the ponderous words coupled together that the Chorus sings in imitation of Aeschylus just before the entrance of the judges and the contestants. And—given their knowledge of Euripides' lack of traditional religious beliefs—they would also be amused by his atheistic prayer.

The contest itself falls into five scenes, each with a different topic of literary criticism: the purpose of poetry (905–1098), the language of poetry (1119–1250), the nature of lyric verse (1261–1364), the gravity of content (1365–1410), and the necessity of good poetry for the very survival of the state (1417–81).

Euripides speaks first, and he argues that poetry should present everyday life in a realistic manner, using ordinary conversational speech, and people modeled on actual life rather than on exceptional heroes; the poet, he concludes, must be able to think, to write, and to teach virtue. Aeschylus agrees that writers should follow Homer and Hesiod in teaching virtue, but the virtue they teach should be the virtue of heroes, bravery in combat, and audiences should not be taught to imitate Euripidean lovesick women. Euripides falsely replies that Aphrodite did not interest Aeschylus: given Aeschylus' insightful portrayal of Klytemnestra's sexuality, this is not fair fighting. This section concludes with Euripides' argument that he shows truth, and Aeschylus' rebuttal that poets should not show scandalous truth, that boys at one time had instructors but, now that they are men, they must be taught the useful and the good by poets.

Euripides opens the second round of the battle, devoted to the language of poetry, with the accusation that big words, ponderous phrases, and language used primarily for sound effect rather than meaning are not useful—they are not the way real people talk. Aeschylus argues a position that many future writers will observe: that larger-than-life actions of heroes demand a high mimetic mode—grandiloquent words and phrases to match the magnificence of the action. He charges Euripides with hurting the war effort by teaching citizens how to pretend to be poor, techniques they use to avoid outfitting warships. Further, he maintains that Euripides teaches disputatious, phony intellectual talk, and he quotes a Euripidean line well known and mocked even then: life is death and death is perhaps life. Then Aeschylus presents the age-old argument that the intellectual life makes people unprepared for decisive action. This is terribly sad, and shows how far the Athenians have sunk when one recalls Pericles' boast in the funeral oration in the first years of the war that the Athenian citizen's love of the beautiful does not cause him to be extravagant, and that his love for intellectual matters does not make him weak.

Following another choral interlude—and Aristophanes makes clever use of these to provide divisions as well as respites between the rounds of the contest—the topic changes to the nature of lyric verse. Euripides makes telling use of the opening lines of Aeschylus' *Libation Bearers* to point up the repetitious nature of Aeschylean lyricism. Although a somewhat accurate criticism of the predictability of Euripidean meter, Aeschylus' use of the "little bottle of oil" becomes somewhat predictable itself. If Euripides does score a point in arguing that Aeschylus' bombastic language prohibits lyricism, then Aeschylus is also correct in his contention that Euripidean lyricism is sometimes overdone, romantic, and lush.

The fourth round, the weighing of lines of verse, is hardly amusing after the first few weighings of the "gravity" of the lines, as a great deal of the humor derives from the Athenian audience's recognition of lines from plays no longer extant; in any case, this is hardly literary criticism to be taken seriously.

The fifth and final round is the crux of the contest, and the sudden seriousness of the argument shows its importance to Aristophanes.

The first question asked—What is to be done about Alcibiades?—was the most argued matter in Athens at that time. This brilliant, handsome, arrogant, devious aristocrat, a protégé and companion of both Pericles and Socrates, had everything Athens could offer—including the jealousy of his peers. He argued for, and was chosen to lead, the ill-fated expedition to Sicily. This expansion of the fighting would have horrified Pericles, who had warned early in the war that Athens would win if it did not try to extend the empire while fighting battles close to home.

Alcibiades came under the cloud of suspicion as one of the Athenian "playboys" who had mocked the Eleusinian Mysteries and mutilated the statues of Hermes just prior to the expedition. After the fleet had sailed, it became known to Alcibiades that he was being summoned home on charges of impiety and that there was the possibility of a death sentence if he was found guilty. He deserted to the Spartan side instead of returning, and Athens gave him the death sentence *in absentia*.

The speech he made to the Spartans is chilling in its cleverness. As reported by Thucydides in his *Peloponnesian War*, Alcibiades' most persuasive argument is that only a man who truly loved Athens and wanted to see it do the correct thing would have been courageous enough to come over to the enemy side, help Sparta win, and thus be in a position to correct the errors of an Athens he loved so much. Accepted by the Spartans, Alcibiades' advice, based as it was on firsthand knowledge of Athenian strategic thinking, led to the excruciating destruction of a large part of the Athenian navy and the extraordinarily cruel starvation of her entire expeditionary force by the Spartans in the deep stone quarries near Syracuse.

Ultimately—mainly due to suspected intrigues with both the wife of the Spartan king and the Persian satrap—Alcibiades was no longer trusted by the Spartans, and after the restoration of democracy in Athens he was given permission to return in 408. He lost his prestige again by his absence from the battle of Notium in 407, and he retired to his estate in the Chersonese rather than return to Athens and stand trial. Athens had once again lost her brilliant strategist, and a few years later she lost the decisive battle at Aegospotami, the one which brought on the final defeat of Athens.

That battle would be lost only a few months after the audience heard Euripides, in the *Frogs*, being asked the question: What should Athens do about Alcibiades? Euripides' answer is a vague dodge, but Aeschylus boldly advises that cities who rear lion cubs should learn to live with them when they grow up to be lions.

Shortly after the first performance of *Frogs*, Alcibiades was assassinated in Phrygia. There are conflicting versions of who actually killed him, but many think that it was done by the Persians acting on a request by the Athenian rulers. He was forty-six years old. By the time of the second production of

Frogs, the question asked Euripides and Aeschylus was no longer pertinent. The lion was dead.

The second question asked the two playwrights concerns the best way to use leaders and citizens. Euripides again is witty but vague in his answer, whereas Aeschylus urges that leaders and citizens be warlike, that they protect their city and attack the enemy—primarily with what was left of the navy, always the Athenian strong point. Here the Chorus, speaking for Aristophanes, attacks Socrates and his associates as being capable only of politically and morally damaging chitchat rather than needful action. (A few years later an Athenian court would rid Athens of Socrates' dangerous "chitchat" by condemning him to death and executing him. Because of attacks on Socrates by Aristophanes in both *Clouds* and *Frogs*, part of the blame for the execution has unfairly been placed on his writing table.)

The final decision is made by Dionysus, and, choosing Aeschylus for reasons of his good sense and integrity, he is sent to the world above complete with a piece of rope to use in hanging the ruinous rulers of Athens so that they will go down to Hades, where, presumably, Pluto will take care of them. In an appropriate farewell Pluto sends Aeschylus off in a processional—reminiscent of the one Aeschylus himself wrote for the conclusion of the *Eumenides*—complete with torches, songs, and dances. The play ends with one of Aristophanes' strongest antiwar statements as the Chorus prays that Aeschylus will be successful in bringing peace to Athens. What began as a parodic journey to Hades, complete with comic defecatory, sexual, and anal obscenities, ends in the utmost seriousness.

Such seriousness is in tune with the multifaceted Athenian spirit: all the major texts illuminate Aristotle's definition of man as an animal that lives in a city. The Athenian does not suffer from dissociation of sensibility, but lives a complete life in which the philosophical, comic, tragic, obscene, sensual, political, and ethical are in harmony, intertwined and indivisible.

Aeneid

MANY AGREE with the complaint that Virgil is difficult to read correctly—with or without an interpreter. The *Aeneid* has been read both as a poem of the affirmation of the spirit of man, and as a sinister poem of darkness made visible. The hero has been considered either a model intellectual Roman stoic exerting enormous control over his emotions, or an inconsistent, emotional scoundrel whose final action in the poem is an explosion into flaming rage. This epic by Publius Vergilius Maro, the poet known to us as Virgil, has been subjected to more varied and contradictory interpretations than any of the texts we have looked at thus far.

According to some, Aeneas is a heroic figure who demonstrates that man can become like a god in will, strength, and wisdom. To others this "pious" Aeneas is something of a bore and, because stronger gods are constantly watching over him, he is not the heroic figure his opponent Turnus is. After all, they suggest, Achilleus and Hektor have equally powerful gods protecting them, so the contest is even—it comes down to which is the braver and stronger warrior; Turnus, on the other hand, gets the sympathy of some readers because, abandoned by the gods, especially Juno, he nonetheless fights with courage.

Some contend that it is an unabashed piece of propaganda for the Roman empire that was written to please Virgil's admirer, the Emperor Augustus Caesar, who, although he may have modestly discouraged worship as a god, is certainly presented as divine by Virgil. At the other extreme are those who hold that the *Aeneid* is the supreme literary epic, one whose refined and polished poetry has never been matched in world literature. To still others it is a pale imitation of Homer's epics, full of borrowings that never approach the thrust and power of either the *Iliad* or the *Odyssey*.

But why all the borrowings from Homer? They are certainly numerous: wanderings, complete with storms, shipwrecks, and monsters; banquets where women fall in love with the wandering heroes (Nausikaa with Odysseus, Dido with Aeneas); visits to Hades, where old men (the prophet Tiresias and the father of Aeneas, Anchises) forecast the future; identical battle scenes, attacking ships and setting them afire; catalogues of ships, troops, and leaders; funeral games (Patroklos, Anchises); midnight spying expeditions (Diomedes and Odysseus, Nisus and Euryalus); slaying of Patroklos by Hektor and of Pallas by Turnus; single combat at the climax (Hektor and Achilleus, Turnus and Aeneas). Moreover, not satisfied with using plot details and episodes from Homer's epics, Virgil pays further homage to his predecessor when he freely borrows words, lines, images, and entire phrases.

Virgil, of course, was making a parallel between the world of the Roman empire and the classic world of Homer. The effect on us of reading the *Aeneid* is the pleasurable creation in our imagination of a parallel between the antiquity of Homer and the antiquity of Virgil. One of the distinctive features of twentieth-century modernism has been the re-creation of this classic device by Eliot, Joyce, and Pound. Those three writers, along with Virgil, Coleridge, and many others, are not just unabashedly borrowing, but rather enhancing and deepening the meaning and pleasures of their own works.

Placing oneself too firmly in either the Homeric or the Virgilian camp is an unwise strategic exercise, as it is possible and best to place oneself in both camps at the same time. The literary terms that have been applied to Homer's epic are: oral, natural, and authentic; to Virgil's: written, literary, and artificial. These contrasting terms are obviously loaded in favor of Homer. How many authors want their poems to be "literary" and "artificial" when they could be "natural" and "authentic"? The only valid distinction to keep in mind is the one between oral poetry and written poetry. The oral epic had many composers, each, one would imagine, improving the poem as both poetry and story; the written epic was composed by one poet over a period of years during which he also polished and improved his poem. Because of the differences in composition, the oral epic has a directness, speed, and thrust not always found in the sophisticated, intellectual elegance of the written epic.

Written epics usually have a more tightly knitted structure— one that does not consist of the loosely woven set pieces used by the oral epic singer. The overall emphasis in the written epic is more on national spirit and the fate of a complicated society than on the fateful actions of individual heroes in a simpler society. The oral epic is frequently the product of a culture that does not even have a word for art or literature, whereas the written epic is the product of a culture in which art is considered one of the highest endeavors of man. As a consequence, oral epics—like plays—are composed to entertain audiences that represent a wide variety of social and intellectual spheres, whereas the author of the written epic has a specific audience in mind, one that is his equal in education and taste.

To read one type of epic and criticize it for not having the qualities of the other is to make a basic critical error that effectively cuts one off from the pleasures of both Homer *and* Virgil.

Aeneas, the leader of the Dardanians in the Trojan War, appears in the *Iliad* as early as Book 2, when Homer tells about the Trojan hero's parents, but his major exploits are in Books 5 and 20.

In Book 5 he fights with Diomedes, who overcomes Aeneas only when he throws a stone and wounds him in the hip. Aeneas falls to his knees, "black night" comes over both his eyes, but Aphrodite, his mother, carries him away from the battle. Strangely enough—the *Iliad*, like most oral epics, is not always consistent— Diomedes attacks him again shortly thereafter, but Aeneas is protected by Apollo, who carries him away to his shrine. There he makes an image of Aeneas, who then miraculously reappears in the battle (as image? as Apollo in disguise? as the actual Aeneas?), where he begins fighting and killing. He is even about to attack Menelaos when that warrior is joined by Antilochos and Aeneas wisely refrains from fighting two such warriors.

Except for brief notices of his fights in Books 13, 15, and 16, Aeneas does not appear again until his final exploit, the most important of them all, in Book 20. There he challenges Achilleus himself to single combat, warning Achilleus that either his or Aeneas' parents will mourn that day. Then follow sixty tedious lines of ancestral history delivered by Aeneas, in which we find that Zeus was the beginning of his family line. (And also, interestingly enough, that Zeus was the great-great-grand-father of Ganymede—another ancestor of Aeneas—making that relationship a celestial incestuous one.)

In the actual fight each man fears the other: Achilleus is protected from the spear-throw of Aeneas only by his god-given shield, and Aeneas only when he is about to lose and is lifted up by Poseidon, who hurls him to the edge of the fighting and then warns him not to fight further with Achilleus, assuring him that after Achilleus is dead he will be stronger than any of the opposing heroes.

The adjective most frequently linked with Aeneas by Virgil is usually translated "pious," an unfortunate word with conno-tations of insincere and excessive religiosity. The Latin word being translated is *pietas*, devotion; and Virgil is employing it to stress Aeneas' devotion to everything—himself, his warriors, society, the gods, and his purpose: the founding of Rome.

The *Aeneid*, then, like the *Odyssey*, is a quest book: Odysseus has to overcome obstacles in order to return home safely, and Aeneas is struggling to fulfill the command of the gods that he establish a home for the Trojans in Italy. There are powerful and related similarities and differences between the two men: Odysseus, as we saw, had to be purged of his war spirit and turned again into a father and a husband; Aeneas has to be purged of all of his attributes as a man in order to be turned into a god, the divine ancestor of Augustus Caesar.

Odysseus chooses humanity; Aeneas chooses divinity. Kalypso offers Odysseus eternal life if he will stay with her on the island; when he leaves her, he is choosing humanity over a godlike condition. It is important to remember that in the early stages of Greek religion heroes became gods: Achilleus was given his shrine on the Hellespont, to which pilgrimages were made, and because of the extraordinary heroic sufferings of Oedipus a shrine was built at Colonus for the worship of that hero-god.

In Books 1–5 of the *Aeneid*, Aeneas rejects Jupiter's election of him as a god; in Book 6, the journey to Hades, the vision provided him by his father of the glorious future of Rome reconfirms his acceptance; and in Books 7–12 he fights valiantly to achieve his destiny and the destiny of Rome. In the process of being stripped of his humanity, he must lose all human attachments—his wife, Creusa, his father, Anchises, and his dear friend Palinurus, his steersman. Aeneas must steer his own way to godhood, and no other human being can help him do this—indeed, they would, like Dido, do everything to prevent it. The personal vision of Aeneas must be replaced by a spiritual vision, and the individual must be subordinate to the vision.

That knowledge comes through suffering was one of the consistent themes of the Greek playwrights; in epic poetry it is not knowledge that comes from suffering so much as it is strength of character. Aeneas, even more than Odysseus, is being tested, and through that testing he learns and his character is formed. Testing, *exercitatio*, is one of the principles of the Stoic philosophers, who believed that man is not born wise but becomes so through *exercitatio*, thus enabling him to foresee, *praecipere*—another Stoic philosophical term. The Stoic philosophers were fond of quoting Virgil, and from Book 6 in particular—the turning point for Aeneas—in which he says to the Cumaean Sibyl, *Omnia praecepi atque animo mecum ante peregi*:

"I have foreseen and thought all in my soul" (vi.105:157–58. As there is sometimes as much as a hundred-line difference between the Latin text and English translations, I will first give the Latin text lines, followed by the Fitzgerald translation lines. Lines are, of course, preceded by the Book number in Roman numerals).

Not everyone agrees that Aeneas is worthy of praise, or even that his character is strengthened; his faults have been named and criticized. His behavior during the fall of Troy is not exactly heroic, and one can question, even given night and fog, a hero losing track of his wife. One can see the hand of the poet at work here, as he wants the future race of Romans to be a mixture of Trojan and native Latin. Other readers have problems with the Dido-and-Aeneas love story; after all, Aeneas is so overwhelmed by Dido that he forgets his destiny and duty and begins work improving Carthage rather than founding Rome. When he is reminded of his duty, some readers consider his treatment of Dido shabby, ungentlemanly, and unfeeling. In Sicily, so very close to his destination, he is so distraught over the burning of his ships that he considers settling there and has to be urged on to his true destination. Finally, the battle scenes in Italy are really no contest, as the god Jupiter himself is on the side of Aeneas, particularly in the final single combat between Aeneas and Turnus.

A frequently held opinion of Aeneas is that his mind always exerts control over his passions, but it seems to me that the reverse is the case: Aeneas is very much a man of feeling who is ruled by passion; he has to force his mind to act in order to subdue his passions. Indeed, the first words we hear from Aeneas are his groaning wish for death and release from suffering. What is perhaps the most famous episode in the epic, the love story of Dido and Aeneas, offers ample evidence of Aeneas' emotions taking precedence over his will.

Virgil demonstrates the devastating power of love when he shows what it does to Carthage itself when that city is overwhelmed by love. Just before the arrival of the disguised Aeneas,

Virgil shows the men of Carthage working on the walls of the city, a citadel, and houses, while others are making laws, establishing judges and a senate; still others work at excavating a harbor and constructing a theater (i.418–40:572–96). Dido herself is busily giving laws, judging, and deciding on work and workers (i.502–08:685–93). But once love has assumed command, all work stops. The towers of Carthage no longer rise, the young give up their armed exercises and the building of harbors and armed embankments: everyone becomes "idle," the ramparts stand unfinished, and even the building crane lies unused (iv.86–89:121–26). There is no question about Virgil's meaning: the passions of love hinder the rational progress of civilization; love will prevent the founding of Rome.

We saw how Homer in the *Iliad* cleverly plays on the name Patroklos and its reverse, Kleopatra, in the story old Phoinix tells during the embassy to Achilleus. Virgil transforms an ancient legend into a story about an African queen, Dido, who becomes a threat to the founding of Rome. This episode would certainly recall to Roman readers the disastrous effects that Cleopatra, another seductive African queen (actually, she came from a long line of Macedonian Ptolemaic queens) had on Caesar, Antony, and Rome. His readers would make the connection between a Carthage that threatens to abort the founding of Rome, and the Punic War between Carthage and Rome. Virgil has the disguised Venus tell her son Aeneas the actual origin of Carthage in her story of Dido's flight from Phoenicia (i.335–70:460–503). The English word "Punic" derives from Latin *Punicus* and *Poeni*, Phoenicia. Roman readers of the *Aeneid* used a rather common expression in their everyday life: *Punica fides*—Punic faith, meaning treachery.

Both Dido and Cleopatra are passionate women with treacherous brothers who overrule and deceive them. Although Dido breaks her vow to her murdered husband by falling in love again, Aeneas appears to be an unfeeling villain—perhaps because the pathos of Dido's unrequited love has gained the sympathy of readers, beginning with writers as early as Ovid and Saint Augustine.

Dido's brother, Pygmalion, not only killed her husband in order to steal his gold, but kept the murder a secret so that Dido, continuing to love Sychaeus, was sick with longing for him. In future texts we will see writers using many such proleptic—foreshadowing—devices: these repetitions become echoes as well as variations on a theme, and they suggest inevitability as well as completion. Dido continues to love Aeneas after his love for her is as dead as her husband; and her unrequited love for Aeneas leads to sickness and death.

The two great themes of Virgil in this epic are strife and love, and they echo a connection already becoming visible in the *Odyssey* when Homer sings of the mutual sexual attraction of Ares, the god of War, and Aphrodite, the goddess of Love, in his story of their intercourse in her bed and the golden net-trap devised by her husband, Hephaestos, to catch his wife in her infidelity. In the *Aeneid* Dido represents Love and Turnus represents Strife: the verb so frequently used to describe the condition of both of them is "to burn"—not only does Dido burn with the consuming passion of love, but she actually perishes in flames, and Turnus burns with the uncontrolled fury of strife. Of course, the extensive use of the verb in describing Dido also becomes proleptic for the appearance of Turnus: these two burning souls are both destroyed by Aeneas.

Virgil, in making a careful distinction between Aeneas and Turnus, is underscoring his viewpoint of the nature of a hero appropriate to the Augustan Roman empire. Whereas Aeneas hates war, but reluctantly fights for the common good, Virgil presents Turnus' desire for individual glory as a quality that would be dangerous to the welfare of the contemporary Roman empire. Turnus represents the Homeric hero as he was defined by Sarpedon's speech to Glaukos about fame and glory. Aeneas has no Homeric parallel in that he himself is in that epic, whereas Turnus combines the qualities of Hektor, fighting to defend his homeland, and those of Achilleus, the brave and fierce war-lover.

The connection between Jupiter and fate is much clearer in Virgil than in Homer. Zeus in the *Iliad* does not always know himself what a warrior's destiny is until he weighs the death portions on his scales. In the opening pages of the *Odyssey* Zeus complains that mortals are always blaming the gods for their troubles, whereas they actually bring misfortune on themselves through their own recklessness—the first indication that character, rather than the will of the gods, is fate. In the *Aeneid* Jupiter *is* fate, they are one and the same: Jupiter is another word for fate. This is not to say that Jupiter cannot change his mind: fate is not fixed, as when he announces that matters have become so confused it would be best for all the gods to withdraw from the conflict, but then later changes his mind. Neptune also vacillates in his interferences, and Juno herself comes to a position of compromise with Jupiter over the future: she agrees to a dual nationalistic composition of the Romans—a mixture of Trojan Aeneas and Latin Lavinia—and abandons the unfortunate Turnus.

It was necessary for Virgil to satisfy his associates' conceptions of the divine nature of the Roman emperors, and their special relationship to Jupiter, by presenting a unique partnership between Jupiter and Aeneas. Virgil composed his poem for the Roman empire, but there was no one nation of Hellenes at the time Homer was writing, only a collection of warring tribes— among them, Danaans, Myrmidons, and Myceneans—and the gods and goddesses could more freely associate themselves with one tribe or another, or even with the Trojan enemies.

There were encounters with Hades in both the *Odyssey* and *Frogs*, and, in addition to the one in the *Aeneid*, they will occur in works by Dante, Rabelais, and Joyce. In the classic texts of Homer, Virgil, and Dante there is a growing elaboration of both the geography of Hades and the intricacy of its punishment, particularly of the punishment suiting the crime.

Homer presents conceptions of the afterlife when he tells in the *Iliad* that souls wander restlessly until they are given proper burial, and Patroklos tells Achilleus that in the afterlife one is but a shade with no real life. Odysseus himself in the *Odyssey* does not actually enter Hades, but rather digs a pit in the earth into which he then pours a strangely interesting mixture of honey, milk, wine, water, barley, and sheep's blood, after which the souls of the dead come swarming up to the pit and speak with Odysseus.

The only souls actually suffering physical punishment in Homer's epic are Tityos, Tantalos, and Sisyphos, all of whom participated in earthly rebellion against the gods: vultures are eating the liver of Tityos because he abused Leto, a favorite of Zeus; Tantalos is suffering hunger and thirst because of stealing nectar from the gods and revealing their secrets—among other deeds; and Sisyphos, noted for his cunning (post-Homeric Greeks made him the father of Odysseus), continually rolls a stone up a hill for, among other matters, trapping Death in chains when he arrived to take him to Hades—Ares had to come and rescue Death before Sisyphos could die. The myriad other personages Odysseus speaks with in Hades are receiving neither reward nor punishment.

Because of Virgil's vividly imagined experience of the underworld, Dante chooses the Roman poet to guide him through that region, and Dante follows his master in inventing a landscape of various regions: trees, rocks, circles, fortresses with walls, solid pillars, and towers of iron, as well as peaceful meadows. Virgil roughly divides Hades into regions corresponding to later Christian concepts of Hell, Purgatory, and Heaven: there is a place where sinners are being horribly punished; one where there seems to be neither pleasure nor pain, inhabited by Phaedra, Dido, and others; and, finally, a beautiful, blessed grove where we find priests, poets, other artists, and Anchises, the father of Aeneas.

No wonder early Christians believed Virgil to be one of them, for Virgil has populated his Hell with sins they condemn (although Virgil is actually referring subtly to crimes of known

Roman citizens): hate, envy, lying, adultery, rebellion, blasphemy, and oath-breaking. However, Virgil was not alone among pre-Christians in his conception of an afterlife of punishment and reward. Fifth-century Greeks, especially the Orphics and the Pythagoreans, first developed those ideas.

One of the striking Virgilian echoes of Homer is in the pairing of Tiresias, who tells Odysseus of his ultimate mystical journey of redemption (*Odyssey* xi.90–137), and Anchises, the father of Aeneas, who relates to him the future glories of the Roman empire (vi.679–898:910–1218), demonstrating once more the paramount difference between these two epics: Homer is concerned with the relation between the hero and his soul, and Virgil with the obligations of the hero to society.

The *Aeneid* has many features that make it strikingly modern. Our first picture of Aeneas and his men (i.208–10:284–86) is one of human beings rather than heroes: they are caught between hope and fear, that modern predicament unknown to Homeric heroes, who knew either hope *or* fear, and not the wasteland in between. Aeneas himself has more in common with the "heroes" of twentieth-century novels than he does with Homeric heroes, in that he hides his inner fears and displays to his men a hope he does not feel.

Art also assumes an importance unknown in Homeric times; even fifth-century Greeks did not have words for art and literature, only terms for craftsmanship.

There is an early, powerful scene (i.441–63:605–72) when Aeneas and some of his men, in disguise, enter the city and discover that Dido and her citizens have already memorialized the Trojan War and its heroes on the walls of a shrine to Juno, the patron deity of Carthage, that has not yet even been completed. Aeneas stops and weeps as he looks at the frieze, and exclaims to his companion Achates that all the world knows and honors their sorrows. Virgil pays high tribute to the power of art to nourish the soul of Aeneas as he "feasts" on a "mere image." This is the very definition of civilization: a collection of citizens who remember the past, and who honor history through the creation of art.

The creation of images as an act of tribute occurs again and again in this epic. The cunning craftsman Daedalus, for example, is remembered as one who carved history on temple walls (vi.14–33:12–50). Virgil even foreshadows Eliot's notion that the man who suffers is not the same man when he creates: he pictures Daedalus twice failing in his attempt to carve the trials of his son Icarus in gold because the grief he still felt prevented him from achieving a Wordsworthian poetry of "emotion recollected in tranquility."

Virgil himself apparently felt, in his dying request that the poem be destroyed, that he had not yet sufficiently transformed his epic into art. All unbiased readers of the text realize, as Augustus did, that the poet was mistaken: art is at its highest when it transfigures men and events and, as Joyce writes in *Ulysses*, engages in "the eternal affirmation of the spirit of man in literature."

Tristan

*T**ristan* is a bridge from the medieval world to the modern world of individuality, personality, and the divided self. As a literary form, the poem is also a romance that forms a bridge from classic epic to modern novel in its combination of elements of epic, romance, and novel. In addition, so many early medieval and high medieval cultures flow into the work that it becomes emblematic of various ways of living in Ireland, Wales, France, and Germany from the period of at least A.D. 500 to A.D. 1210, the date usually assigned—roughly—to the composition in German of the poem *Tristan* by the man we know of as Gottfried of Strassburg.

Is this to say that Achilleus, Odysseus, and Aeneas had no individuality, no personality? Yes, or at least not in the sense in which those terms acquired meaning beginning with medieval works, for the classical-epic heroes were distinguished by outstanding solitary attributes: the wrath of Achilleus, the resourcefulness of Odysseus, the piety of Aeneas. Moreover, the Homeric heroes did not consider themselves as being separate from the world; rather, the world was an extension of their own bodies.

The heroes of classical epics were locked into a society and a heroic code in which there was no mobility and limited freedom of choice. They were seldom confused or puzzled by a world which was merely an extension of themselves: that world was not split into self against self. Homeric heroes cleave *to* the world; heroes of medieval epics are cleaved *from* the world. Homeric heroes are spirited doers; medieval-epic heroes are suffused with despair. Odysseus ponders, decides, and acts; Tristan, Isolde, and Mark puzzle, worry, and delay. Young men in Homeric times were born into an economic and social class from which they could not move; an ambitious young man in medieval Europe could become a knight or a cleric, or set off to the Orient to make his fortune in the spice trade.

Achilleus, as we saw, did not know how to behave in a divided world: when in conflict with Agamemnon, he could only react by retiring to his shelter—separating himself from a divided world and the possibility of a divided self. With the exception of that rare and shining moment when Achilleus breaks the heroic code and gives over the body of Hektor to Priam, the Homeric heroes did not have freedom of choice, any more than did Aeneas. The heroes and heroines in the epics we have encountered thus far believed that the gods, and not their individual characters, were designing and controlling their destinies.

An individual personality is acquired through multiple and varied encounters, accompanied by the conviction that one is determining one's own future. In that sense Odysseus in the *Odyssey* is the closest we have come to a modern man so far, and his individuality is one of the reasons some consider that work to be a romance rather than an epic. To learn by having varied experiences away from the safety of home is to become an individual with a distinct personality, and, in the twelfth and thirteenth centuries, this was precisely what was provided a young man of nobility. Tristan is sent by his foster parents to be tutored in the home of a nobleman, where he learns foreign languages, books, and music, as well as riding, fencing, wrestling, running, jumping, throwing the javelin, tracking, hunting, and courtly behavior. After his return home he is abducted and then left stranded on the Cornish coast, where he has to prove his own worth without benefit of name or family.

What *Tristan* reflects is the beginning of Medieval Humanism, a belief in the worth of the individual and in the possibility of individual development and change: an acceptance of life in the world as something other than preparation for eternity. This meant an acceptance of one's earthly body as well as one's divine soul, and the dawning of the Renaissance idea that man is not permanently "fixed," as are the angels above and the demons below, but is a free agent who is both angel and demon, one who, by his own striving, is capable of becoming one or the other or both: an *ange-bête*.

Medieval man is learning the terrors of trying to live with God, Man, and Self, as the mutilated bodies of Peter Abelard (1079–1142) and Saint Thomas à Becket (1118?–1170) testify. Tristan and Isolde are representative of this conflict as they tragically attempt to satisfy the demands of God, society, and their own individual personalities.

A rather mundane miracle brought about this development of individuality: the rise of a middle-class merchant society. For some five centuries preceding the thirteenth century, Europe had been effectively isolated from the rest of the world by the antagonism of Islam on its southern and eastern shores, and the dangers offered by the Vikings on the northern and western shores. During the twelfth and thirteenth centuries the trade routes to the Orient were again opened, and at the same time the Viking threat diminished. It could be said that the renewed spice trade with the East almost alone created the rise of the merchant class, the founding and enlargement of cities, and a new element unknown to the preceding feudal society: money and leisure time for education and for reading—a financial situation that opened up the world of learning to young men for purposes other than a religious vocation.

The signing of the Magna Charta, the building of the Cathedral of Notre Dame, the rise of the universities in Paris, Bologna, and Oxford, four crusades, and, in the world of literature, the flowering of *Parzival, Tristan,* and the *Nibelungen-lied,* as well as numerous other poems, all occurred during the astonishingly brief period of fifty years—from 1180 to 1230.

With these poems we are once again in the Homeric territory of oral performance, for the medieval *conteurs* operated in much the same fashion as the early Greek bards, going from court to court earning their bed and breakfast by singing after-dinner tales. Depending upon the singer, the Tristan stories varied in detail until we reach Gottfried, who composed a version so superior to the best-known previous renditions that it came to be the one most highly regarded.

There are, from this period, at least five authors of Tristan stories. In examining the *Iliad*, when we looked at the problem of determining which society was being reflected in the work, we realized the poem had been handed down from singer to singer over a period of centuries. The history of *Tristan* is even more fascinating and puzzling: it is a Celtic story that originated in Ireland, passed on through Wales, crossed the Channel to the Breton coast of France, and then made its way to Germany to become Gottfried's version.

The migratory nature of *Tristan* is also true of much of the literature of this time, in particular the tales of King Arthur, much sung about by the French Bretons, perhaps because they were descendants of peoples driven out of England by the Anglo-Saxon invasion who hoped for the return of Arthur and restoration to their native land. Indeed, the stories of Arthur linguistically reveal their migration in the transformations of the Irish word *Caladbolg* into the Welsh *Caledvwlch*, then into the French *Calibourc*, and finally into the English *Excalibur*. The names of many of the characters in *Tristan* are Celtic in origin.

These medieval romances frequently offer instances of myth becoming history to the people who sang and heard the stories, and it is worth looking briefly at some of the qualities these myths have in common with one another, as well as with the poem *Tristan*.

One of the earliest Irish myths is the story of Ériu. A disheveled hag in the month of March, she represents Nature in her transformation from harsh winter into a lovely spring goddess in April, when, representing the land of Ireland, she marries MacGrene ("son of the son"). Tristan, a son of three fathers, and Isolde, the Irish princess, appear to be manifestations of Ériu and MacGrene.

Many of the elements of *Tristan* are to be found in early Celtic stories, such as the tests of the hero in the eighth-century Irish *Feast of Bricriu*, as well as in *Sir Gawain and the Green Knight*.

As with Thebes before the arrival of Oedipus, in some of the stories the land of Ireland is under a spell or plague that can be lifted only by a hero: this is paralleled by Tristan's relief of Cornwall from the yearly tribute sent to the Irish king.

Potions and magic are also elements in Celtic stories, as well as in native European folk tales, and the recognition of the hero while he is in a bath occurs in the *Wooing of Emer* when Drust, a hero much like Tristan, undergoes ordeals and wounds and is recognized while bathing.

Drust, a direct forerunner of Tristan, was a real person; he was the son of the King of the Picts in northern Scotland toward the end of the eighth century; in the later Welsh version of the story his name becomes Drystan. The connection is even more apparent in his love for Essyllt, the wife of his uncle, King Mark. The name Mark is the Celtic root for horse (Irish *marc*, and Welsh *march*), and the humor in some of the early tales derives from Mark's attempts to keep his horse's ears a secret—not only from his subjects, but from his barber.

The Irish stories involving the lovers Diarmaid and Grainne, the wife of Finn, also provide elements of the Tristan story, such as the lovers' placing a cold stone (sword) between them when they are sleeping in the forest in order to prove their innocence to Finn. Diarmaid, it turns out, is a most unwilling suitor, refusing to have intercourse with Grainne during their sojourn in the forest (another Tristan element) until the persistent Grainne insults him by saying, when muddy water splashes on her thigh, that the water is more forward than Diarmaid is. With this insult to his manhood, Diarmaid relents. This is more than the equally reluctant lover Tristan does with Isolde of the White Hands when muddy water splashes on her thigh and she makes the same remark about him to her brother.

Joyce, in his modern comic masterpiece *Finnegans Wake*, uses the story of the youthful Diarmaid stealing the young bride away from the older Finn as a basis of his novel—Humphrey Chimpden Earwicker's fear that his sons will steal his daughter Isabel (Isolde), for whom he has incestuous desire, away from him. And, of course, Joyce sets the Earwicker pub and residence in Chapelizod, the section of Dublin named for the legendary location of the Chapel of Isolde.

The various Tristan stories, as well as many other tales, contain such traditional elements as voyages for healing, substitutions of a virgin on the wedding night, trysts under a tree, flights to a forest, vows of truth, island combat, rudderless boats, quests for a princess, and laying of traps for a suspect. This last occurs in stories as early as those told by Herodotus.

A wound which can only be healed by the enemy, or by the person who inflicted the wound, is also ancient. In one of the legends of the Trojan War, Achilleus and his men arrive at Mysia; mistaking it for Troy, they fight the inhabitants. Achilleus wounds Telephos in the leg before departing for Troy. After making a pilgrimage to Delphi, Telephos goes to Mycenae disguised as a beggar; there he is aided by Klytemnestra: she assists him in his abduction of her young son, and he takes Orestes to a Mycenean altar. The cunning Odysseus, who also oddly enough happens to be in the neighborhood, discovers the identity of Telephos, that Troy cannot be taken without the wounded man's aid, and that Telephos can only be healed by Achilleus. When Achilleus is approached (apparently everybody is in the neighborhood), he claims to be no physician, but Odysseus interprets the directions to mean that the "author" of the wound—the spear of Achilleus—is the only physician that can heal Telephos. Achilleus applies rust from his spear to the wound and Telephos is healed. In a later treatment of this legend, Sophocles changes the name of Telephos to Philoctetes, and, in his play of that title, turns Odysseus into a villain who will use any trick to get the bow of Philoctetes that is necessary for defeating the Trojans.

Healing by the enemy also figures in the Norse sagas *Harald Hringsbane* and *Aliflekkrsaga*, as well as in the Irish *Táin bó Cuálnge*, and other tales about the famous Cuchulainn.

In addition to occurring in Norse, Old Irish, and Old French folk tales, the love potion makes early appearances in Latin literature, primarily in Horace, Juvenal, Pliny, Suetonius, and Plautus.

There is a striking parallel in the Irish story of Deirdre, who, married to King Conor, runs away into the forest with the young Naisi. Naisi is slaughtered in a meadow when the two of them are captured, but Deirdre is spared; a year later she kills herself by striking her head against a stone when her husband taunts her about a suspected new possibility of infidelity.

Earlier and less sophisticated versions of *Tristan* tell of barbarisms by Isolde, who laughs as she watches Tristan being whipped with lashes, and by Mark, who not only has Tristan killed but comes close to punishing Isolde by turning her over to a hundred lepers who wish to satisfy their lust with her.

Tristan possesses elements of Oriental, as well as Celtic and European, literature. The substitution of a virgin maid for the deflowered wife, as when Isolde sends Brangane to Mark's bed as her substitute, is common in Sanskrit (Hindu) tales, as is the Act of Truth, in which Isolde has to grasp the red-hot iron. In the Arabic story of Kais and Lobna, the husband marries a second time, but remains faithful to his first wife; when he becomes ill, he sends for her and they die together, as do Tristan and Isolde. Apparently these Oriental stories made a roundabout trip from India to China, then back to Arabia and Persia, and thence to Europe by way of the Islamic invasion of Spain and Arabic settlements in southern France.

Tristan is a story about love, and in many ways it establishes itself in a privileged position by becoming a paradigm for the Western novel: it is about a love triangle that involves adultery. At the same time, it defines the Western world's vision of love: the European and, later, the American experiences of love are presented in literature as mixtures of spirituality and sensuality, joy and sorrow, exaltation and pain, and the temptations of the forbidden. Love must have obstacles to survive: the love potion must contain both love and death, and Tristan and Isolde must be both patients of love and physicians to each other.

Love truly alienates the two lovers. Their misery anticipates the modern condition of a feeling of homelessness, as the life of the court makes them unhappy in their subterfuge and deceit. At the same time, it is impossible for them to live the life of simple folk, as they discover when they return without protest from their idyllic but isolated Cave of Love. They have no home, and they can find happiness neither in society nor in togetherness apart from the world. They are in the condition of death, and have been since they drank the love potion.

Love turns Tristan and Isolde into creatures who cannot live with God, with society, or with themselves. They have been overwhelmed by the modern version of the Dionysian force of love, which does not allow the integrated life known by the Athenians, but rather demands that love be either spiritual or sexual.

Their cave, the Temple of Love, is described in technical terms applicable to a medieval church, and the raised bed, placed where the altar would be, is dedicated to the Goddess of Love. They lie on it together, with the sword (cross) between them, and from the three symbolic windows stream down the three lights of loving kindness, humility, and breeding (propriety and reputation). Their bridled lust for each other is not loving kindness, their treatment of King Mark has in it no humility, and their propriety and reputation are but a sham.

Given the familiar ethereal Wagnerian treatment of the two lovers, this hardly seems fair. However, following the drinking of the love potion, they are certainly not suffering from unrequited love, but rather from unrequited sex. This is made evident when they confess their love to Brangane and politely ask her to disappear so they can consummate their mutual attraction—which they do that evening—and the sexual union is described as an act that heals the sick "patients." Throughout the rest of the poem they are not scheming to be together—they *are* together in the society of the court—but rather scheming for sexual contact. This is not to denigrate either their feelings or what the society of the time thought of them. After all, love can be adulterous sex and unadulterated love at one and the same time. It should also be remembered that Tristan is barely eighteen and, given the customs of the time, Isolde probably no more than fourteen.

There are revealing variations on the time span of that love in at least three authors: Thomas, whose work Gottfried transforms into art in his version, holds that the love potion wasn't needed, as the two were in love already; the cynical storyteller Béroul relates that the love potion lasted for three years; the romantic Gottfried presents it as lasting for eternity.

And so, in Gottfried's version, Isolde is not responsible for her infidelity to her husband, and Tristan is not responsible for betraying Mark's friendship: the love potion gave them no choice. Further, it was commonly held among the nobility in this period that true love could not exist between married persons, as family-arranged marriage, or even the obligation to love, prevented it. This was so declared at a Court of Love held at the castle of the Countess of Champagne in 1174: these courts were a popular feature of medieval life. Moreover, Christianity is a religion of love, in ways that the Greek and Roman religions were definitely not. Indeed, does not the loving God of Christianity condone the adulterous relationship—and put His blessings on it—when He protects Isolde from being burned by the red-hot iron when she is deceptive in the sacred oath about her fidelity to Mark? No wonder many readers find this episode puzzling, if not sacrilegious.

Isolde's infidelity is magnified not only by her vows to Mark, but also by the deep friendship that exists between Tristan and her husband, as Mark, in Celtic society, became Tristan's father upon the death of Rivalin. Isolde is thus not only Tristan's lover but legally his teenage stepmother: Phaedra, whose love for her stepson, Hippolytus, remained unrequited, was hardly in a worse position.

Mark's early feelings for Tristan are so deep that he entrusts him with the keeping of the sacred royal regalia—his sword, spurs, crossbow, and golden horn—and bestows upon him untold wealth, vowing to leave the castle and all his wealth to him. Mark addresses Tristan in the language of lovers: "You will be mine, and I will be yours." Tristan, then, is placed in the impossible position of choosing between his father-friend and his stepmother-lover. He initially complies with the code of honor when he turns Isolde over to Mark for marriage instead of eloping with her. However, the deceptions begin immediately, and Tristan makes the fateful choice between his love for Isolde and his friendship for Mark.

Mark's behavior in Gottfried's telling of the story is considerably more civilized than his barbaric actions in earlier versions—killing Tristan after luring the lovers back from the forest with false promises of safety, and threatening to turn Isolde over to the sexual pleasures of the hundred lepers. Indeed, he becomes more than sympathetic in his frustrated efforts to trick the lovers into revealing themselves. We sense throughout that he knows of their love—in spite of the lack of concrete evidence—and this makes him a very sad character indeed. After all, Celtic law very much resembled primitive Hellenic customs in that women were property, like fields, to be leased out to farming by neighbors if so desired, or to be burned: from the eighth to the twelfth century, burning was the usual punishment for the unfaithful wife.

Irish storytellers produced a large body of tragic stories— particularly in the tenth century—that were far superior to the productions in France. These stories, as can be seen from *Tristan* and those concerning Parzival, Gawain, and Lancelot, were not just stories of love. They were also *Bildungsromane*—adventures in the physical, intellectual, and moral development of a young man—as well as *Künstlerromane*—documentations of the growth of the artist. In fact, much is made of Tristan's skill at playing instruments and in musical composition. In scenes recalling the ancient story of Pygmalion and Galatea, Tristan teaches Isolde not only Latin and other foreign languages, but how to read, write, and play musical instruments; if they did fall in love before drinking the love potion, then it would have been during these intimate sessions.

But Tristan differs from other heroes in that up until the age of eighteen he is neither cleric nor knight. Whereas other youths became knights at the age of puberty and immediately thereafter began their exploits, Tristan spends his time receiving an education away from his foster parents, being abducted, and having, at the age of fourteen, to demonstrate that he is worthy of acceptance to the court of King Mark. He is not knighted until he is eighteen.

Tristan has to develop *edeler muot*, the words in Gottfried's poem signifying nobility of spirit and soul, as well as *lip*, excellence of body and life spirit—a quality similar to the Homeric *areté* and *áristos*. *Lip* is acquired primarily through physical, intellectual, and moral education, and it shines through rags, as we see in the appearance of Rual before King Mark, when, like the naked and salt-caked Odysseus before the Princess Nausikaa, he has to validate his worth.

One is born with *lip*, but it must then be properly developed. (Aristotle, as is evident from his *Ethics*, would have approved of the idea: good fortune is present at birth and must then be nurtured.) Tristan is fortunate in that he has three fathers: from his actual father, Rivalin, he inherits *muot*, nobility of spirit; from his foster father, Rual, he receives *lip*, education; and from his third father, Mark, he acquires *guot*, wealth.

The combination of these qualities makes Tristan *quadrare*, square and thus flawless. Symbolic fours appear throughout this poem and other medieval works, and the aim of every hero was to be foursquare. Tristan goes to fight Morold armed with God, Right, Himself, and a Willing Heart. Plato in his *Protagoras* uses the symbol of foursquare when he applies it to hands, feet, and mind. The metaphor is drawn from architecture: man must be a perfect building, with both his exterior and his interior structures in perfect harmony.

The episodic nature of *Tristan* is unified and bound together by the proleptic device of doubling, one that Joyce makes considerable use of in his *Finnegans Wake*, where he even puns on Dublin and doubling with the word "doublin." A few outstanding uses of doubling among the many in the poem are: Rivalin and his son both fight Morgan; father and son both have a cherished friend in Rual; Tristan fights Morold and slays him, and is later slain by Orgillus; Queen Isolde is the Dawn and Princess Isolde is the Sun; Isolde prefigures Isolde of the White Hands; Tristan makes two healing voyages to Dublin; he slays a dragon and later a giant; the treacherous steward in Dublin is echoed in the one at King Mark's court; the rescue by Tristan disguised as a minstrel is matched by his rescue as pilgrim; Gandin woos Isolde and then Cariado woos her; the assignation by the brook is followed by the assignation in the orchard; Tristan is banished twice by Mark; Mark loves Isolde and Isolde loves Tristan; and, at the end, Tristan is wounded by the poisoned spear of Orgillus, just as earlier he had been wounded by the spear of Morold: but this time he cannot make a journey of healing to Queen Isolde, and he dies of sorrow from the lie told him by Isolde of the White Hands before Isolde can arrive with the healing medicine.

Tristan reveals many similarities to episodes we have seen in classic Greek and Roman works. Disguise, which figures prominently in the poem—Tristan (Tantris) is frequently in disguise as a beggar or a pilgrim—makes an early appearance when Blancheflor comes disguised as a beggarwoman to visit the dying Rivalin: the warmth of their comforting embraces both heals Rivalin and sexually arouses them, and Tristan is conceived.

Blancheflor is a life-giver and is proleptic for the two Irish Isoldes in the poem. When the pregnant Blancheflor discovers that Rivalin is leaving the court of King Mark without her, she faints "as if dead," and is revived by his kisses. The love-death theme is thus strongly stated from the very beginning: Blancheflor tells Rivalin that if he does not take her with him as his love, then her brother Mark will "destroy" her, will "put her to death" for bringing dishonor to him. She is, like Tristan and

Isolde, a love-death symbol: she "bore death" away when she conceived Tristan, and she dies giving birth to him. The infant Tristan joins the numerous mythical and classical heroes who had extraordinary births.

To be raised by foster parents is another heroic attribute not limited to Orestes and Oedipus. Indeed, such an experience was the norm rather than the exception for young nobles in Celtic and Germanic societies. Moreover, Rual and his wife form Tristan's name from "triste" (an obvious French addition to the Celtic tale)—again in the traditional manner of epic and tragic heroes who receive names that are emblematic of their lives: Odysseus (giving pain) and Oedipus (swollen foot).

Just as God watches over the ordeal of Isolde at the testing, He sends the storm that causes Tristan's abductors to promise to set him ashore in Cornwall, reminiscent of the storm-battered Odysseus after he leaves Kalypso. And, like Odysseus washed up on the shores of the Phaiakians, Tristan has to prove, as he does to the hunters, that he is an accomplished and civilized person. When he arrives before Mark, they are both in disguise, and neither knows the true identity of the other—not very much different from the meeting at the hut of the swineherd Eumaios in the *Odyssey* when Odysseus knows Telemachos but not vice versa, or when Odysseus knows Penelope and she pretends not to know who he is. And Tristan establishes his *lip*, his prowess, just as Odysseus does on the island of the Phaiakians in the athletic competitions.

After Rual arrives and reveals his identity—there are an extraordinary number of recognition and reversal scenes in this poem—he relates the story of Tristan's childhood, bringing tears to his own eyes as well as to Mark's, a scene reminiscent of the banquet of the King of the Phaiakians when Odysseus hides the tears brought on by the tale of Troy that Demodokos sings.

The yearly tribute sent by Mark and his barons to King Gurman of Ireland—bronze one year, silver the next, then gold, and finally, every fourth year, the tribute of young boys—has its counterpart in the human sacrifices of seven youths and seven maidens imposed yearly upon Athens by Crete. The associated story of the Minotaur, the monster in the Daedalian labyrinth who eats the youths and is slain by Theseus, finds its echo in Tristan's killing of Morold, who has come from Ireland to collect the tribute, as well as in his slaughter of the dragon that is terrorizing Ireland. King Gurman, in a remarkable piece of Celtic irony, has promised his daughter to the man who slays the dragon, and it is indeed Tristan who wins her. And on his return to Cornwall with Isolde, the heroic Tristan brings with him all the young hostages.

Tristan's rebuke of the cowardly barons, when he finds them drawing lots to determine which of them will fight Morold, recalls Sarpedon's speech to Glaukos in the definition of a hero. Tristan describes a hero as one who fights with honor because he knows he will thereby gain the regard of God throughout eternity, and if he loses, he knows that God values earthly sorrows and the quick death of a youth in single combat; moreover, he has God and a just cause on his side.

Combat on an island where no one can interfere is traditional throughout heroic literature, but Tristan's brave gesture of setting his boat adrift after he lands because, as he tells Morold, only one of them will be returning, is a nice Celtic touch.

Tristan's arrival on the Irish shore in a drifting boat containing only the hero and a harp has all the elements of a mythic journey, as indeed it is, along with his winning over the populace as well as the court through his skill with both music and words.

Following this journey of healing, Tristan returns again to woo Isolde for King Mark. After slaying the dragon, he submerges himself in a pool in the forest, and when brought back to the castle for his second healing, he is placed in a bath.

These bathing scenes, so reminiscent of the numerous cleansings of Odysseus and Telemachos in the *Odyssey*, culminate in Isolde's recognition of the identity of the naked Tristan, as the maid Eurykleia discovered the identifying scar of Odysseus while she was bathing him. An elderly maid with a naked hero is one matter; a young girl in a room with a naked male youth is emblematic of the frankness of Celtic and Nordic un-ashamed acceptance of the human body. This disregard of the nakedness of the youth and the long conversation between him and the three women in the room—Isolde, her mother, and Brangane—further illustrate the Celtic open acceptance of the body. (These were of the same stock as the European Celts who terrified their enemies by attacking them naked on horse-back.)

Some commentators find it puzzling that the Celtic Princess Isolde does not kill Tristan in the bath; however, just as Tristan is torn between manly honor and love, Isolde states quite clearly that she is divided between womanhood and anger: the poet tells us that womanhood triumphs. (She will later display her Celtic ferocity when she orders that Brangane be killed by having her head cut off.) In any case, she must have been somewhat charmed by the naked Tristan in the bath delivering his carefully composed, courtly speeches. Brangane, as usual, brings her wise counsel to the solution of the dilemma.

After all is resolved at the Irish court and Tristan and Isolde have set sail and consumed the love potion, Isolde is oppressed by her love, as she does not know if it is returned. When Tristan asks what she suffers from, she replies, "Lameir," a word that, in its various spellings, contains all the major thematic images of the poem: love, bitterness, and the sea.

From this point on, the poem consists of a series of traditional adventures, primarily involving ruses and tricks, and we need not subject them to further analysis. A few, however, deserve attention, either because they are quite curious or because they provide further revelations of the poet's conception of art.

Readers unfamiliar with early Celtic and Nordic customs may be puzzled by the sleeping arrangements; these took a variety of forms. In some cases the king and all his followers, both men and women, lived, ate, and slept in the same room. Following the evening meal, they would pull back the benches from the table, someone would spread thatch on the floor, and they would all sleep by their places at the table. Some form of light was left dimly burning in order to discourage unlawful sexual intercourse, but, presumably, lawful intercourse proceeded in some kind of unabashed fashion. In more sophisticated courts the king and queen slept in a central chamber which separated the men in the sleeping hall on one side from the women on the other.

In some versions of *Tristan* the king and queen sleep in a central bed with all the knights arranged in beds around them. It is in one of these stories that Tristan tries to enter Isolde's bed while Mark is away, and is wounded by the swords Mark has carefully hidden around the bed. In order to protect their comrade, the other knights all wound themselves so as to prevent Mark from identifying the guilty one. In Gottfried's poem this has been made somewhat more sophisticated by having Tristan the only knight sleeping in the room, and by the sprinkling of flour on the floor as a substitute for swords.

This sleeping arrangement leads to a strangely ritualistic wedding night for Mark and Isolde, as Tristan is in the room with them. Being Mark's heir and favorite, he has the honor of first leading the substitute bride (the virgin Brangane, who has been persuaded by Tristan and Isolde to take Isolde's place) to the darkened wedding bed, and then Isolde, his beloved and the real bride. Following this, he brings wine for Mark to drink, the traditional toast offered to the deflowering of a virgin.

This would all be heartbreaking except for two reasons: to a modern temperament, the entire stately ritual can become somewhat amusing when one realizes there are four people in the room, each of them now sexually involved with one or more of the other three in a thoroughly modern fictional—and sometimes realistic—way. The other reason is that no one in the room has a heart that is breaking. This is high Celtic control, and it is deadly serious: Tristan's mother, Blancheflor, does not cry out in lamentation when she learns of Rivalin's death, nor when, four days later, she gives birth to Tristan. Nor does Tristan weep when Rual and Mark are both in tears over Rual's recital of the earlier woes of Tristan. This Celtic nobility, both men and women, had more in common with the Greek tragic heroines Klytemnestra, Antigone, and Medea than with the weeping Achilleus and Odysseus.

Tristan is probably not exerting any great control when he finds one excuse after another not to consummate his marriage with Isolde of the White Hands: her raucous and demanding behavior is not very endearing, and she is, after all, the only real villainess in the poem. One cannot help but be amused by his four-page interior meditation about whether or not to have intercourse with her—and, when she insists, his lame excuse that he has a pain from an old wound, an excuse that is figuratively, if not literally, true.

The major preceding instances we have had in these essays to show the effect art has on life are Achilleus' substitution of songs of fame for acts of fame in the *Iliad*, Odysseus' tears at the court of King Alkinoos in the *Odyssey* when the bard sings about the Trojan War, the entrance of Aeneas into Carthage, when he weeps over the carvings of the Trojan War on the walls of that city, and the discussion of the function of poetry in *Frogs*. *Tristan* adds to this concept with the Hall of Statues that Tristan orders fashioned in the cavern, a gallery of art with statues of Isolde and Brangane where he can remember and relive the past, bring it as much as possible into the present. The poem then has Tristan's friend Caerdin fall in love with the statue of Brangane, demonstrating the ability of art not only to recapture the past and vivify the present, but to influence and direct the future.

This, of course, has been Gottfried's intention throughout his version, as he advises us that love stories from the past can afford comfort and warmth in the present, and direct future acceptance of the joys and sorrows of love.

Although some have contended that Gottfried has his tongue in his cheek, that he is telling an outrageous story of impatient and licentious lovers, and that he is mocking the entire chivalric establishment, I prefer to believe not—although I did at one time. It seems to me that this intelligent, gentle, and sensitive poet (we know him only from his work) is smiling wryly over his own foolishness in love—he reminds us of this in his poem— and is adding courtly gentility to the state of love without totally abandoning the primitive and barbaric nature of love handed down to him by a tale that may have been conceived as early as the first century of our era.

Gottfried seems to me to be saying, in the episode of Isolde's ordeal of truth by fire, that God knows the foolishness of lovers when He sees it, and He prefers not to burn her, especially as He knows that Tristan will die from the wound of a poisoned spear in his groin, and that Isolde, lying beside her dead beloved, her body to his body, her mouth to his mouth, will die as she is kissing Tristan.

Inferno

To BEGIN with a comedy of absurdity before discussing Dante's comedy of sublimity, Lady Bracknell, in Oscar Wilde's *The Importance of Being Earnest*, asks Jack his qualifications for engagement to her daughter, Gwendolen. A man about to be married, she says, should know "either everything or nothing. Which do you know?" After some hesitation over which answer she wants, Jack hazards that he knows nothing. "I am pleased to hear it," Lady Bracknell replies, "I do not approve of anything that tampers with natural ignorance. Ignorance is like a delicate exotic fruit; touch it and the bloom is gone."

I agree with Eliot when he says that it is better to know nothing about the *Divine Comedy* before reading it than to know everything; a "natural ignorance" will allow for an appreciation of the exotic delicacy of the poem which a substantial amount of literary and historical scholarship might prevent. If you asked how to get to the World Trade Center in New York and were handed a map which, when unfolded, was exactly the size of Manhattan, you would still be as ignorant of the location of the building as you were before being given the map. I intend to provide a small, hand-drawn map of Dante's political and literary life, which will be of aid in following Dante and Virgil through the geography of Hell. For later visits to favorite locations, the tourist can consult the more than extensive scholarly "maps"—some of them actually larger than the poem—that are available in any good library.

Many of the poems we have examined have been quest poems in which the hero is searching either for a lost home or for a new home. Both Odysseus and Aeneas, during the course of their journeys, make dangerous, hero-validating trips to a Hades where their own future is predicted. Dante is on a quest for salvation, and he also is told his future during his trip to Hell. The beauty and the details of the poem engage the involvement of another quester: the reader.

Aristotle is one of the primary influences on Dante, but to Dante man is not an animal, and he lives not just in a city, but in the world and in eternity. The last two territories are both immediate to Dante, and they are the major concerns of his mature work.

Dante was born in 1265 in Florence, a city that had been divided for generations by the struggle for supremacy between the Holy Roman Emperor and the Pope. Dante's parents were middle-class and among the adherents to the Guelf party, many of whom supported the idea of equality between the Emperor and the Pope. As a young man Dante dedicated himself to poetry, especially Virgil's, and to philosophy. He fought as a soldier for Florence, and served on various councils, including the important Council of the One Hundred, and he also held the high office of Prior. In 1302 he opposed the Pope's attempt to exert secular rule, and, on an embassy to appeal to the Pope, he was detained, banished by the leading politicians from his beloved Florence, and sentenced to death.

He lived a life of exile, earning his living as mediator between various noble houses in an Italy that was in constant turmoil over the conflict between Pope and Emperor. His wife and children remained in Florence, the children were later condemned to death because of their father's beliefs and had to flee, and he spent the last eight years of his life with his family in Ravenna, probably teaching poetry, where he died in 1321. He had spent most of the previous ten years working on his poem.

The purpose of his poem grows out of his religious and political life: to set the Emperor and the Pope on the straight path, one bringing order to the world, the other bringing order to man's eternal soul.

The philosophy and theology of his poem were set out earlier in his *De Monarchia*, a work about universal empire.

Founding his ideas upon Saint Paul's, which followed those of Jesus, Dante holds to the duality of the life of man, in that one should render proper dues to the always separate spheres of church and state. The Emperor was to reign over the Earthly Paradise: mortality, the blessedness that comes from using all one's faculties, philosophy, moral and intellectual virtues, and reason. The Pope was to reign over the Heavenly Paradise: man's immortal soul; theology; wisdom and power; the virtues of faith, hope, and love; and the Holy Spirit.

In the *Divine Comedy* Virgil symbolizes earthly Reason and Beatrice the eternal Holy Spirit. Dante first saw Beatrice (she was probably a Florentine gentlewoman named Bice) in his early youth, and, though they perhaps never exchanged words, she was to become a major symbol in his life and poetry. She was young when she died, and she became the Platonic path for Dante from philosophy to beauty, from beauty to love, and from love to Divine Goodness. She initiates Dante's journey through the afterlife, watches over him in the *Inferno*, and guides him through the uppermost region of *Purgatorio* and then through *Paradiso*, territories inaccessible and thus unknown to the pre-Christian Virgil.

The poem is a celebration of free will, and it reflects the medieval rather than the coming Renaissance world, particularly in its theology, structure, and use of symbolic numerology.

The poem is composed of three canticles (the Trinity), each canticle containing thirty-three cantos, except the first, whose prologue-type canto makes a total of one hundred cantos (a "perfect" number) in the entire poem. In a final veneration of the Trinity, the stanzas are tercets written in *terza rima*, an interlocking rhyme scheme of *aba* in the first tercet, *bcb* in the second, and so on throughout each canto.

As Dante wanted his work to be read by all his compatriots, and not just scholars, he chose to write it in Florentine Italian rather than in Latin. He called it a *Commedia*, not only because it had a happy ending but because he thought the term was derived from Greek words meaning village and song, and his poem was to be a song of the people, written in the "careless and humble" language of everyday speech. It acquired its present title in 1555 from an editor who truly considered the poem to be Divine: the purpose of the poem is the salvation of human souls.

Dante draws heavily on both Plato and Aristotle in determining the nature of sin—a word, of course, unknown to those two philosophers.

Plato constructs his *Republic* on his analysis of a political and human psyche consisting of reason (mind), spirit (heart), and appetite (stomach and sexual organs). The citizens of his state fall into one of those categories: philosophers of the mind, vigilant guardians of the state, and common people, who are ruled by their appetites. Dante is presenting the path to an ordered world, and he uses these three elements of the soul to show the disorder that results when appetite overcomes reason, spirit overcomes reason, and—most heinous of all—reason overcomes reason.

Dante considers appetites such as lust and gluttony to be innately human, as they are an excessive pursuit of something intrinsically good, and he locates those guilty of lust and gluttony, along with the other incontinents, in the upper circles of Hell, where their punishments are not as severe as those endured farther below.

Distortion of man's spirited element into violence against others, self, God, nature, or art is much more serious to Dante than sins of appetite, and he locates the violent sinners in a lower circle. Although the combative and spirited element in man is necessary to his survival, it must be controlled by reason.

What Dante considers most sinful of all is to use the one faculty of man which distinguishes him from animals, reason, in order to distort or betray reason. These sinners, the fraudulent and treacherous, occupy the eighth and ninth circles, the very bottom of Hell, where their punishments are greater than any others. It is there we find the wily and crafty Ulysses.

Dante also makes use of Aristotle, who, of course, uses Plato. In his *Ethics* Aristotle propounds the values of moderation, a mean between extremes, as, for example, courage is a mean between the excess of rashness and the deficiency of cowardice. Dante has peopled his Hell with sinners guilty of a lack of moderation, but particularly so in the upper circles, where he even pairs the avaricious and the prodigal in the fourth circle. Aristotle would have recognized all the sinners in Dante's Hell except for two groups he could never have conceived of— heretics and those guilty of original sin.

Dante agrees with Aristotle that good is the end at which nature aims, that this is the aim of God for the soul, and that, consequently, no man could hate God. He believes with Aristotle that man's faculties are not intrinsically evil, and that it is disorder in the soul which causes evil. Aristotle and Dante share with Plato a recognition of the importance of the harmony of the soul.

Christian theology, for Dante, thus develops from Plato's ideas about looking beyond the world for the highest good, Aristotle's presentation of moderation and final purpose, and the Hebraic prophets, who looked behind and blamed bad conduct in the past for present and future evils. Dante projects these concepts into a world created by providential design and presided over jointly by Emperor and Pope. He peoples his Hell with those who bring disorder to either the political or the sacred world created by God.

Finally, Dante inherits the great gift of allegory from Provençal poetry and medieval hermeneutics.

The poets of southern France, in their devotion to love and to beliefs the Church considered heretical (Albigensian), almost made a goddess out of their devotion to, and need for, secrecy. These poets of Provence flourished from around the years 1000–1200, writing in a tongue that combined the languages and cultures that had been pouring into the area for centuries: French, German, Italian, Spanish, Greek, and Arabic. Their Courts of Love and veneration of love certainly contributed to

Tristan, but what Dante seems to have learned most from them, in addition to allegory, is the conversational directness of their poetry, their gift of lyricism, and the ingenuity of their complicated poetic forms. Their culture and spoken language, but not their large body of phantasmagoric poetry, were wiped out by the Church in the war against the Albigensian heresy.

Two of the best Provençal poets are in Dante's poem. Bertran de Born appears in one of the most horrifying scenes in Hell: as he severed families and political ties on earth in the family of Henry II and Eleanor of Aquitaine, he carries his own severed head, using the eyes as a beacon to guide his way. Dante puts Arnaut Daniel in Purgatory, where he is in a fire that refines him. T. S. Eliot pays his homage to Daniel in *The Waste Land,* and Ezra Pound offers his courtesy in a number of poems. Pound translated a great many Provençal poems and was responsible for a renewed interest in Provençal poetry among a large number of readers and poets in the twentieth century.

Another of Dante's allegorical methods is a direct inheritance from interpretive practices of medieval theologians, who read Biblical passages on four levels: literal, allegorical, moral, and anagogical. Dante himself was fond of applying this method to Psalm 114, which begins "When Israel went out of Egypt . . ." (King James Version).

Although there can be many readings of the psalm, Dante, in a letter to his patron, Cangrande della Scalla, considers the opening line of the psalm to signify four journeys: a *literal* Old Testament journey of the Jews out of Egypt, an *allegorical* New Testament journey from sin to salvation, a *moral* journey of the soul from grief to a state of grace, and an *anagogical* journey of the soul from temporal corruption to eternal glory. (In *Ulysses* Joyce uses the opening line of the psalm, when Stephen exits from Leopold Bloom's kitchen, to indicate his release from the bondage of Dublin into the life of an artist.)

The poem begins with the directness, vivacity, and visual clarity that will continue throughout; and, like other epic poems—for that is what *The Divine Comedy* is—it begins in the middle of the action. And not only in the middle of the action, but in the symbolic middle of Dante's journey through life, for the time is the year 1300, when Dante is thirty-five, and the journey through Hell lasts from late Friday evening (the day of the crucifixion) until early Easter morning—the time of Christ's own journey to the afterworld to bring His message to the dead.

The three major divisions of the *Inferno* are represented by the leopard, the lion, and the wolf that prevent Dante from achieving salvation—the sins of incontinence (appetite), violence (spirit), and fraudulence (reason). Let us look at four of the most vivid episodes, representing all three divisions: Paolo and Francesca in the Second Circle of the Incontinent, Farinata and Cavalcante in the Sixth Circle, which lies between the Incontinent and the Violent, as heretics partake of both sins; Brunetto Latini in the Seventh Circle of the Violent, and Ulysses in the Eighth Circle of the Fraudulent. These four episodes also illuminate the poet himself in the human sympathy he shows toward all six of the sinners.

Francesca reveals her sin through words, and it was words—reading a book—that caused her sin with Paolo. Indeed, the first action of a newly arrived sinner in Hell is to speak, to confess his sins to Minos, who then determines the appropriate circle of Hell. So many of the sinners were brought to their condition by the distortion of speech, the faculty that separates man from animal: heretics, blasphemers, panderers, seducers, simonists, diviners, hypocrites, thieves, false counselors, sowers of discord, and, in the very mouth of Satan himself, Brutus, Cassius, and Judas, those who have been treacherous to benefactors.

The speech of these sinners has brought them to the great "throat" of Hell, to the mouth of Satan, who is himself silent throughout eternity. The *Inferno* illustrates man's failure to use language properly; *Purgatorio* is a place where language is refined and purified through fire; and in *Paradiso*, Dante glories in a heavenly language that is pure light rather than sound, the perfect silence of God. Dante has conceived the extremes of good and evil as being beyond human speech.

In addition to being intentionally banal, much of the language in Hell is inarticulate: submerged and garbled speech, gibberish, gurgles, moans, and curses. There are silent falsifiers, prophets who cannot speak, schismatics with split tongues, their throats cut, their heads severed, and the crafty Ulysses himself transformed into a tongue of flame. Even such masters of language as Virgil and Dante misunderstand each other when they find themselves among the false of speech.

Speak and hear, *dicono e odono*, echo throughout a poem which is as aural as it is visual; Hell overwhelms Dante with the sounds of shrieks, cries, groans, and lamentations. And the geography of the lustful in Canto 5 rushes at Dante in a tempest of bellowing seas and hellish storms of conflicting winds that whirl the sinners about with fury. The sinners, who were made helpless on earth by their passion, are compared to birds driven by uncontrollable winds. And there we find Dido, Helen, Cleopatra, Achilleus, Paris, and Tristan, and we realize that the geography of Hell is actually the geography of earth, and that the poem is not so much about existence in Hell as it is about life on earth.

Dante, the youthful poet of love who equated love with a gentle heart but believed that the nobility of love derived from the virtuous contemplation and worship of woman, is overwhelmed by the desire to speak with the spirits of Francesca and Paolo, who are—to him—so recognizably lovers. Throughout the conversation between Dante and Francesca (the weeping Paolo is unaccountably and mysteriously silent) the two practice the ideal courtesy of their times: Francesca calls him *grazioso e benigno*. She is so touching when she reveals that she would pray to God if He were her friend and would allow it. Dante shows more sympathy for these lovers, whose families he knew and

whose love he admires—even though he has to condemn it—
than for anyone else in Hell. He weeps for "grief and pity," and
provides Francesca with echoes of his own great sonnet from
his *Vita Nuova*: "Love and the gentle heart are one."

The book Francesca and Paolo were reading was about the
illicit lovers Lancelot and Guinevere, from the Arthurian chivalric stories, and Dante's own idea of the cause of their sin
joins other works we have read which suggest theories of the
purpose and dangers of literature: *Iliad, Odyssey, Frogs, Aeneid,*
and *Tristan.* Withholding the explicit, Dante understates the
emotion in a powerful way when Francesca says that Paolo's
kisses replaced the book, and "that day we read in it no further."
Dante makes a forceful claim for the hegemony of poetry.

The presentation of lovers who have let desire overcome
reason, and who have both been killed by Paolo's older brother
(Francesca's husband), echoes many of the maxims of courtly
love: love quickly takes fire in the gentle heart, love absolves no
one who is beloved from loving, and love brought Francesca
and Paolo to one death. Faced with the pitiful condition of these
lovers, a condition of his own imagination, Dante can only faint
and fall to the ground of his own artistic creation, "like a dead
body."

In the tenth canto Virgil leads Dante through the byways of
a "secret street" to reach Farinata and Cavalcante, heretics who
spend eternity in their tombs. On the allegorical level of the
poem, these are heretics whose secret life was like life in a tomb
when they were living. Language again assumes a primary role
when Farinata recognizes Dante by his Florentine accent and
Virgil advises Dante to let his "words be fitting." Farinata is
haughty, proud, full of disdain, and, as he rises breast-high in
his tomb, he seems to be all breast and brow and raised eyebrows.
"Who were thy ancestors?" he demands imperiously of Dante,
using *tui*, the familiar "your," in his address to a fellow citizen.

Farinata had been a leader of the Ghibellines in the civil war
with the Guelfs in the generation before Dante. The Ghibellines

had supported the Emperor and opposed the Pope, whereas Dante, in his generation, belonged to a faction of the Guelfs who wanted equality between Emperor and Pope in their respective domains.

Cavalcante, Farinata's companion, was a Guelf, but Dante objectively considers the extremism of both parties equally sinful. He treats them respectfully, especially the father of his friend, the poet Guido Cavalcante. Cavalcante's brief appearance is touching in the father's concern that his son may be dead, for he is surprised to see Dante without his beloved friend Guido.

Following this brief encounter, Farinata and Dante return to their political argument, and Dante makes the surprising discovery, one that has puzzled many commentators, that the dead know the past and the future but not what is currently happening on earth. Dante perhaps intends to suggest that the sinners in Hell did not properly know the present when they were alive and so cannot know it now, and that they are forced to face a future temporal time that will one day end, whereas they will remain in Hell for eternity.

As with so much in the *Inferno*, the motif in this canto is one of speaking and hearing and, in this case, remembering, when Virgil advises Dante to remember what Farinata has said about him, as all will be made clear to him when Beatrice becomes his guide.

Dante is respectful to both Farinata and Cavalcante; in his final words to Farinata he asks him to assure Cavalcante that Guido is still alive, although Dante knows that he is on his deathbed. These two great Florentines are in Hell's upper division, along with the lovers Francesca and Paolo, and they have Dante's sympathy, for it was their excessive love for Florence, and not sinful nature, that overcame their reason.

Most of the souls in the second and deeper division of Hell, the violent, are punished with much greater ferocity than those in the first, but Dante, even though he can locate his respected teacher Brunetto Latini there, apparently cannot bring himself to do more than have him walk naked across the hot, barren sand that symbolizes the infertility of sodomy. Brunetto has been "baked" and "scorched" by his sexual practices on earth and his sojourn in Hell, and Dante has been much criticized for publicizing Brunetto's private life. However, that life was hardly private to the knowing and gossipy Florentines, in whose city homosexuality, perhaps in imitation of the Greeks, had become widespread among scholars and poets.

But Dante, as he is with Paolo and Francesca, Farinata, and Cavalcante, is deeply respectful of this honored teacher and poet, whose *Little Treasure*, a poetic account of an allegorical journey, may well have inspired Dante's poem. (Note that Dante treats many other sinners with great scorn, and can even cheer their punishments.)

He addresses Brunetto with the politely honorable question "Are you here, Ser Brunetto?" and explains with reverential attitude the presence of Virgil, who, he says, is leading him home. Brunetto is still the teacher, and he gives Dante moral, ethical, and political advice. Although his speech is not as lengthy as those of the shades of Tiresias to Odysseus and of Anchises to Aeneas, it serves the same function in that Brunetto prophesies Dante's future. Virgil underscores the importance of this when he sees that Dante, like a schoolboy, is writing down what his teacher says, and he comments: "He is a good listener who takes notes." The teacher's final word to the student is that he read his book, and Dante concludes the canto with a touching comparison of his teacher to the winning runner of a footrace.

We find Ulysses in the eighth *bolgia* (ditch) of the Eighth Circle, the *bolgia* reserved for the false counselors, and he is one of Dante's greatest creations as well as one of the most puzzling. The only person actually named in the canto as evidence of Ulysses' false counsel is Achilleus, whom Ulysses lured away from Deidamia and back into the fighting, concealing from him the fact that he would be killed in the battle. But Dante would consider Ulysses a man of many disguises who was false both to himself and to others. It would also seem that Ulysses is there because he was an enemy of Virgil's heroes, the Trojans. On the other hand, Dante specifically credits Ulysses with actions which led to the dispersal of the Trojans and the consequent founding of Rome. In any case, Dante portrays Ulysses as crafty and brave up to the moment of his death, and he is condemning Ulysses, perhaps because he considers him a man who continually lusts after new experiences rather than consolidating and learning from the old.

Upon arriving at the eighth *bolgia*, Dante sees that there are multitudes of the fraudulent: their firefly-like flames flicker by the thousands on the horizon, and they restlessly move along the ditch. Again and again he uses the word *dentro*—within—to describe them as being consumed by living, and thus living eternally within the flames they themselves created. Ulysses speaks with Virgil, as a classical hero would respond only to a classical poet who had written about heroes.

In a remarkable metamorphosis, the flame that is Ulysses, tossing and murmuring, waving to and fro in the wind, becomes all tongue, flinging forth a voice. The shade of Tiresias had told Odysseus that death would come to him in old age from the sea in some way that was not warlike (*Odyssey* xi.100–37). Dante transforms the prediction into a warlike journey by sea, in which Odysseus, always questing for knowledge, attacks the island of Purgatory, and God Himself has to create a storm to prevent the hero from physically entering His spiritual territory. No Homeric poet or later Athenian playwright ever endowed Odysseus with the godlike powers that Dante attributes to him.

Ulysses tells Virgil and Dante that even his ardor for home and Penelope could not keep him there, because of his more powerful ardor for experiencing the world: his desire to know the vices and virtues of mankind. Dante, also a man who wanted to know everything, cannot but admire this man who shares his desire to know the entire world.

Setting off on his final voyage, Ulysses sailed past Spain and Morocco and on to the Pillars of Hercules, landmarks erected by that hero-god to prevent men from going beyond the limits of the world. But in this poem these Pillars are allegorical barriers God has placed to limit man's knowledge, much as He did with the forbidden tree of knowledge in the Garden of Eden.

In his final crafty speech to his potentially unwilling sailors—to Dante a speech of false counsel—Ulysses called on them to consider their proud heritage and not deny experience. Men are not born to live as brutes, he said, but rather as seekers after virtue and knowledge. Ulysses and the crew sailed on, and would have succeeded in storming Purgatory but for God's storm. The hero concedes defeat, but only, he concludes, because "One" willed his death. This is the same One who was no friend to Francesca and Paolo, One who will not yield, in Dante's belief, His power but rather demands that man submit to His love.

Dante's conception of Ulysses is a large step into the modern Faustian world of admiration for, and condemnation of, power and knowledge, a world in which Einstein can look with horror at the powers created by his own Odyssean craft and knowledge, and wish to put Dantean limits upon it.

Essays

A T THE AGE of thirty-eight Michel Eyquem de Montaigne retired from public life to devote the remainder of his life to what he considered the only proper study of mankind, oneself. This is less egotistic than it appears, for Montaigne shared Terence's belief that *Homo sum, humani a me nil alienum puto*—"I am a man, I consider nothing human foreign to me." At the beginning of his study he thought he was only learning about himself; later, deciding that each man contains all men, Montaigne arrived at the conviction that by knowing himself he would know all men. In the process he revealed to us more about himself than any other writer before him, including Saint Augustine.

As the *Essays* are the autobiography of a soul and a body, not the story of a man's particular circumstances—no "to begin with, I was born"—some facts of the life not always presented by him will help in reading the essays.

Montaigne was born in 1533 in the Château de Montaigne. The château, which had been in his family for three generations, was thirty miles from Bordeaux, and he spent all but a few years of his life at either place. For Montaigne, the internal life was more important than the inconsequential external one. He had little use for the worlds of politics and society, and retired from them as soon as he could.

His mother's family was equally as important as his father's. They were Spanish Jews who had converted to Catholicism, as had many Jews—willingly or unwillingly—during the long period of the Inquisition. Montaigne's mother receives very little attention in his essays, but we learn much about his devotion to his deceased father.

Although his father received only an ordinary education, he

had great admiration for learning, and specific ideas about the raising of children. The infant Montaigne was sent by his father to the home of poor villagers so that he might be nursed in circumstances not only foreign to him but beneath his station in life. When the infant returned home, and before his French was formed, his father employed a German doctor who spoke no French but was fluent in Latin to care for Michel; the mother and father learned enough Latin to be able to converse with the child. Montaigne's native tongue, then, was Latin, and he confesses that this was the language that automatically came forth—even late in his life—in moments of surprise or stress.

The schools he attended were no more than average, but his love of books began when he was hardly past infancy, and he early impressed his teachers with his analyses, as well as his corrections, of noteworthy commentators. Like all young men, he served his time as a soldier, and he continued into old age his love for the active outdoor life.

But, until his retirement in 1571 at the age of thirty-eight, Montaigne's main occupation was the fourteen years he gave to civic duties, primarily in the Parlement at Bordeaux. Certainly, it was there that he formed many of his notions of the follies and injustices of mankind, and he was relieved to retreat from that external world to the internal world of his library in the secluded tower of his château. The remaining nineteen years of his life, until his death in the château where he was born, Montaigne spent analyzing his experiences.

Some things did not change: his Catholicism, his conservatism, his honesty and frankness, his dismay at injustice, his respect for self-control, and, following his retirement, his preference for an uneventful life.

He greatly loved books, horseback riding, animals, talking, his own inconsistency, unpredictability, and the strange and unusual—freaks, tricksters, and criminals. One of the high points of his life was a conversation in Rouen with a cannibal from Brazil. (He later decided that the cannibal was more noble than the representatives of the nobility in the room.)

He disliked arrogant and obstinate conversationalists, anti-Semitism, the then common practice of legal torture, those who offered unwanted advice, men and women of any religious persuasion who elevated faith above works, and sexual intercourse while standing up.

Sex, ethics, religion—all things were equal to Montaigne: he could inject a humorous anecdote into the middle of a meditation on death. He began the essays a stoic, continued them briefly as a skeptic, and concluded them an epicurean. We know all this—and much more—not from what others wrote about him, but from his own self-portrait.

Montaigne invented the term *essai*, deriving it from the French verb *essayer*, to try. The essays would be attempts, not conclusions, in which experience would be tested and tried through writing. He would "try" to understand himself through analyzing and judging his own experiences and his *attitudes* toward those experiences. Montaigne knew that he might not know the truth, but that his attitude toward, and feeling about, that "truth" was indeed a certainty.

He suffered many misfortunes around the time he began to write, and the early essays are consequently much more pessimistic than the later ones. His father died, as did his dear friend La Boétie, and his infant daughter died at the age of two months; he himself was nearly killed in a horseback-riding accident. All of these events caused him to determine that one must think ahead about pain and death, and come to terms with them. This is the same stoic philosophy we saw Virgil transmit to Aeneas, in its insistence on the importance of anticipating and planning the future.

The accident on horseback, from which he nearly died, and the further "accident" of painful kidney stones, which he knew Pliny had called an unbearable disease and a primary cause for suicide by its sufferers, taught Montaigne the futility of anticipating pain or death. He would live in the present.

In later life Montaigne came to agree with Socrates that

death was not really all that important and was not worth considering. But Montaigne would value pain all of his life for the fortitude, bravery, and self-control that it taught; death, he concluded, did not have all that much to teach.

Indeed, as he continued with his essays, Montaigne came more and more to distrust philosophical logic and to admire the uncomplicated bravery of ordinary people. Reason, he decided, did not necessarily make one happy: the simple life preached by Saint Paul was the best one.

This was the time when "What do I know?" became his motto, when he accepted the unreliability of the senses and the limitations of intellect. He came to the conclusion that all was flux, that not only the world but the individuals in it changed from moment to moment. Sense impressions of interactions between a changing self and a changing world were thus totally unreliable.

This crisis of skepticism was the period in which Montaigne tried out and rejected the ideas he had previously held. He was now ready to use the essays for re-composition. "To compose" means both to put together in an artful pattern and to make calm, free from agitation.

In 1580 he published the essays written up until that year, spent a year in Italy, and then agreed to return to public life for four years as Mayor of Bordeaux. Following this, he returned to the seclusion of his beloved library in the tower, where he wrote the final book of essays in the years 1585–1588.

He is less skeptical now, more apt to see the pleasures in life rather than the pains, even to the extent of carefully observing his own aging body. And in this final period he arrives at a new realization, one that does not occur in the preceding essays: each person contains within himself all other human beings. To know oneself is to know all humanity.

The emphasis in the essays is now on the equality of body and soul, of effecting a careful balance between the two, and of the importance of each taking care of the other. He explores the vanity of those who exaggerate their own importance, who in private cannot remove the mask of their public lives, or, worse, lead public lives of rectitude and private lives of disorder.

Through self-analysis Montaigne comes to such an acceptance of himself and others that some have accused him of moral permissiveness. With the emphasis on his own strong efforts to maintain self-control, he seems to be recognizing the inevitability of human folly rather than judging it. In the final few essays he accepts the comic, the obscene, and the absurd, not only in himself but—of course—in all human beings.

There is not much exaggeration in the commonly held opinion that reading a few pages of Montaigne selected at random will give an accurate picture of the man. It is true that the titles of the essays are somewhat misleading: he does like— as he tells us—to let his mind wander where it will. His inconsistency, however, has been much exaggerated. He does seem to change his mind in some of the essays from moment to moment; actually, given his extensive rewriting, any one of the later essays can contain adjacent sentences written many years apart. It is to be hoped that, given that span of time, any reasonable person open to experience would change some opinions. But it must be remembered that Montaigne accepted inconsistency as one of the delightful characteristics of the human condition.

Rather than trust to a random selection of a few pages, the beginning reader of Montaigne should, after reading "To the Reader," start with a few representative essays: "Of Idleness," "Of Cannibals," "Of Democritus and Heraclitus," "Of the Inconsistency of our Actions," "Of Practice," "Of Giving the Lie," "Of Repentance," and "Of Experience."

"Of Repentance" was written four years before Montaigne's death, and it is from the "epicurean" stage that followed his stoic and skeptical periods. He does strongly suggest Epicurus,

with his emphasis on pleasure being the only good, the importance of harmony of body and mind, and the virtues that come
from living the simple life.

The essay begins with his assertion that he would make
himself quite different if he could live his life again, a contra-
diction of his later statement in the same essay that if he had
his life to live again, he would live as he had lived. The second
sentence was written some years after the first; Montaigne has
not contradicted himself—he has changed his mind. In the
second paragraph of the essay he offers the explanation that he
does not portray being but, rather, passing. And, he goes on to
explain, he is concerned not about the "passage" from "one age
to another," but rather about his own life from "minute to
minute."

Then comes the new—for Montaigne—idea that every individual contains the entire pattern of human nature. In inves-
tigating and understanding himself, he is exploring all of
mankind. Since Freud, some have objected to Montaigne's claim
in this essay that he is the most learned man alive when it comes
to knowing and understanding himself, and that no one before
him has engaged in such thorough self-examination. But Montaigne is not interested in analyzing unconscious states—with
the exception of the one after his fall from the horse. We do
not get in these essays much attention to dreams, wishes, or
fantasies. He is interested only in the workings of his conscious
mind, and even in that area there is a distinct peculiarity in his
thinking: he has very little of the later scientific and psychological
concern with cause and effect, with the "whys" of human
behavior. Although he seems to the modern mind to be totally
lacking in curiosity about the external world, he is vigilant in
observing the workings of his own mind and body *in the present*.

Montaigne says that he rarely repents because, being neither
angel nor animal, he accepts a fallible human condition in which
errors are inevitable. He is not as permissive as some charge
him with being. He does believe in vices, in good and bad
behavior in himself and in others, but he contends that man is

a mixture of both angel and beast, and should recognize his behavior on both those levels. He considers as vices those "that reason and nature condemn, but also those that human opinion has created, even though they be false and erroneous opinions, if it is confirmed by law and custom." Because we live in a society of fellow human beings, Montaigne believes that we must accept their rules. He is in agreement with Aristotle, who thought that what everyone believed to be true was true. Aristotle certainly knew that wasn't the case, but it was to him a practical way to live in a world where majority opinions ruled.

But Montaigne offers a balance to that idea when he writes that "I have my own laws and court to judge me, and I refer myself to them rather than anywhere else." He will conform in his behavior to the norms of society, but he will not allow that society to judge him: they see only his external actions and not his more important internal actions. He admires the Roman who offered his construction workers more money if they would build his house so that everyone might look in from all sides.

"The worth of the soul consists not in soaring high, but in orderly movement." This placid statement disappoints, given the admiration we have for the soaring adventures of Achilleus, Odysseus, Oedipus, Antigone, Tristan, and Isolde. It seems to advise a dull, boring, unheroic life—and it does. But Montaigne is referring to external existence; he does not deny the soaring possibilities of a heroic life of the mind. Even fifth-century Athenians warned that one should avoid the mountaintops of ambition, and it is Creon who assures Oedipus that he would rather be the power behind the throne than be king. Indeed, the advice that "moderation is best" first appeared in the *Odyssey*, was reiterated to the point of monotony by the Athenian playwrights, and found its way into a logical philosophical system in Aristotle's *Ethics*.

Montaigne has as much faith in the intuitive as in the logical workings of his mind. This is certainly what he is doing when he writes that one should not judge persons virtuous or vicious when they are acting impulsively, but rather when they are in "their settled state" and thus are "nearest to repose and to their natural position." One is not judged by actions, but rather by one's state of mind—an Aristotelian "disposition" to perform a particular kind of act. Aristotle and Montaigne arrive at similar conclusions, one logically and the other intuitively. Indeed, Montaigne's ultimate illogic in this essay is to weigh pleasure and sin on a balance scale: the pleasure might be sufficient, he decided, to outweigh and thereby excuse the sin, especially "as in intercourse with women, where the impulse is violent, and, they say, sometimes irresistible."

He supports his view with the example of a man in Armagnac nicknamed "The Thief," who, when he was young, had to choose between poverty and theft. As an older and wealthy man, he spends his time reimbursing the relatives of those from whom he stole. The man, Montaigne concludes, obviously recognized that theft was wrong, and hated it, but he hated the idea of poverty even more. The end, comfort, justified the means, theft.

Because his actions are guided by reason and careful judgment, Montaigne believes that his judgment should be awarded the praise or blame his actions deserve, and there is thus no reason for his soul to repent. As to others who practice lives of constant vice, he cannot believe in the sincerity of their repentance. In an essay entitled "Of Repentance," Montaigne comes to the conclusion that repentance doesn't exist for most people.

But he admits that we do feel sorrow over behavior that was not, in the Aristotelian terms to which he adheres, in "conformity" with man's "natural condition," and this he terms "regret" rather than repentance: "My actions are shaped and conformed by what I am and by my condition in life. I can do no better. And repentance does not properly apply to the things that are not in our power, but regret certainly does." But even then, Montaigne admits that "I have little regret," for he still accepts the stoic view that events were bound to happen the way they turned out. And, most of all, he accepts the role of chance in his actions and in their consequences: bad luck calls for no act of repentance.

He concludes an essay on the topic of repentance with a meditation on old age and the ages of man. Contrary to what Antisthenes believed, Montaigne considers it better to live happily than to die happily. And, although he does not refer to it, Montaigne is arguing against a position that goes back as far as Solon's "Count no man happy until he is dead" in Herodotus. Montaigne rejected this by the time he had finished his first book of essays: for him, each day of life is a preparation for another day of life, not for death.

In the final pages of the essay he writes beautifully and simply about his grateful acceptance of old age and of the "seasons" of man: "I have seen the leaves, the flowers, and the fruit; now I see the withering—happily, since it is natural."

King Lear

K ing Lear opens on a bare stage, bare except for an unoc-
cupied throne, a throne that will become empty and remain
so after the end of the first scene. The crown will be split
between the husbands of two daughters: whenever anything is
divided in half in this play, only the nothingness of barren space
remains.

The physical action of the play itself occupies many spaces:
throne rooms, courtyards, moors, hovels, fields, cliffs, and it
spreads across the island of Britain, the early scenes leaving
behind them only vacant space, and the later scenes only vacant
bodies: Gloucester, Regan, Cornwall, Goneril, Edmund, Cordelia, and Lear.

Power and speech are vast presences and absences in this
play, and they are welded together, just as the masks everyone
wears are fixed to their very souls. Power is won in the beginning
by Regan, Goneril, and Edmund, those who distort speech and
writing, and lost by Cordelia, who is silent. The Fool has the
powers of truth, but he must express that truth in distorted
speech. Lear soars over them all with the power and poetry of
his speech, but, like Othello, he is doomed by his inability to
interpret the speech of others. At the end Lear speaks to
Cordelia's speechless lips, and then joins her in speechlessness.
Edmund's plunge into evil, as well as his attempted redemption,
comes through the act of writing. Once Cordelia returns, the
speech of the Fool is absent from the play, and they may well
have been played by the same boy actor, in disguise as both
voluble Fool and silent Saint.

There is mystery in the power this play holds over both
spectators and readers, a power that was voided for over a
hundred and fifty years—during the eighteenth and nineteenth

centuries—when a happy ending was substituted for the final scene. The mystery is that we do feel for this proud, irascible, cantankerous, demanding, and foolish old man; he is impossible, and Goneril and Regan do have just cause for complaint. We can more easily understand our relations to Oedipus, Antigone, Hamlet, and other tragic figures: we respond to them because we recognize in them something of ourselves. But what is it about Lear that so moves us? It may well be that our Western Judeo-Christian culture is violently disrupted by the violation in this tragedy of our traditional beliefs about honoring parents, that it is more blessed to give than to receive, and that there is always some hope. Oedipus, after all the horrors of his life, is translated painlessly to an afterlife where he joins the immortals as a hero-god; even Antigone exits with her "ungovernable will" intact, and Hamlet probably does go to his rest accompanied by flights of singing angels. Cordelia and Lear die a pagan death in a pagan world, where the most powerful goddess is untrustworthy Nature.

Two other aspects of the play may be responsible for our inability to cope with the disasters it presents.

Aristotle in his *Poetics* defined tragedy as having a beginning, a middle, and an end, and death was the final end, after which there was nothing more than a shadowy existence in Hades. But it has been said that tragedy ended in the medieval period, as, given the possibility of Heaven, there can be no such thing as a tragic ending for a Christian tragic hero—even for Hamlet. But Shakespeare has carefully placed Lear in a non-Judaic and pre-Christian world where there is no hope for redemption. *Holinshed's Chronicles* of 1587, one of Shakespeare's sources for this play, gives the 3105th year of the world as the time in which Lear ruled over the Britons and came into conflict with his daughters, Goneril, Regan, and Cordelia. But even this "historical" account has a happy ending. Shakespeare, however, is determined to give us no hope.

The belief that we have some conscious control over our destinies is disturbed by the "wheel of fire" in this play, and by the presentation of life as a torture "rack" from which there is no release. The play brutally reminds us that we are all born with a terminal illness—mortality.

King Lear has as much in common with fifth-century Athenian tragedy as it does with Elizabethan. It continues from the male-female rivalry for power between Klytemnestra and Agamemnon in the *Oresteia*—the resisted "female force"—and the bloodthirsty generational conflict between Klytemnestra and her children. As we saw, Aeschylus' play consists of a series of three trials; in Shakespeare's play there is no possibility for justice in a meaningless world where a mad, self-dethroned king, reduced to seeking shelter in a hovel, presides over a hallucinated trial of Goneril and Regan. *King Lear* is an *Oresteia* that ends with Agamemnon's death.

The Theban plays of Sophocles can also feed our understanding of Shakespeare's play. Oedipus, like Lear, is "more sinned against than sinning," and the two tragic heroes share a quickness to anger and to action. Each new piece of information causes Oedipus to send immediately for another source of information, and Lear's immediate response to Goneril's inhospitality is "Saddle my horses!" But Oedipus is superior to his antagonists, whereas Lear is overwhelmed by his. Oedipus almost breaks when confronted with the powerful silence of Tiresias; Cordelia's silence totally destroys Lear.

In *Antigone* a stubborn king confronts a stubborn princess in a struggle for power, and the princess kills herself, as does Goneril in *King Lear*, although for inglorious reasons. But the conflict is similar: Goneril tells Albany just before her final exit that "the laws are mine, not thine," and the two daughters are engaged throughout the play in a contest of law with Lear.

In his long exile Oedipus learns that he is guiltless of wrongdoing, and the physical and mental storms of Lear's exile teach him that he is nothing but a "foolish fond old man." But King Oedipus goes to live with the gods, and, centuries later, Athenians continued to offer libations at his hero-god shrine.

King Lear is—to borrow a phrase from Joyce's *Ulysses*—"beastly dead."

But *King Lear* has more in common with the *Bacchae* than with any of these other tragedies. In both, a mysterious, powerful, irrational, and unknowable Dionysian force is let loose upon the universe, and the good and the evil are equally destroyed. However, in Euripides' play there is meaning to Dionysus—he represents human forces which must not be repressed or denied, whereas in Shakespeare the force is inhuman and meaningless and there is no justice in the universe.

In these plays, neither tragic hero knows himself, but in the *Bacchae* Dionysus tells Pentheus, "You don't know who you are," whereas in *King Lear* the world tells Lear, "You don't know who I am." To the existentialists in the 1940s and 1950s this was "their" play, but even Camus' "stranger" somehow managed to conclude that the indifferent universe was benign.

Shakespeare's play shares with Homeric epic and Athenian tragedy the features of man in disguise from others as well as from self. In physical disguise from others: Kent and Edgar; in psychological disguise from others: Regan, Goneril, and Edmund; in disguise from self: Gloucester and Lear. The play allows for heart-rending scenes of recognition and reversal: the recognitions and reversals of Odysseus, Telemachos, Penelope, Orestes, and Oedipus result in redemption, whereas the reversals of Lear, Cordelia, and Gloucester bring about irreversible disasters.

Subplots can sometimes have only a tenuous relationship to the plot, but in the case of *King Lear* both plot and subplot pit helpless and deceived fathers against evil and devious offspring, and each father dies beholding his one faithful child. Gloucester dies in the "modern" intermingling of opposite emotions— "Twixt two extremes of passion, joy and grief"—that we saw with Tristan and Isolde, and Lear dies in a condition that has been subjected to a number of interpretations:

Do you see this? Look on her! Look, her lips,
Look there, look there—
                              V.iii.311–12

Some actors have decided that Lear believes Cordelia to be alive, and their delivery of these lines is ecstatic, so that Lear dies in a paroxysm of joy. Some unwise few have attempted to die of both "joy and grief," but those two emotions are difficult to convey at the same instant, one of the reasons, perhaps, that Gloucester's death is reported—in the fifth-century Athenian mode—rather than shown. Both breeds of actors are, of course, taking unfortunate liberties, as Lear brokenly states that Cordelia has "no life," "no breath at all," and that she will "come no more."

The Elizabethan view of the universe was one of a chain of being, each link in its proper, unmoveable place, descending down from God and the angels and other higher orders, through the orders of man and animals, and finally into inanimate objects. The clearest presentation of this view is in Ulysses' speech in *Troilus and Cressida*. The lines pertinent to *King Lear* are:

> The heavens themselves, the planets, and this centre
> Observe degree, priority, and place,
> Insisture, course, proportion, season, form,
> Office, and custom, in all line of order;
>   . . . O, when degree is shak'd,
> Which is the ladder of all high designs,
> The enterprise is sick! . . .
> Take but degree away, untune that string,
> And hark what discord follows!
>   I.iii.85–110

Lear dares more than "disturb the universe": he totally disrupts the Elizabethan audience's concept of divine order, a disruption especially frightening to a people with a long history of civil wars. He turns the world upside down by removing his public mask, but insists upon wearing it in his daughters' houses. ". . . what discord follows!" when Lear discovers that men and women do not hold the high rank he thought, but rather belong among the animals and senseless stones.

For a sane King Lear begins his doubts by questioning the naked Edgar about the nakedness of the human condition:

Is man no more than this? . . . Thou art the thing itself; unaccommo-dated man is no more but such a poor, bare, forked animal as thou art.

III.iv.97–102

and a later, broken King Lear speaks to Cordelia about the naked foolishness of the human condition, begging her:

Pray, do not mock me.
I am a very foolish fond old man.
IV.vii.59–60

To know self in the world of this play is to know the nothingness of self. We find no long soliloquies here, no meditations on the nature of man, no logical reasonings, but rather "O reason not the need!" (II.iv.259). There are no intermediate stages with these people: they live in a world of either/or, and they do not know the world of humanity that lies between angels and the beasts. "Who is it that can tell me who I am?" (I.iv.220) Lear cries, and there is none to answer, no present gods, not Nature, and certainly none of the other characters: they don't know who they are, either. Regan might as well be speaking for herself when she says of her father:

'Tis the infirmity of his age; yet he hath ever but slenderly known himself.

I.i.292–93

and somewhat later to her father:

You should be ruled and led
By some discretion that discerns your state
Better than you yourself.
II.iv.143–45

Because Lear and many of the other characters in the play act before they think, their impulsive behavior does not allow for intellectual discourse with self. At the end of the first scene Goneril says to Regan:

> You see how full of changes his age is . . . with what poor judgment he hath now cast her off appears too grossly.
>
> I.i.288–91

Goneril tells Regan in the last line of the first scene that they must act quickly, and they do, without thinking of the consequences either to themselves or to their father. They have learned well from their father, who rashly banishes his beloved Cordelia and the trustworthy Kent. We see how quickly Gloucester turns against Edgar. Lear and most of the other characters act like impetuous children.

There is one exception, Edmund, and he is the major topic of conversation in the playful sexual banter that opens the play, a truly strange beginning for such a dark tragedy. Reversing the last words of Mary, Queen of Scots, T. S. Eliot writes in his *Four Quartets* that "In my beginning is my end," and this is truly the case with the begetting of Edmund, the bastard son who, in revenge, tries to overthrow his father. We know that scenes similar to this one must have occurred many times before, scenes in which Edmund had to listen to his misguided man-of-the-world father boast about his sexual exploits.

And so Edmund has learned to "study deserving" (I.i.30), learned to live in a world where he has no legal standing, and where his father jokes about his mother's pregnancy; he has no choice but to be manipulative.

He is not only lover but "brother" of Regan and Goneril, who have learned not only how to "study deserving," but how to express their findings in exceptionally pretty speeches to their father. However, their fears that Lear will impulsively disinherit them cause them to act rashly, and their wild passion for

Edmund causes conflict between them and leads Goneril into poisoning Regan and killing herself.

These characters do not know how to sit still, how to be patient—one of the words that echo throughout the play. They do know the importance of patience, as they advise others to employ it, and Lear can even admonish himself early in the storm scene: "No, I will be the pattern of all patience" (III.ii.37). But patience requires that action be thought about and delayed, and the characters in this play are incapable of that: they all demand instant gratification.

They are not in control of themselves, and over and over Shakespeare tells us that they live in a world where an inexorable goddess Nature, who is so fiercely primitive that she has not yet acquired any anthropomorphic traits other than gender, is, along with some other vague, unnamed gods, merely playing games with them:

> As flies to wanton boys are we to th' gods;
> They kill us for their sport.
> IV.i.36–37

By the time human beings have made their gods and goddesses anthropomorphic, they know where they stand with them: the gods have been defined. But Homeric Greeks left the powers of Nature, Delusion, Necessity, and Fortune without human characteristics. The world of *King Lear* is presided over by these hidden enemies of mankind, and we know they are not benevolent when the villainous Edmund identifies himself with Nature in the opening line of the second scene of the first act: "Thou, Nature, art my goddess."

The evil children of Lear and Gloucester are vicious and cruel to their elders, deceive their fathers, deprive Lear of the familiar and comforting trappings of a king, close their doors against him and drive him into the storm, gouge out Gloucester's eyes, and order Lear and Cordelia hanged. They are primitive evil powers who are the enemies of parents, and Shakespeare has made them human personalities without humanity. In *King Lear* abstract nature and human nature are equally barren:

> . . . as of unnaturalness between the child and the parent
> I.ii.140–41

Unnaturalness abounds in Lear's world, a world in which

> . . . thou mad'st thy daughters thy mothers
> I.iv.163–64

and

> The younger rises when the old doth fall.
> III.iii.23

Depraved sexuality is also a part of the conflict between children and fathers in *King Lear.* The sexual element appears in the play as early as the opening lines of Gloucester's lewd banter about his intercourse with Edmund's mother, and continues almost immediately with the speeches of the two daughters, in form and content speeches of love and suggestive sexuality more appropriately addressed to a future husband than to a father. Regan's protestation of love is almost shocking in its tactile sensuality, and she blatantly labels her love for her father an act ("deed") as well as a feeling; moreover, the "precious square of sense" to which she refers might well be her sexual organs, and in any case has just the right touch of suggestive ambiguous intimacy she knows Lear wants to hear. No wonder Lear is enraged by Cordelia's paralegal speech.

Lear's violent response to her speech brings up the motivation for the entire scene: he is making a public spectacle out of an intimate scene that could have occurred (onstage) in a private room in the castle with only Lear and his daughters present. Cordelia's speech not only disappoints, it humiliates Lear in front of the court, especially as he has previously proclaimed that her "ample third" of land is "more opulent" than her sisters'.

———

Why Cordelia does not play the game her father is asking for is not given in lines in the play, and can only be found in her character as we come to know it later. Some have called her the Christ figure in the play, but I rather think she is the Lear figure. Lear is a straightforward, outspoken, frank, impulsive, and honest man, and she is a woman with those same characteristics. Lear won't play other people's games, and in this particular case he wouldn't have played his own game any more than Cordelia did. Lear and Cordelia, though they can be wrong-headed, have a pride and an integrity that make their fall even more brutal.

Because Cordelia is absent for much of the play, we do not see with her, as we do with Regan and Goneril, Lear's obsession with the feminine sexuality of his daughters. There are a variety of curses a king might bring down on his daughter when she has asked that he remove his knights from her premises, but Lear's is not only addressed to the dangerous goddess to whom Edmund prays, but is unwarranted, wildly excessive, and, moreover, is directed at her sex:

> Hear, Nature, hear; dear goddess, hear:
> Suspend thy purpose if thou didst intend
> To make this creature fruitful.
> Into her womb convey sterility,
> Dry up in her the organs of increase,
> And from her derogate body never spring
> A babe to honor her. If she must teem,
> Create her child of spleen, that it may live
> And be a thwart disnatured torment to her.
> Let it stamp wrinkles in her brow of youth,
> With cadent tears fret channels in her cheeks,
> Turn all her mother's pains and benefits
> To laughter and contempt, that she may feel
> How sharper than a serpent's tooth it is
> To have a thankless child.
>   I.iv.266–80

When he has been totally severed from his daughters, he turns to an extreme of disgust at female sexuality in a speech to Gloucester:

> Die for adultery? No.
> The wren goes to't, and the small gilded fly
> Does lecher in my sight.
> Let copulation thrive; for Gloucester's bastard
>   son
> Was kinder to his father than my daughters
> Got 'tween the lawful sheets.
> To't, luxury, pell-mell, for I lack soldiers.
> Behold yond simp'ring dame,
> Whose face between her forks presages snow,
> That minces virtue, and does shake the head
> To hear of pleasure's name.
> The fitchew nor the soiled horse goes to't
> With a more riotous appetite.
> Down from the waist they are Centaurs,
> Though women all above.
> But to the girdle do the gods inherit,
> Beneath is all the fiend's.
> There's hell, there's darkness, there's the sul-
>   phurous pit; burning, scalding, stench, con-
>   sumption. Fie, fie, fie! pah, pah! Give me an
>   ounce of civet good apothecary, to sweeten
>   my imagination! There's money for thee.
>   IV.vi.110–30

The peak of wrath that is reached with the charge that women's sexual organs are occupied by a fiend of hell can go no higher in intensity, and must fall over into ugly, disjunctive rhythms.

The play presents us with three different kinds of madness: the knowing madness of the Fool, the pretended madness of Edgar, and the actual madness of Lear. The presence of madness

in the play is announced as early as lines 145–46 of Act 1, Scene
1, when Kent responds to Lear's rejection of Cordelia with: "Be
Kent unmannerly/When Lear is mad," and when Lear cries out
at the end of Act 1:

> O, let me not be mad, not mad, sweet heaven
> Keep me in temper; I would not be mad.
>
> I.v.40–41

During the first two acts of the play Lear worries a great
deal about the possibility of going mad—this before he even
fully realizes what his daughters are up to; when that realization
comes, both the universe and Lear become a storm of madness.

The commands to the storm to commence show that Lear
himself is directing his own descent into madness, that it is his
conscious choice as a way of avoiding an unacceptable reality.
This is clearly stated later in the play when Gloucester envies
Lear's madness:

> Better I were distract;
> So should my thoughts be severed from my griefs,
> And woes by wrong imagination lose
> The Knowledge of themselves.
>
> IV.vi.276–79

As the storm grows in intensity, Kent asks the mysterious
Gentleman the whereabouts of Lear and is told:

> Contending with the fretful elements;
> Bids the wind blow the earth into the sea,
> Or swell the curled waters 'bove the main
>
> III.i.4–6

Lear has become commander of the universe, director of
the elements, as he cries out for the world itself to be flattened,
and Nature herself cracked. The two speeches hurled at the
universe are charged with imperatives: "Blow . . . crack . . .
Rage . . . blow . . . spout . . . singe . . . strike . . . Rumble . . .

Spit . . . Spout. . . ." He directs his own transformation into nothingness, fulfilling his own words to Cordelia in the first scene, when he warns her that "Nothing will come of nothing." The word "nothing," along with so many other stark negatives, echoes throughout this tragedy, in which each inhabitant of an empty world becomes "an O without a figure" that the Fool calls Lear early in the play (I.iv.183–84).

The Fool could not save him, and Lear remains a magnificently mad cipher until the Fool returns as Cordelia, and Lear, discovering blessedness and forgiveness, wishes to reject temporal existence for a prison in which he and Cordelia can become "God's spies" and live in eternal truth rather than in temporal mutability.

The tragedies of Shakespeare and the Athenian playwrights are similar in their essential six-part psychological structure. A tragedy is set in motion when the hero or heroine makes an initial choice; this is the traditional exposition of the play. In the second stage, usually the first half of the play, all the developing choices succeed until a crucial choice is made which leads to the failure of the choices in the second half of the action. Whereas the initial choice was an act of free will on the part of the hero, the final choice—death—is controlled by external rather than internal forces. The tragedy concludes with an evaluation by others of the choice.

Applying this structural analysis to *Hamlet* points up the highly unusual structure of *King Lear*. I will refer to the divisions as: Initial Choice, Successful Choices, Crucial Choice, Losing Choices, Final Choice, and Evaluation of Choice.

The action is set in motion by Hamlet's Initial Choice to avenge the murder of his father. Following this, he controls a series of Successful Choices that culminate in the staging of the play to trap Claudius. Going up the stairs to his mother's bedroom, he has the opportunity to kill Claudius, but makes the critical error of choosing not to, as Claudius is praying and his soul would immediately go to Heaven. Following this, each scene consists of Losing Choices until Hamlet's death, a Final Choice that is not under his control. Following Hamlet's death, Horatio and Fortinbras present the Evaluation of Choice, a structural period that becomes a sort of Recovery Room for the audience or reader.

Hamlet is representative of Shakespeare's tragedies in that the Initial Choice requires a number of scenes, and the Crucial Choice falls midway between the Successful Choices and the Losing Choices. The Initial Choice occurs following the revelation to Hamlet by his father's ghost in Act 1, Scene 5, and the Crucial Choice is Hamlet's decision not to kill the praying Claudius, in Act 3, Scene 3.

Many of the plays of Sophocles and Euripides that were written to be presented alone also follow this structure. For example, Pentheus in the *Bacchae* makes an Initial Choice to defy Dionysus, he engages in seemingly Successful Choices in restraining him, and then makes the Crucial Choice to spy on the Theban women on the mountain. There follow the Losing Choices and the Final Choice—a death out of his control—described by the Messenger; ironically, Dionysus delivers the Evaluation of Choice.

The structure of *Oedipus the King* is striking in that the Initial Choice to discover the murderer comes before the play begins, and it is also the Crucial Choice; all of what Oedipus thinks to be Successful Choices are known to the audience to be Losing Choices; and the Final Choice to blind himself is totally within his control.

The compact structure of *King Lear* is, like that of *Oedipus the King*, shockingly different from other plays. Act 1, Scene 1 embodies the Initial Choice *and* the Crucial Choice. There are no scenes of Successful Choices for Lear; the Losing Choices are anticipated at the end of Act 1, Scene 1, in the planned machinations of Goneril and Regan, and commence immediately, beginning with Lear's next appearance in Scene 3. The characters begin to fall and "rot" in the very first scene.

Following Hamlet's death there are almost fifty lines of

Evaluation of Choice, while following Lear's death there are a bare fifteen lines. The bodies of Cordelia and Lear go directly to barren graves; unlike *Hamlet*, *King Lear* offers no Recovery Room for the reader or the audience. Hamlet's body is borne off in state, to be accompanied by music and farewell gun salutes; Lear, who "usurped" his life—wrenched it unnaturally from his truer self—is merely "gone indeed," and Albany directs simply that the gored bodies of Lear and Cordelia be borne "from hence."

The closing barrenness of *King Lear* is reminiscent of the closing barrenness of Euripides' *Bacchae*, in which everyone has been banished from Thebes, and all that remains on the stage is the broken body of Pentheus, which his grandfather has so pitifully attempted to put together again. And, as with the *Bacchae*, there is nothing left at the end of *King Lear* that can be put back together again. The world has been sundered, and all that remains are the empty souls of Albany, Edgar, and Kent.

Don Quixote

THERE ARE two novels called *Don Quixote*.

In the first one, a country gentleman, who is around fifty years of age, has read so many chivalric stories that he decides to become a knight-errant, and he sets out to restore the world to that golden age of perfect gentle knights rescuing damsels-in-distress and righting the wrongs of the world. He is not mad, but only imitating chivalric behavior; as he himself says, "I know very well who I am." He acquires a witty and sensible squire, and the two of them have many uproarious adventures in which the knight doesn't always win—although he thinks he does, and that makes all the difference. At the end of the story this gentle, kindly knight is forced to give up his quest, and he returns home to die. The novel glows with warmth and tender understanding for the human condition.

In the second novel another country gentleman, also around fifty years of age, has gone insane reading ridiculous stories of knights-errant, and decides to become one himself. When he says, "I know very well who I am," he is referring to the chivalric knight he is obsessed with at the moment. His squire is a dull oaf who tells many boring stories, and his talk, full of platitudes, is tiresome. About half the time the knight overcomes his opponents, frequently accidentally, but in his attempt to right usually nonexistent wrongs he seriously injures other people. The knight is tricked into returning home, where he decides, before dying, that he will give up knight-errantry and instead found an Arcadian paradise of pastoral shepherds and shepherdesses. He is insane from beginning to end. The novel is not funny, there is no warm humor in it, many of the interjected stories are as tedious and long-winded as old Nestor's in the *Iliad*, and the cruelty of the would-be knight, and of others to him, is extraordinary, as is the author's belief that physical suffering is hilariously funny. The only sides that are split in this novel are those of sensitive and affronted readers.

Readers who find themselves distinctly recognizing one or the other of the two preceding paragraphs are reading the novel in the wrong way. But then, so have many readers throughout the centuries, including commentators who have called this "the greatest novel ever written." Much damage is done by that kind of hierarchical evaluation, as no novel can be the greatest novel ever written.

Certainly, the first readers of the novel—and it was widely read throughout Spain within six months of its publication—found it side-splittingly funny, but that was in a country undergoing a period that was among the cruelest the world has ever known. We are not seventeenth-century Spaniards, however, nor other Europeans of the time (Spain was not alone in its tastes during this period). Neither are we eighteenth-, nineteenth-, nor early twentieth-century idealists who warmly sympathized with those who tilted against windmills. The novel has been a powerful presence since its publication, and Don Quixote and Sancho Panza have become mythical figures who have inspired great works of music, ballet, and painting, as well as an enormously successful Broadway musical comedy. The novel itself has been called the "first novel," and it has indeed strongly influenced the direction of the Western novel.

While Shakespeare, a contemporary of Cervantes, was mirroring the wide range of individuals and societies within an entire Elizabethan world through his Trojan warriors, Italian lovers, and ancient British kings, Cervantes seems to present two unique individuals rather than a society. Certainly, the fantastic array of outcasts, criminals, fanatics, lunatic would-be shepherds and shepherdesses, and childishly cracked nobility are in no way representative of the depth and variety of Spanish society in the years around 1600. Even the geography is sometimes inaccurate, and the descriptions of the landscape are not reliable, written, as they are, in a pseudo-literary chivalric style.

Although tastes in humor and storytelling change, basic human nature does not change, and readers in all periods have responded to Don Quixote's foolish idealism, for we recognize the desire of people everywhere and at all times for a perfect and ideal world, and we realize the impossibility of that dream. When this visionary idealism is paired with a Sancho Panza, a down-to-earth realist who only hopes for a better life for himself rather than for the world, then we realize that Cervantes has represented, not society, but two conflicting views of reality. Some readers (I include myself) consider that the intellectual brilliance outshines much of the dated and cruel humor in this book.

Self has been pitted against Other—the world—in all of the works we have been examining in these essays, and the Other has frequently destroyed the Self in an unequal contest. Up through the very last moment, with his plans for a pastoral paradise, the Self of Don Quixote has been larger than the Other, or at least he thought it was, and in this novel that amounts to the same thing. Readers respond to such supreme confidence, recognizing that they probably have more in common with Don Quixote and Sancho Panza than with Achilleus, Odysseus, or Aeneas.

Readers delight in the superbly imaginative ways this novel deals with the problematic relations between reality and illusion, and in an author who realizes that we invent both the world and ourselves through language. Cervantes is at his best when characters are reinventing themselves through language, as Don Quixote does when he adopts the language of chivalric novels, and as the delightful Dorotea does, whether she is relating fact or fiction.

Further, readers who believe that God is dead are apt to respond even more fully to a novel and an age in which it appears that God has recently turned His back on the world in disgust and occupied Himself with better projects. What He has left behind in this novel are two symbols of restraint: an apparently incompetent barber-surgeon to care for the body, and a priest who cares more about the slippery world of literary criticism than about man's slippery soul.

Finally, readers respond, as they do in *Faust* (Part 2), to Goethe's dictum that "striving is all." That attitude toward life saves Faust from eternal damnation, and it is true that most people do want to die with their boots on, or, as Gary Cooper says, in probably more than one western movie, "A man's gotta do what a man's gotta do." Don Quixote has that attitude up until his death, and we admire him for it.

The life and character of the creator of *Don Quixote* share many of the features of his hero.

Miguel de Cervantes Saavedra was born in 1547. The family was never well off, as his father was a rather unsuccessful barber-surgeon without a degree, and when Cervantes was five years old, creditors seized all the family possessions. They moved to Seville, where Miguel and his brother attended an excellent Jesuit school. Cervantes published his first poem at the age of twenty-one, and he also got into a quarrel with a Don Antonio Sigura. The duel they fought was, unfortunately, on forbidden royal palace grounds.

Cervantes fled to Rome rather than have his right hand cut off as punishment, and served in the office of a cardinal until, at the age of twenty-four, he joined an army regiment. He fought bravely in the famous naval battle against the Turks in the Gulf of Lepanto in 1571. Not only was he brave but he was foolish and idealistic: as he was seriously ill, he had to plead to be allowed to come from belowdecks to fight. His left hand was mangled and ruined in the battle, and he received a severe chest wound. Afterward, the four years he spent in southern Italy and in Naples allowed him the opportunity to become acquainted with scholars and poets, and to immerse himself in the works of Ariosto, Petrarch, Boccaccio, and Dante.

In 1575 he was on a galley sailing from Naples to Spain, the ship was attacked, and Cervantes and his brother were taken prisoner and sent to Algiers to be sold as slaves. During his five years in prison there, Cervantes made four escape attempts, anticipating his future imaginary hero by saying about them, "One should risk one's life for honor and liberty." His impoverished family was finally able, along with Spanish citizens living in Algiers, to raise the ransom money. He feared that a treacherous informant—a defrocked priest who had ruined one of his escape attempts—would write letters to Spain falsely denouncing him. Thanks to that, we have the biographical and autobiographical *Información*, a document drawn up by Cervantes and twelve witnesses that testifies to his moral goodness in providing food and assistance, as well as spiritual comfort, to other prisoners.

The years from age thirty-three to fifty-eight were times of extreme poverty for this ex-soldier whose services had been forgotten. He was thirty-eight when his pastoral novel of shepherds and shepherdesses, *Galatea*, was published, but most of all he wanted to be a playwright, an unfortunate and unrealistic aspiration when Lope de Vega (1562–1635) commanded the stage. This period lasted for a quarter of a century, and Cervantes wrote at the end of his life that creative ideas "miscarry" when one is poor and has to earn one's "daily bread." (However, he did manage to have more than twenty plays produced during the period 1581–1587.)

In 1584 he married a woman from a good country family who was much younger than he. They had no children, but he had a natural daughter, Isabel, from a previous relationship. Twenty-five years later his wife would write of their life of "love" and "friendship" together. But others say that it was an unhappy marriage; who is to know the reality?

During some of these years he worked as a commissary requisitioning wheat from reluctant farmers for the Armada of 1588, and as a tax collector, but the government delayed his salary, he was accused of inaccuracies in his account books, and in 1597 there were questions from the Treasury. Cervantes was innocent; a banker absconded with his money. He went to jail for almost three months, and there, among criminals and outcasts, it is commonly believed he developed the idea for his novel.

From 1603 to 1605 he lived in Valladolid, where he wrote *Don Quixote*, a book that was soon read throughout Europe, but one which did little to relieve his poverty. Two-thirds through the Second Part—for which there was great demand—an Alonso Fernández de Avellaneda published his own version, which included such nasty personal attacks on Cervantes as calling him an incompetent, one-handed writer. At least that version, published in 1614, caused Cervantes to push on with his own work—and to include jibes at the false work in his Second Part of *Don Quixote*, published in 1615.

This poor, broken man wrote a book hoping to make money, but he saw little of it, and had to live with his wife in the house of a Franciscan priest. He died on April 23, 1616, the same date as Shakespeare, although Shakespeare actually died ten days later—the English calendar had not yet been reformed. The fact that the unwary—and they are as numerous today as they were in the seventeenth century—believe they both died on the same day is, of course, marvelously quixotic.

Cervantes shares with his hero the fictional quixotic world of idealism and impracticality, of optimism in defeat, of persistence and determination against overwhelming odds, and—most of all—the successful struggle to maintain one's own individuality.

Cervantes' and Don Quixote's concentrated determination to persist and survive in a tricky and deceitful world causes them both to see that world from an isolated position that restricts their vision. The novel itself also becomes isolated from the world.

Spain had fought the Moslem world for so long that orthodoxy in religion came to be equated with patriotism, and heresy was punished by a new inquisition that became even more widespread under Philip II (reigned 1556–1598). Medieval

Christianity still lived on in Spain, and the monarchy controlled the Church.

Cervantes' novel reflects little of this, nor should it: his novel is, as Samuel Beckett says of *Finnegans Wake*, "about itself." There are numerous historical sources to inform us of the events taking place while Cervantes was working on *Don Quixote*: Shakespeare was writing *Hamlet, Othello, Macbeth*, and *King Lear*; a revolutionary new scientific world was being discovered by Tycho Brahe, Kepler, Galileo, and Vesalius; Rubens and Frans Hals were painting; and Monteverdi brought about innovations in music. Spain was culturally isolated from the rest of Europe, Cervantes was socially isolated from the rest of Spain, and Don Quixote, who was created ten years after Montaigne died, shares with the essayist an isolated but lively internal world that is more real than the narrow and unimaginative external one.

Don Quixote does, however, share many of the features of an earlier imaginative work, the *Odyssey*. It abounds in transformation stories along the lines of the magically changing Proteus. As in the *Odyssey*, which might also be called the "first novel," there are many episodes involving disguise, delusion, and deception, as well as scenes of recognition and reversal. Both works delight in *burlas*—tricks that can be burlesque, serious, or both—as well as in a fascination with the grotesque, and both essentially take place "on the road." Cervantes even goes Homer one better: Homer presents himself as a singer at the court of King Alkinoos in the *Odyssey*; Cervantes presents Don Quixote presenting himself as a double, both a "real" and a fictional character, in the Second Part of that work when he is at the court of the Duke and Duchess.

Don Quixote outdoes Odysseus in that he undergoes at least forty encounters, far too many to analyze outside of a book solely about this novel. Everyone remembers the encounters with the windmills and the sheep, as well as many others in the First Part. The relations between reality and imagination are much more subtle in the Second Part, and two of the more complicated ones are particularly worth examining for their revelations, as is one of the structural devices in a novel that has been accused of having no structure.

In Chapter 25 of the Second Part, Don Quixote and Sancho Panza encounter a Puppet Master, actually Ginés de Pasamonte, one of the prisoners on their way to becoming galley slaves that Don Quixote had freed in Chapter 22 of the First Part. A previous illusion (that the thieves were honorable) thus returns in disguised illusion as a man who earns his living by creating illusions with an ape and puppets.

In his *Republic* Plato criticizes art because it is so removed from the truth, being a reflection of reality which is itself only a reflection of ideality. As he did with Homer, Cervantes is here bounding beyond Plato in his presentation of reality and illusion. Reality is transformed into actors who have been transformed into puppets whose deeds are transformed into narration by a boy who is not very skilled at what he is doing. Moreover, he is corrected by Don Quixote, who is actually acting as Cervantes' illusionary surrogate in settling old scores with Lope de Vega's theatrical illusions. Above all, given the number of curves offered by the interpolated stories in his novel, Cervantes needs to follow the advice Don Quixote and Pedro give the boy: go straight ahead in telling your story, and tell it in plainsong, not in counterpoint. However, Cervantes' story would have been marred by plain, straightforward storytelling, as it would if he had kept it "real" and "truthful."

Don Quixote, who has always had difficulty distinguishing between reality and illusion, is so caught up in the illusion of the play that it becomes real to him, and he jumps onto the stage to save the damsel-in-distress, mangling or destroying the puppets in the process—damage more easily remedied than the broken leg suffered by one of the earlier victims of his illusions.

Pedro, apparently affected by Don Quixote's madness, begins

to mourn the loss of his illusion-creating objects as though they were all real, as if he had been the "lord" of "kings and emperors" and of stables and horses, and is now a poor man.

Just when all seems to be well, and Don Quixote, who has now blamed the entire affair on the usual enchanters, is paying Pedro for the damaged puppets, he draws back at paying for the now eyeless and noseless Melisendra, the damsel-in-distress who had been rescued by her husband on horseback. No, the Don exclaims, that cannot be Melisendra, for the horse "seemed to fly rather than gallop," and by now she and her husband must be safely in France. Pedro, seeing that Don Quixote is once more beginning to depart this world, relents, and they soon go off, full of good fellowship, to a peaceful supper—for which Don Quixote gladly pays the bill.

The Duke and Duchess are the most degraded and jaded characters in a book crammed with devious liars. They are cruel, bored, and childish, and the twenty-eight chapters (30 through 57 of the Second Part) allotted to their involvement are so full of undeserved pain inflicted on Don Quixote and Sancho Panza that they become distasteful, perhaps an indication of Cervantes' condemnation of their behavior.

The episode of the Flying Horse in Chapter 41 cleverly portrays illusion interacting with reality, and it was suggested earlier that this novel be appreciated for its intellectual brilliance rather than for its cruel humor.

Don Quixote and Sancho Panza have fearfully seated themselves on the huge wooden horse; they are blindfolded, and Sancho touchingly removes his blindfold for a moment in order to have a last look at the world. When they are ready for their journey, Don Quixote puts his fingers on the wooden peg, and the witnesses begin to shout, employing the power of suggestion as they describe to the two riders their soaring swiftness. Sancho, always the realist, wants Don Quixote to explain why, if they are so high in the air, they can so plainly hear the voices of those below. Don Quixote, ever the willing subject of illusion, assures him that it is no ordinary flight, that it is, indeed, one where it is possible to hear voices thousands of miles away. In any case, he assures Sancho, he has never had a smoother flight: it seems as if they haven't even moved from the spot where they mounted.

The carefully planned illusion is continued as bellows blow air on them, and lighted wicks hanging from canes are held near their faces to make them believe they have come near the hot place. The heat reminds Don Quixote of a story, which he relates to Sancho Panza, to the great amusement of the Duke, the Duchess, and those watching and listening in the garden. There is further glee when the firecracker-filled horse is exploded and poor, frightened Don Quixote and Sancho Panza fly through the air and fall to the ground "half-scorched."

I admit there is some humor in this cruel joke, but what is most interesting and clever here on the part of Cervantes is that the illusion created by the Duke and Duchess turns into reality for Don Quixote and Sancho Panza, and they elaborate the invention in ways unanticipated by the royal couple. This is truly improvisational theater, and would be great fun except that Cervantes is showing someone else controlling Don Quixote's imagination. Up until now he has usually been in charge of his own illusions—creating them for himself—and to see this brave knight and his trusting squire duped by bored and vicious royalty for twenty-eight chapters is one of the sorriest sights in the book.

It has been said that this novel has no structure, that it is rather a series of encounters, no single one of them gaining meaning because of its location, or in any way necessarily causing the next episode. This may be true, but Cervantes has undoubtedly provided both the hero and the reader with relief and rest from adventure by allowing Don Quixote three returns home.

On one of them, the return from his "knighting" at the inn in Chapter 3, Rocinante stumbles when Don Quixote charges the merchants who resist swearing to the beauty of Dulcinea, and the recently dubbed knight is injured. A neighboring farmer brings him home, but thoughtfully and kindly waits until dark so as not to embarrass the new knight in front of the villagers.

This is the broken knight's first return. After a brief stay, long enough for the first attempted cure—the burning of his books and walling up of his library room—to fail, he and Sancho Panza avoid possible hindrance by starting out secretly at night on the knight's second foray. His first journey also began at night—"before daybreak"—because it was a hot July.

After his wild series of adventures in the First Part, Don Quixote is then tricked by the curate and the barber into returning: they have pulled him out of bed, trussed him, and locked him into a cage like an animal. This is pitiful, with the poor, "patient" Don leaning against the bars, not "flesh" but a "statue of stone." Don Quixote, without his imagination, is object, not subject. Later released, he fights with the goatherd, is seriously wounded, and is unceremoniously placed on the back of the cart that carried the cage. Then comes a most cruel action on the part of the barber and the curate: they bring him into town in full view of the villagers, not only at high noon but on a Sunday when everyone is in town and just coming out of mass; the implied cure will be public humiliation. This is the second return of the broken knight.

The Second Part begins with Don Quixote in bed, still recuperating, and anxious about what the villagers think of him. He thus discovers from Sansón that there has been a book about his adventures. At this moment, Don Quixote becomes both reality and fiction, seemingly detaching himself from his author's pen to lead both a life of his own and the life of a character in a book. ("O Jamesy let me up out of this," the independent Molly cries out to her author in *Ulysses*.)

Sancho, in one of his most charming and original statements, boldly declares that the two of them will go out and have enough adventures not just for a second part, but for a hundred parts.

This visit at home has been lengthier than the earlier one, and they again start out at nightfall in order to avoid detection—

but this time it is with a difference: they do not know that Sansón, who is escorting them for a few miles, has already plotted, along with those other two restraining figures, the curate and the barber, the final humiliation and deknighting of Don Quixote.

He is vanquished on the beach in Barcelona by Sansón, in disguise as the Knight of the White Moon, who makes him swear to return home for a full year. The Knight of the Rueful Countenance is now no longer a knight-errant and, both "sad and happy"—in the "modern" condition of Tristan and Isolde—he returns to the village in broad, unromantic daylight. The broken knight has made his third and final return, and the time of day is not given: as his knighthood has ended, it is no longer important.

Aeschylus and Sophocles taught that through suffering comes knowledge. Cervantes, who was working on *Don Quixote* while Shakespeare was writing *King Lear*, joins him in leading us back into the world of Euripides' *Bacchae*, where out of suffering comes only further suffering. The arrogant and power-hungry young Pentheus, the imaginative and middle-aged Don, and the trusting and wrathful old Lear are all broken on the rack of the world by inflexible gods. All three works present the dark dangers of illusion to the individual, and the terrible consequences of drawing others into that illusion. In reading *Don Quixote* we should end by worrying about our own laughter at the illusions.

Gulliver's Travels

THE HOUYHNHNMS are self-controlled, generous, truthful, well balanced, just, civilized, quick to learn, neither mean nor petty, neither boastful nor cowardly, and they have no fear of death.

Swift applies these traits to his cultured horses as Socrates applies them to his true philosophers in Plato's *Republic*. This and further evidence leads me to believe that Book 4 of *Gulliver's Travels* is a biting satire on Plato's ideal state, in which Swift shows that an ideal rational republic is so much horse-culture.

Although the resemblance between Houyhnhnm society and the *Republic* of Plato has been suggested by others, what has been neglected is the extent of the correspondence between the *Republic* and the entire island of which the Houyhnhnms are only a part. The Houyhnhnms are the philosophers whose lives are guided by reason, Gulliver represents the courageous auxiliary soldiers, and the Yahoos are commoners controlled by their appetites.

Focusing on the real object of Swift's attack helps in dealing with the two-hundred-and-fifty-year-old problem of Gulliver's disgust with himself and the problem of the humane Portuguese Captain. Swift is, above all, a political writer, and he has his hero become disgusted not so much with his humanity as with human social organizations in which he has no place: there is no room on either the island of the Houyhnhnms or the island of Britain for the simple, honest, courageous individual named Gulliver, but only for human institutions, in which there is room only at the unemotional, inhumane top or at the emotional, inhumane bottom. In the *ange-bête* world of *King Lear*, only nothingness remained, with no place for Lear's newly discovered humanity; Gulliver finds that there is no place for his courageous but gentle humanity, and so he repairs to his stable to sleep with unintelligent English horses.

Gulliver is forceful in his attacks on human greed, and it is greed that is the basic reason for Plato's construction of his state: larger states will always greedily eat up smaller ones, and so he builds his state on the education of its citizens as soldiers. Plato believes that the state is the individual writ large, and therefore it will be easier to locate justice in the state rather than in the individual. The examination leads to the conclusion that justice is present when reason controls spirit, and spirit controls appetite. However, instead of determining, as Aristotle does, that the best individual is one in whom these faculties are in moderated balance, Plato proceeds to propose a dehumanizing division of his ideal state into a rigid class structure. He will separate (and isolate) the citizens into the intellectual class (the philosopher-kings), the spirited class (the soldiers), and the appetitive class (people who are unsuited for "higher" education). Many of Plato's ideas are satirized by Swift, but the primary target is this division of the state into three faculties, and then the application of those three faculties to Plato's proposed reorganization of the individual.

Dante uses this threefold division in the *Inferno* when he designs a geography of Hell in which the descending circles of sinners are occupied by those who placed appetite over reason, then those who placed spirit over reason, and, in the lower depths, those who used reason to distort reason. Certainly, it is a truism that books talk to books, and, since Plato, many writers have addressed the *Republic*—particularly Dante in his *Divine Comedy*, Swift in *Gulliver's Travels*, and, as we shall see, Dostoevsky in *The Brothers Karamazov*.

Plato's philosophers, like the Houyhnhnms, live lives of wisdom controlled by reason; the soldiers, like Gulliver, are controlled by the good emotions of spirit, honor, and courage; and the commoners, like the Yahoos, are controlled by the base emotions of appetite and must be trained and regulated by the state. Not only does Swift endow his three social divisions with these characteristics, he physically indicates them by having Gulliver's shelter located between the House of the Houyhnhnms and the Kennel of the Yahoos. Swift demonstrates that when man aspires to a life of pure reason, and in that process becomes disgusted with his animal nature, he comes to reject what makes him truly human—his honorable and courageously spirited nature.

Aristotle's man—an animal that lives in a city—is the one who satisfies his animal appetites and at the same time lives a life of spirited rational inquiry in that city. What is truly pitiful about Plato's idea of a state is that, after locating his three divisions of the soul, and indicating that the best, most just, and happiest life is one in which reason, spirit, and appetite are in balance, he then proceeds to build a state with the most severe separation of those three qualities that he can possibly imagine. Plato suppresses human nature; Gulliver attempts to do so, and the calmly smiling god of the Dionysian force shows him that that way madness lies.

Gulliver's essential nature does not change throughout his four voyages into an unreal world, any more than does Don Quixote's in the three voyages he makes into *his* unreal world. Both return home for rest and recuperation, but then, dissatisfied with a life lacking in spirit and adventure, they set off again. But neither sees himself—their eyes are constantly fixed on the external world. They do not come to know themselves, but only to reject themselves, as Don Quixote does when he gives up the life of chivalry and dies, and Gulliver does when he is denied a place in what he considers the ideal rational society and rejects his humanity for life in a stable. They are both marvelously curious about stimuli, but don't question their own responses.

In each of his previous voyages Gulliver has investigated various political states, and Swift shows the folly of them all, primarily satirizing contemporary ideas and practices in England and France. The wonder is that readers for hundreds of years have decided that he suddenly abandons satire and turns to admiration for the society of the Houyhnhnms in the fourth book.

Swift uses the voyages that frame Gulliver's four travels, in particular the initial incidents of each one, as part of the meaning of the adventure itself. With the overall aim of satirizing man's political order, each voyage concentrates on a particular aspect of man: the physical in Book 1, the political in Book 2, the intellectual in Book 3, and the moral in Book 4. The sequence of the voyages of discovery thus mirrors Dante's use of Plato in the *Inferno*: the sinners who elevated appetite over reason, such as Paolo and Francesca; the sinners who allowed lust and violence to overcome reason, frequently in political ways, such as Farinata and Cavalcante; and finally those who used reason to distort the two faculties which above all others should, according to Plato, be guided by reason—the intellectual and moral faculties—such as Ulysses, Judas, Brutus, and Cassius.

The inhabitants of the territories Gulliver visits have been overwhelmed by *húbris*, arrogant pride, a fault not always recognized by characters in works since Athenian literature, perhaps because, given the extent to which Saint Paul and other New Testament figures preached against this sin, it has become hidden rather than nonexistent. We must remember that Jonathan Swift was Dean of St. Patrick's Cathedral in Dublin, and that he himself preached against the sin of pride in that pulpit as he does in this novel. And Gulliver, who moves through the dangerously prideful territories of the first three voyages without succumbing to the sin of pride, catches it from the insidiously hidden *húbris* of the Houyhnhnms, and denies the animal nature he shares with the Yahoos.

Gulliver sees everything but himself in the first three voyages. When he finally accepts his kinship with the Yahoos—but only when it is forced upon him in a command that the Houyhnhnms euphemistically call an "Exhortation"—he goes through powerful and moving scenes of recognition and reversal; *Gulliver's Travels* is a mock epic that ends in mock tragedy.

The climactic incidents of each of the four outward-bound voyages become increasingly violent as Gulliver's journey progresses, until, on his final expedition, he suffers the most extreme misfortune of all when he is overcome by his own sailors, put in chains, and made a prisoner. On the island of the Houyhnhnms he will be worse than a physical prisoner, he will be enchained by spiritual aspirations to achieve a purely inhuman rationality. Not only does his experience on the ship foreshadow his experience on the island, but Swift is planting a later comparison to the physical violence of the Yahoos as well as a contrast to the equanimity of the Houyhnhnms. What actually takes effect here is an equation between the physical violence of the sailors and the calm violence done to the spirit by the Houyhnhnms' excessive rationality.

Gulliver is overcome by the sailors and bound by "fastening one of my Legs with a Chain near my Bed," and he is made a "Prisoner in my Cabbin." This is an outrageous parody of Plato's myth of the cave, with his prisoners chained in darkness, seeing only (a subsequent analogy) the shadow of the bed—probably all that poor Gulliver can see—instead of Plato's Idea of a bed. The prisoners freed from Plato's cave, where they are trapped in the world of sense imagery, are led through education to climb upward to the highest possible conception, the Idea of the Good. Gulliver will be released from his prison house of the senses, and his immersion in horse-culture will lead him to the prison of the totally rational soul.

Gulliver has so rejected the animal in himself that he fails to recognize the first Yahoos he sees as being of his own species: they represent the idea of man as essentially animal, and they are no more to be imitated than the Houyhnhnms, who also deny their animal and spirited nature and represent the idea of reason devoid of spirit and feeling. "I never beheld, in all my Travels so disagreeable an Animal," he says of the Yahoos, reacting to them with "Contempt and Aversion"—his response when he doesn't recognize himself in them, and his response to self when he does recognize them in himself. One of the Yahoos lifts up his forepaw to touch Gulliver (a Houyhnhnm makes the same gesture), Gulliver strikes the "Beast," whom he thinks of as "Cattle," and a "Herd of at least forty came flocking about me from the next field."

Gulliver's response to the horses is different because he perceives that they "confer" together in some kind of "Language" that seems "almost articulate." Already he has erroneously begun to respond to them as creatures similar to himself.

When Gulliver goes to the home of the Houyhnhnms, Swift reveals the two-pronged attack of this episode: he is satirizing Plato *and* the Enlightenment thinkers, for both shared a belief that a perfected state would result in the creation of a perfected man—in Plato's case, the philosopher-king.

Although the satire on Plato is a topic of the book that makes its first appearance in Part 4, the satire of the Enlightenment is continued from the previous three parts, and that historical period needs some brief consideration in order to appreciate fully how Swift is denigrating the Houyhnhnms.

Traditionally, the Enlightenment began with the English revolution of 1688 and continued through the American and French revolutions of 1776 and 1789. Reason, of course, was the key word, with the conviction that progress would continue until man and state were perfected. Much of this belief was founded on new scientific inventions which allowed man increased control over nature—particularly agriculture—and industry, as well as refinements in the weapons of war.

As far as Swift and many others of the subsequent Counter-Enlightenment were concerned, these improvements in science unfortunately led to ideas about the scientific improvement of man through social engineering, primarily by refining social institutions. The emphasis was to be on groups of individuals rather than on the individual, and truth would be scientifically established. As with Plato, the belief was that the scientific analysis of human nature would lead to the organization of the best society. If scientists and legislators could improve nature, then they could improve man: rational laws would control irrational man and make him rational. The study of human nature was—for the first time—considered a science, and humanity could be disciplined through the hegemony of institutional structures over spirit.

Swift believed that a science of human nature only ended by codifying behavior, as he demonstrates with the Houyhnhnms when he shows that their rigid codes have eliminated spontaneity, inspiration, feeling, religion, mysticism, happiness, and the knowledge that comes through self-examination. They are creatures of habit, and they reject Gulliver because, like Plato in his *Republic*, they cannot deal with difference, change, or chance.

Gulliver discovers that the first Houyhnhnm he meets uses "various Gestures, *not unlike those of a Philosopher*, when he would attempt to solve some new and difficult Phænomenon" [emphasis mine] and that the "Behaviour of these Animals was, it seemed to him, orderly and rational, acute and judicious." And so he accompanies them home, where Swift shows that—to pure reason—Gulliver is a mere object, as there is no warmth or offer of food or comfort until this strange object has been scientifically defined. This they proceed to do by (1) close and careful scrutiny of the found object, Gulliver; (2) comparison with a similar object, the Yahoo in the yard; and (3) objective experimentation by offering Gulliver the food of a Yahoo. Although they will always place Gulliver in the category of Yahoo because of (1) and (2), Gulliver's rejection of Yahoo food in (3) will, along with later revelations, cause them to put him in the category of exceptional Yahoo.

Gulliver sets out to learn the language of the Houyhnhnms, and, as they represent Plato's philosopher-teachers, they are anxious to teach him; Gulliver wants to "imitate a rational creature." Although later we are told that the horses have poetry, it is obviously oral epic, as Gulliver here discovers that "the Inhabitants have not the least Idea of Books of Literature."

Of course they don't: they have progressed to the culmination of Plato's state, where literature is outlawed.

The horses are astonished by Gulliver's "Capacity for Speech and Reason." Swift is here making the distinction between *animal rationale*, man as rational animal, and *rationis capax*, man as capable of rationality. These terms are used by Swift in a letter to Alexander Pope, and he holds that *capability* of rationality—not rationality—is what distinguishes man from animals. Gulliver is capable of rationality, but he errs in accepting reason devoid of spirit or appetite as rational behavior instead of as the unbalanced behavior it is.

Plato and Aristotle hold that no man would knowingly perform wrong actions, as no man guided by reason could make choices that he knew would harm himself. Swift's horses have progressed so far in this direction that they have no word for lying, only the expression "said the thing which was not." Plato, in his *Republic*, contradicts his devotion to truth when he advocates a "noble lie" to be told to the citizens—that they have sprung from the earth: the city-state is their mother, not human parents. In the manner of this "noble lie," Swift has his Houyhnhnms also believe that they are returning to their first mother, the earth, when they die.

Chapters 5 and 6, the critique of European political states, perform the same function as Book 8 of Plato's *Republic*—the critique of the inferior societies of timarchy, oligarchy, democracy, and tyranny.

Chapters 7 and 8 continue the parallel between the Houyhnhnm society and the society of Plato's state. In both: the highest good is the "Contemplation and Practice of every Virtue"; reason and virtue are identical; there is only one truth, and it is not arguable; the distinction between knowledge and opinion, in which the horses come to agree with Gulliver on the "Sentiments of *Socrates*, as *Plato* delivers them; which I mention as the highest Honour I can do that Prince of Philosophers"; a belief in the importance of exercise; the need for neither physicians nor lawyers; a dispassionate attitude toward both life and death; love for fellow citizens; common ownership of children; genetic engineering; and a society "wholly governed by Reason."

Two paragraphs after the one in which the Houyhnhnm society is described as "wholly governed by Reason" (Chapter 9), Swift shows how ridiculous this all is when he describes the dexterity of the horses in using their hooves to make and use tools, milk cows, and thread needles. This is climaxed by the visit of the horse-woman, widowed only that morning, who apologizes for arriving late for a visit because her husband had happened to *"Lhnuwnh"* that morning—he had departed *"to retire to his first Mother."* As was the code, she expressed "neither Joy nor Grief" at his death. The inhuman rational coldness of this particular scene makes it even more shocking that for hundreds of years some readers determined that Swift was presenting the ideal society in this final part.

The "Exhortation" decreed by the General Assembly when it determined that Gulliver presented a possible threat to future tranquillity is a marvelous example of Orwellian doublespeak. They cannot compel him to leave: as "no Person can disobey Reason," Gulliver should know that his departure is in his own best interest, and he can only be "exhorted" to leave. But the Exhortation is undeniably an order, and Gulliver certainly doesn't believe it is in his own best interest. But then, he is somewhat better off than a citizen of Plato's ideal state, where infants with slight deformities are killed at birth, the seriously ill are hastened to their death—as are the old and infirm—and anyone with a difference is dispatched to exile or death.

And so Gulliver, who can no longer tolerate the "Reflection of my own Form in a Lake or Fountain," kisses a horse's hoof and departs. He is dressed in the skins of Yahoos, and has built a canoe the bottom of which is lined with Yahoo skins and which has flexible sails put together from the carefully selected tender skin of a Yahoo—the "youngest I could get." Gulliver's humanity has been totally suppressed: he has apparently murdered a child.

Gulliver only desires an uninhabited island, but the one he lands on is inhabited by barbarians who fall neatly, in his mind, between the Yahoos of Houyhnhnm-land and the Yahoos of Europe, and he reacts to the sailors who rescue him with "Fear and Hatred."

Readers who decide that Swift is presenting the ideal society in this part have great difficulty in accounting for the human nobility of the Portuguese Captain. However, when it is seen that the Houyhnhnm society is ridiculous and absurd, then Gulliver's repugnance for the Captain, who is a "courteous and generous Person" and a "wise Man," serves to point up his blindness to all that is spirited and spiritually human in his rejected self.

When he arrives home, his self-disgust leads him to reject "Wife and Family," and to total delusion when he spends four hours a day conversing with horses who cannot possibly engage in conversation or even understand Gulliver "tolerably well."

"Fortune made Sinon miserable, but not one who is untrue and a liar" (*Aeneid* ii.79–80).

By having Gulliver, in the final chapter, repeat the false oath of Sinon—the treacherous Greek left behind to deceive the Trojans into taking the deceptive horse within their walls—Swift tells the reader that the society Gulliver considered ideal was no more than another version of the noble lie devised by Plato and the Enlightenment thinkers.

There was no place in the structure of the Houyhnhnm society or soul for Gulliver: the Houyhnhnms were pure reason without spirit or appetite, and the Yahoos were pure appetite without reason or spirit. Sadly, Gulliver, the man of reason, spirit, and appetite, rejected all three because he could find no human place in the *ange-bête* world of Plato's and the Enlightenment's—and some Moderns'—dreams of utopian societies and perfect individuals.

Socrates insisted that the unexamined life is not worth living. Swift shows that if the self-analysis is limited to pure rationality, then the examined life isn't worth living either.

The Brothers Karamazov

F IND OUT whether it's possible to lie between the rails with a train passing over you at full speed."

This is the first entry Dostoevsky made in his working notebooks for *The Brothers Karamazov*, and, although it is evident he already has the incident with Kolya in mind, he is about to write a novel in which God's locomotive passes over the bodies and souls of all the characters. And it is to be both a murder mystery and a spiritual mystery.

In the murder mystery a greedy and domineering father, whose life has been ruled by money and sex, is killed by one of his four sons—all of whom have a conscious or unconscious desire for his death and who are therefore, in varying degrees, responsible for the murder. The story of the crime is developed in a carefully constructed plot in which the victim, the suspected criminal, and the actual criminal are all clearly identified in the first one hundred pages—clearly, that is, on a second reading: as with all great murder mysteries, the reader responds to the revelations in this one with the exclamation "Of course!"

All of the complicated threads of the murder mystery are tied together at the end of the book; the spiritual mystery remains a mystery of God's grace. The grace that Dostoevsky is concerned with in this novel is God's gift of freedom. The Athenian tragedians, living in the intellectual fifth century B.C., were concerned with cause and effect—the suffering they saw, and the wisdom that came from and justified that suffering. They did not know how to look at a person's life before that life even began. Dostoevsky looks to God, Who causes everything, and sees that He has justified man by giving him the freedom to choose between good and evil, and that God does not cause suffering but rather man does, for he is responsible for all. God did not create the "dark," but rather, in creating the "light," he separated it from the "dark" forces and gave man freedom to fight those forces. In Dmitri's words, "God and the devil are fighting on a battlefield that is the heart of man."

In the spiritual mystery that is the novel, God's gift of freedom leads to suffering, suffering leads to spiritual death, and that necessary fall leads to rebirth. Beneath the dedication of the novel to his wife, Dostoevsky quotes the Book of John 12:24:

Verily, verily, I say unto you, except a corn of wheat fall into the ground and die, it abideth alone: but if it die, it bringeth forth much fruit.

Dostoevsky indicates the importance of the verse to the spiritual mystery of the novel by having Father Zosima quote it first in regard to Dmitri's suffering, and again when he is advising the suffering, unconfessed murderer. In the first instance Father Zosima is speaking to Alyosha, and in the second he is dictating his life story to the scribe Alyosha. The novel is about the spiritual suffering, death, and rebirth of Dmitri, Alyosha, and Ivan. The father and the illegitimate son who murdered him did not know spiritual suffering in this story, and they thus come to know only death.

Dostoevsky's novels are epic tragedies that closely parallel Homeric epic and Athenian tragedy. Those works also dealt with suffering, death, and rebirth, and they did so by combining both narration and dialogue in their presentation of psychological and physical action.

Achilleus enacts his own symbolic death as he rolls on the ground, covering himself with dirt, mourning for the death of Patroklos. He is spiritually dead until, in a momentous act of rebirth, he returns Hektor's body to Priam. Odysseus' ten-year journey homeward is an act of purification that is part of his own symbolic death and rebirth when he encounters, among others, the souls of the dead. His rebirth is complete when he is united with Penelope and afterward makes his redemptive final journey to the place where the inhabitants know only peace, not war. Orestes has suffered in enforced exile—the most painful life known to the ancient Greeks—and returns in the *Libation Bearers* to undergo more suffering in planning and carrying out the murder of his mother. His symbolic death follows immediately, when the Furies descend and he is put on trial for his life. His rebirth is a momentous rebirth both for him and for a new form of justice in the city-state. The sufferings of Oedipus are beyond bearing, but he endures the fulfillment of the prophecy, his own free act of blinding himself, his self-exile, and his rebirth in the sacred glade of the Eumenides, a rebirth that is also redemption. Euripides, in the *Bacchae*, shows the suffering caused by the vengeful Dionysian force.

In *The Brothers Karamazov*, Dmitri and Alyosha are reborn; Ivan's rebirth, as I will show, is foreshadowed. But, before that, the three young heroes must each experience spiritual, intellectual, and physical sufferings akin to their epic and tragic forefathers, Achilleus, Odysseus, Orestes, Oedipus, and Pentheus. For Dostoevsky, the Dionysian force is God's grace.

Dostoevsky, like Dante, Virgil, and Swift, is using the division of the soul from Plato's *Republic*—but in a distinctly Russian fashion. Certainly, the troika of the three brothers, all pulling in different directions, is Platonic in that Dmitri represents appetite, Alyosha is spirit, and Ivan embodies reason. However, unlike Dante, they are elevating these faculties not above reason but, rather, above faith.

Dmitri's lust for Grushenka has prevented him from acquiring loving faith, but this young man achieves it when he, whose name is derived from Demeter—earth-mother—embraces Grushenka as earth-mother rather than as object of lust.

Alyosha is so serious, both in himself and in the way Dostoevsky is using him as an interlocking force for all the other characters, that we tend to forget that he is barely twenty years old. (This is also the case with Ivan, who is twenty-four, and Dmitri, who is twenty-seven.) But that is the entire point: his intense spirituality has no foundation except in the spiritual life—he has not lived—and that is why Father Zosima sends him out into the world, and why Dostoevsky considers his novel only a prelude to his never-to-be-written sequel about the life of Alyosha in the world.

Alyosha's serious symbolic death comes with the death of his double, Father Zosima, and his amusing symbolic death follows immediately when he visits Grushenka, eats sausages and drinks champagne, and she sits on his lap. Oh, what a marvelous fall is contained in this "jocoserious" (Joyce's word) scene, complete with Grushenka's medieval-style story about the onion and the devils.

Returning to the monastery, Alyosha has the dream-vision of Father Zosima at the wedding at Cana. His rebirth comes when he wakes up and walks out of the monastery while it is still night, looks up at the stars, sees that the universe and all the people in it are connected in a community of love, and falls down to embrace the earth. For Dostoevsky, and for the brilliant young scholar V. S. Solovyov, from whom Dostoevsky learned when they were both very young men, belief in God is not enough, and belief in man is not enough: there must be love for God, love for man, and love for God-manhood, Christ. That kind of love can only be learned from "active love," and this is why Alyosha must go into the world.

Ivan's suffering is caused by his inability to justify the ways of God to man. As he tells Alyosha (Part 2, Book 5, Chapter 3), he accepts God's mysterious wisdom and purpose, believes that eternal harmony will eventually come to be, and accepts God—but not the cruel and evil world created by God.

His mind is torn between love of mankind and love/hate for the "sticky leaves of spring" that represent the world to him, and this schizophrenic condition is manifested in his alter-ego Grand Inquisitor, who despises mankind, and a worldly and sophisticated Devil, who gives every indication that he loves

mankind and will one day love God. Ivan's suffering leads to a
symbolic death in the coma of his brain fever, from which he is
not reborn in this novel. The fact that the Devil, who is certainly
a very real Devil as well as an alter ego of Ivan (he knows things
Ivan could not possibly know), says that he will one day be
reconciled with God, and that Father Zosima's atheist brother
(one of Ivan's many doubles) becomes reconciled also, suggests
to me that the author has the Author working in mysterious
ways by visiting Ivan with a symbolic death, and that both have
every intention of providing means for the rebirth: her name
is Katerina Ivanovna Verkhovtsev (Katya).

Two significant characters do not have a place in the Platonic
schema of appetite, spirit, and reason, and it is significant that
they are the only two major characters into whose minds
Dostoevsky never takes us. They are, of course, Father Zosima
and Smerdyakov, and they are beyond Platonic and Aristotelian
formulations—and our knowledge—because one represents supreme godlike goodness and the other supreme demonic evil.
(Dostoevsky is perhaps following Dante, who presented a silent
Satan and a silent God—both beyond human comprehension.)
As to the thoughts of the three brothers, Dostoevsky carefully
uses them as one of the structural devices: he focuses on the
mind of Alyosha until the youthful novice falls to the earth in
a rebirth to the love of man as well as God, then on the mind
of Ivan until he falls into a coma, and finally on the mind of
Dmitri as we watch him take the leap of faith into love of God
and man.

Dostoevsky's theodicy, then, is that, by grace, God gave man
a freedom that had to lead to suffering, but through this suffering
comes not knowledge but love of the community of fellow men
in the recognition that "all are responsible for all." God refuses
to answer Job's questions about suffering, in effect replying,
"Don't ask—who are you to question God?" and Father Zosima
contends that, because man has the gift of freedom, it is not
God who causes suffering but rather people, that Hell "is the
suffering of no longer being able to love."

This position underlies many scenes in a long but tightly knit and self-reflective novel. Because so many sections mirror others both in action and in idea, two of them can serve as emblematic of the entire novel: Chapter 2 of Book 6 in Part 2, "The Life of the deceased Priest and Monk, the Elder Zosima . . . ," and Chapters 4 and 5 of Book 10 in Part 4, "The lost dog" and "At Ilyusha's bedside."

The novel was appearing serially, and friends wrote to Dostoevsky after the Grand Inquisitor chapter appeared, disturbed and concerned that the arguments against Christ were apparently irrefutable. And they are: the logic, from premise to conclusion, is masterly and unassailable.

The attack by the Grand Inquisitor is not only against Christ, but against the Roman Catholic Church. Although Dostoevsky feared the temporal power of that church, he apparently supported the idea of a theocracy of the Russian Orthodox Church. But the establishment of a human utopia controlled by mystery, miracle, and authority—one that will give man bread, remain secret from him, and take away his freedom—was also Dostoevsky's attack on the socialist utopian dreams that he once held. The rebuttal, Christ's kiss of grace (if that is what it is) on the "bloodless aged lips" of the Grand Inquisitor, was too full of mystery to offer the satisfying logical rebuttal that some readers—as well as Dostoevsky—felt necessary.

Consequently, Dostoevsky offers the "second culminating" episode, the life of Father Zosima, as a rebuttal of the "first culminating" episode, the Grand Inquisitor. Admitting that no logical rebuttal is possible, he writes that he will answer the negative outlook of reason by offering a positive mystical and religious outlook in an "artistic picture" consisting of "artistic realism." Art will defeat reason. What he presents are four actions that contain and envelop the entire novel, the novel itself being the answer to the Grand Inquisitor: love of man, love of God, love of

God-man, love of the earth, and that we are all responsible for all.

The first chapter of Father Zosima's life is divided by Dostoevsky into four sections: "(a) Father Zosima's Brother," "(b) Of the Holy Scriptures in the life of Father Zosima," "(c) Recollections of Father Zosima's youth before he became a monk. The duel," and "(d) The mysterious visitor." The first section reflects Ivan's condition, the second is Alyosha's, the third is Dmitri's, and the fourth mirrors Smerdyakov.

In section (a) Alyosha is told of Zosima's brother Markel, who died at the age of seventeen. Six months before his death, an important political exile from Moscow had come to live in their town, and Markel, an intelligent young man, fell strongly under the influence of this "freethinker" and became an atheist. The exile left for a post in Petersburg, and Markel became ill. Mysteriously, "A marvelous change suddenly took place in him, and his spirit was transformed." His mother wept over him as he lay in bed with a fever, and he asked her not to cry, telling her that "life is paradise, and we are all in paradise, but we don't want to see it; if we wanted to, we could have heaven on earth tomorrow." When he told his mother that "every one of us is responsible to everyone else for everything," he was, of course, expressing an idea that was later adopted by Father Zosima, Alyosha, and Dmitri. Dying of brain fever, Markel told his mother that "there was such a glory of God all about me— birds, trees, meadows, sky, only I lived in shame, and dishonored everything, and did not notice the beauty and the glory."

The parallels with Ivan are obvious: the fall from grace, the illness, the brain fever, the belief in a future earthly paradise (the Grand Inquisitor), and Ivan's love for the "sticky leaves of spring"—in spite of the fact that he rejects the world, telling Alyosha that he is eager to return to God the ticket of admission to the world that he has been given.

Ivan parallels much of Dostoevsky's own youth (as well as much of Markel's brief life) in his youthful commitment to socialism, then to atheism (Ivan's rejection of God's world is certainly that), then to revolutionary thought—all of this culminating in Dostoevsky's mock execution, imprisonment in Siberia, and reconversion to Christianity. Even Ivan's language is that of the revolutionists of Dostoevsky's youth in the 1840s, rather than the revolutionary language of the 1870s that Rakitin spouts. The novel leaves Ivan in the symbolic death of a coma, but, given the rebirth experienced by his mirror images, Markel and his author, then certainly Dostoevsky is furnishing sufficient proleptic material to support strongly the view that Ivan will recover in both body and soul.

The long first paragraph in Chapter 4 of Book 1 of Part 1 that is devoted to Alyosha's life, and the long second paragraph of section (b) of the chapter on the life of Father Zosima both contain considerable repetition of the words "remember" and "memory," as well as—when both are in the presence of their mothers—memories of the slanting rays of sunlight (grace) streaming through a window onto the child. (When Zosima's brother Markel was dying, "the slanting rays of the setting sun lit up the whole room.")

These opening paragraphs clearly indicate that this section mirrors Alyosha, as the section is primarily devoted to Zosima's meditation on the Book of Job: an examination of a man whose faith (not belief) in God is shattered because it was built upon an unsuffering, self-satisfied view of the condition of suffering in a world created by God. This is precisely the condition of the twenty-year-old Alyosha's spiritual faith, and it is for this reason that Father Zosima sends him out into the world of Dostoevsky's projected serial: to experience suffering and trial in order to strengthen his faith. As we saw, immediately following Zosima's death Alyosha goes to Grushenka's house, where he suffers temptation, trial, and a symbolic fall.

The duel is the major episode of section (c), and we find that Zosima, like Dmitri, has attended a military school. Also like Dmitri, he is living a "free and licentious bachelor life" that is controlled by "wrath and revengeful feelings." Dostoevsky pointedly has the youthful Zosima relate in detail his "ugly and brutal moods," loss of temper, and beating of his servant until the man's face was covered with blood.

This could easily be a description of Dmitri's impetuous rage, especially on the night of his father's murder, but the parallel is even more pointed in the resemblances between Father Zosima and Dmitri before the duel and before the projected parricide: both have intended to kill, and both, through the mysterious workings of the grace of God, are saved from killing another of God's creatures. And yet, in their own eyes, Father Zosima and Dmitri both ask themselves the question "What am I worth?" and come to the conclusion that they are each "responsible to all for all." The young Zosima will enter a monastery, and the young Dmitri will endure his purgation in America and his final redemption when he returns, in disguise, to his beloved native soil.

Section (d), "The mysterious visitor," presents a man who, like Smerdyakov, has committed a murder and escaped detection, and he also feels no remorse: "But he never thought about the innocent blood he had shed, of the murder of a fellow human being."

Both the mysterious visitor and Smerdyakov confess to murder, but the first has the future monk for his spiritual advisor, and the second has his double, Ivan. The results, Dostoevsky demonstrates, are quite different in the two cases. The bodies of both men are stricken with punitive illness, and they both die without anyone other than their confessors knowing of their guilt, but the name of the murderer is finally revealed in the last sentence of his story as that of the archangel Mikhail; his soul is possessed by God. Smerdyakov, who has had a name from the very beginning—and one that means stink in Russian and worse (*merde*) in French—is possessed by Satan.

Dostoevsky's original plans were that *The Brothers Karamazov* was to be a novel about faith and about children; the work became larger than that, but, fortunately, the children are still there.

Kolya, that precocious thirteen-year-old intellectual who perhaps unknowingly quotes Voltaire, hates to be questioned about his age, but loves to talk about God and humanity, predates and prefigures Ivan in that Dostoevsky in his creation of Ivan used notes originally made for Kolya.

Kolya figures prominently in all of Book 10, and one of the first things we discover about him is his correspondence to the Grand Inquisitor. This is established in the fake miracle he concocts when he lies down between the rail track lines, is run over by a train, dies, and is mysteriously reborn, thus secretly establishing his miraculous powers. Moreover, the sequence of apparent suffering, death, and rebirth mirrors the very real suffering, death, and rebirth in the novel.

The incidents in Chapters 4 and 5 of Book 10 primarily concern Kolya's "miracle" of the restoration to life of the dog little Ilyusha thinks he has killed. Ilyusha has been taught by Smerdyakov the trick of feeding a dog a piece of bread in which there are pins, and Smerdyakov is thus, as he is with Ivan, the indirect but efficient cause of Ilyusha's guilt and illness.

Kolya presents the "resurrected" dog to the bedridden Ilyusha, who turns "white as a sheet," with his "large eyes almost starting out of his head." We are told that, had the "unsuspecting" Kolya foreseen what a "fatal effect" his action would have on Ilyusha, he could not have been induced to play such a "trick." The unsuspecting Ivan was tricked into giving Smerdyakov permission to kill their father, and Kolya's trick kills a child. Smerdyakov instigates ideas that lead to death, and Kolya/Ivan becomes an instrument of death.

Kolya has trained the dog in such difficult tricks as "playing dead" (so he can stage a "miracle" of resurrection), as well as the cruel one of holding a piece of meat on his nose until Kolya gives the command to eat. Oh, how the Grand Inquisitor would applaud such subservience and deprivation of freedom: indeed, Kolya is a thirteen-year-old Ivan/Grand Inquisitor.

But Kolya/Ivan becomes also, oddly enough, a Christ figure. When little Ilyusha appears as a new boy in school, he is teased by his fellows, and Kolya protects and defends him. When Ilyusha's father has been publicly humiliated by Dmitri, and Kolya is about to protect him from humiliation by his classmates over the incident, Ilyusha stabs Kolya with a penknife, thus punishing Kolya for the sin of a fellow human being. Kolya further protects Ilyusha by swearing the other boys to secrecy so that the schoolmasters will not discover the incident.

The same day that Ilyusha stabs Kolya, he also throws stones at Alyosha and bites the young novice's finger until it bleeds: Alyosha here becomes the Christ figure, suffering for his brother Dmitri's sin. On the way to visit Ilyusha, Alyosha tells Kolya/Ivan that everyone trusted him to provide the resurrection: "If you could have found the dog and Ilyusha saw that he had not died, then the happiness would have cured him. We have relied on you." Resurrections provided by the Devil end not in happiness, but in death.

The sharpest correspondence between Kolya and Ivan is presented when Kolya tells the story of the goose to the roomful of people at Ilyusha's bedside. In the marketplace one day he spotted a "stupid" young peasant watching geese. Oats were dropping out of a sack in a cart, and a goose had thrust his neck under the cart's wheel in order to feed on the oats. In the suggestive style of Smerdyakov, Kolya told him that if the cart were to move just a little, the goose would be killed. The peasant's face lit up, he took the bridle of the carthorse in his hand, Kolya "winked" at the peasant, he tugged at the bridle, and "crack, the goose's neck was broken in half." This is Ivan "winking" at Smerdyakov, unconsciously giving his permission to kill the father and then placing the responsibility on Smerdyakov. But there were witnesses to Kolya's action. When the two youths were brought before the judge and the peasant claimed that Kolya had egged him on, Kolya became Ivan when he defended himself by calmly answering that he hadn't encouraged him but had simply "stated the general proposition, had spoken theoretically." Kolya and Ivan have achieved their ends through the actions of others; the tough young Kolya, however, feels absolutely no responsibility.

But Kolya's is the last spoken line in the book, and Dostoevsky shows that he, along with all the other major figures, will change for the better.

In the final scene of the novel, Alyosha and the children have gathered around the huge stone that is to be placed as a marker over Ilyusha's grave, and in his brief talk to the children Alyosha uses variations of the word "remember" dozens of times.

Certainly, Dostoevsky has, throughout this novel, captured in imaginative fiction Aristotle's logical proof that memories of good actions performed will belie Solon's advice to Croesus that "no man be counted happy until he is dead." Dostoevsky believes we are "all responsible for all," and through "active love," rather than through inhuman institutions. Dostoevsky thinks that human suffering will be eliminated when everyone, like Alyosha, falls down and embraces the earth.

The final two paragraphs of the book offer the physical nourishment derived from the grain of wheat that falls to the ground, dies, and is reborn (in the epigraph from the Bible at the beginning of the book), and the spiritual nourishment that comes from love of other human beings:

"Well, now we will stop talking and go to his funeral dinner. Don't worry about our eating pancakes. It's a very old custom and there's something nice about that!" Alyosha laughed. "Well, come on! And now we do go hand in hand."

"And always so, all our lives hand in hand! Hurrah for Karamazov!" Kolya cried once more with enthusiasm, and once more all the boys joined in.

The Waste Land

E VER SINCE its publication in 1922, *The Waste Land* has been a popular and special poem to college undergraduates; they feel that it was written for them, speaks to them, and belongs to them. Evelyn Waugh in *Brideshead Revisited* illustrates the poem's early hold on youth. At Oxford, standing at Sebastian's window, Anthony Blanche declaims, to passing undergraduates, memorized passages from the poem—and this only a year after its publication.

There are many reasons for the poem's appeal to first readers, most of whom know nothing of ancient fertility rites, do not recognize the many allusions in the poem to other poems, and are blissfully and innocently unaware of the wealth of intricate interpretations to which this most "difficult" of all modern poems has been subjected. Perhaps their emotive response to the poem is richer than that of their elders, and one that they themselves will also ultimately lose. Before proceeding to corrupt those untarnished first readers who cherish the poem by providing them with a detailed examination prohibited in the other essays by the length of the texts, it might be well to look at the poem's appeal to the blessedly unsophisticated reader.

Each new generation thinks it has destroyed and surpassed the previous one, and that it, in turn, inhabits a world that will be destroyed and surpassed by those who come after. To these readers the poem does not hide the fact that it is about death and resurrection, and it speaks to them about these "grave" matters in emotional rather than in intellectual terms. The poem is reaching down to the deepest roots of ancient Greek mythology and religion—the overthrow of Uranus by his son Cronus, and the overthrow of Cronus by Zeus—as well as to the myriad number of rebirth stories that reach their zenith in Adonis and the Christ.

There is also an unabashed nostalgia throughout the poem and, for the young reader, nostalgia for what is thought of as the happier past each generation feels it will never know—a sense of being lost in an anxious and confusing present over which it has no real control, and a paradoxical nostalgia for the future caused by the belief that there will be no renewal or rebirth. The poem speaks to these deep feelings as it looks at the present as a limbo between an organized past and a disorganized future, and finds it meaningless.

The poem questions the sincerity and integrity of modern man, aspects of self which each person learns early to question. Moreover, the poem seems now to present sincerity and integrity as having been profoundly threatened by the contemporary societies of every period since the poem was written.

Eliot himself was incensed over the early responses of critics who contended that the poem was about disillusionment and melancholy, and rightly so, for how could a poem that so energetically rages against the conditions of life in the twentieth century be labeled withdrawn and defeatist? The poem speaks to young people's sense of disappointment in a world that they find, early on, breaks the promises made to children.

Not many first readers would be able to translate the epigraph to the poem, which tells about the Sibyl's desire to die, but one does not need to know Latin and Greek to know that the poem is about death-in-life. It is when we are very young that we first become aware of the shocking fact of our own mortality.

Academics make a great commotion over the *acedia*—spiritual torpor, apathy—in the poem, but this is hardly one of the primary concerns of youth, and that cannot be what makes the poem personal to them. Rather, they respond to the sense of *urgency* that pervades the poem, the sense that time is flying past, that there is no tomorrow, and that something must be done Now! Today! Although other poems contain this sense of urgency (Marvell's "To His Coy Mistress," for one), they do not possess that combination of simultaneous *urgency* and *languor* that is the essential quality of youth—the feeling that there is both all the time in the world and no time at all. Unfortunately, it is the languorous atmosphere in the poem that has been so frequently read only as apathy, defeat, and disillusionment.

Mr. Prufrock, in that other Eliot poem so beloved by youth, is confused about the relationship between the physical and the spiritual worlds. Similarly, the world of *The Waste Land* is one where lust is mistaken for—or becomes a substitute for—love, and where the spiritual plane cannot be reached because of an inability to make the necessary leap of faith. The people in this poem are incapable of unifying love and sex, and have not the love and faith necessary to participate in the ritual that will resurrect the dead god.

A hero is one who is willing to die; but when the "hero" of this poem finally arrives at the Chapel Perilous—the place where medieval heroes died on the altar-bier and were then reborn—he finds an "empty chapel, only the wind's home." The twentieth century has provided the quester with no chapel for rebirth.

In addition to the subject matter of the poem, the presentation itself is appealing to new readers.

The outstanding feature of a modern work is that it must announce on its first appearance—and keep announcing on future readings—"I am Modern!" Ezra Pound admonished young poets: "Make it New," and "Literature is news that stays news." Certainly, *The Waste Land*—along with other works from early in the twentieth century, such as Picasso's *Les Demoiselles d'Avignon*, Stravinsky's *Rite of Spring*, Pound's *Hugh Selwyn Mauberley*, and Joyce's *Ulysses*—continues to stay new and shocking. To be modernist—and to stay modernist—the surface of the work must be as startling as the content, and it must keep calling attention to itself. One aim of literary production before the twentieth century was to write in accepted modes in which form did not call undue attention to itself. But Pound had come under the influence of the inventive and diverse forms of Provençal poetry, and the world of literature became different:

in Joyce's *Ulysses*, beginning with the Sirens episode, every episode is written in a totally different "voice." Style now announces itself as an essential part of the meaning of the text.

Though there is variation, even "The Love Song of J. Alfred Prufrock" is written in rhymes and meters; and there are certainly no foreign words in the body of the poem. But *The Waste Land* opens with participles rather than rhymes, falls quickly into an almost proselike reminiscence, and continues with patches of German, French, Italian, and Sanskrit. And the style changes not only from section to section, but within each section. The young reader, especially in the sixties, seventies, and eighties, recognizes in this variation the multitude of changes of rhythm and tempo characteristic of contemporary popular music; the readers of the period from the twenties through the fifties responded, of course, to the ragtime and jazz rhythms that are in the poem.

Disjuncture is a characteristic of *The Waste Land*, as it also is of much of the work of Eliot, Joyce, Pound, and other modernist and post-modernist writers. No transitions are provided in these works, no bridges from one section, mood, image, or idea to another, and readers are consequently forced to make their own connections, or—if they have the sense to take the sensible, irrational approach to reading a modernist text—they reject the forming of artificial connections, or of connections that could not and were not meant to be made, representing, as they do, the lacunae, the disjunctures, and the disconnections of twentieth-century life: Eliot's " 'On Margate Sands./I can connect/ Nothing with nothing,' " and E. M. Forster's "Only connect."

In reading literature, one must sometimes be able to maintain two or more contradictory interpretations at the same time without attempting to resolve them. The youthful John Keats formulated the idea of negative capability, the ability to live in mystery and doubt simultaneously. Samuel Beckett was Joyce's secretary during part of the writing of *Finnegans Wake*; when asked what the book was about, he replied that it was about itself. In many ways *The Waste Land* is about itself—poetry, and the relation of poetry to life. As such, it contains mutually contradictory ideas—water and fire as sources of both death and rebirth—and it demands that we make ourselves comfortable in our own mystery and doubt in dealing with a poem that is about mystery and doubt. When one first comes to *The Waste Land*, one is perhaps at the best age for responding to a poem about a world that is recognized as contradictory, mysterious, and concerned more with itself than with its inhabitants. The quester in the wasteland is a stranger in a strange land, and so are we all. Maturity frequently brings with it a distancing from the young person's feeling of awe and strangeness in the universe.

Eliot said about his "Sweeney Among the Nightingales" that all he was trying to communicate in that mysterious poem was a sense of foreboding. He certainly succeeds in doing that, but he overpowers the reader of *The Waste Land* with the reality of a more forbidding and threatening world than Eliot could possibly have imagined when he wrote the poem. One does not have to be young to respond to a poem ("Literature is news that stays news") whose every line is a newspaper headline announcing not imminent doom, but that the Bomb was dropped five minutes ago:

> (Come in under the shadow of this red rock),
> And I will show you something different from either
> Your shadow at morning striding behind you
> Or your shadow at evening rising to meet you;
> I will show you fear in a handful of dust.

The above passage, along with many others in the poem, should be responded to as one responds to overwhelming music rather than solely by the means of rational inquiry. Eliot's famous "objective correlative" theory, in which he states that one of the poet's tasks is to find external images that are the correlatives of internal states, applies also to the music of many of his passages, passages in which the music of the images is all, in which it is fruitless to ask what the images *mean*, because what they mean is to be apprehended, not comprehended—felt with the viscera and muscles rather than with the mind. Although it is certainly true of a great deal of poetry written before this century, it is important to realize that with much modern poetry the poet is reaching for *nonverbal* responses from the reader— responses that will be accessible only to readers who put aside, for the moment, their tendency to understand only through rational inquiry. Much great poetry speaks directly to the reader's unconscious. When it comes to such questions as why the rock is red, and what is the relation between the rock's shadow and "your" shadow, one should respond with Mr. Prufrock's admonition: "Oh, do not ask, 'What is it?'/Let us go and make our visit."

Eliot loved to tell and listen to ghost stories, and *The Waste Land* is a ghost poem, full of unidentified voices of the dead, phantoms, invisible prophets, a wounded Fisher King, the ghosts of the past—Chaucer, Shakespeare, Cleopatra, Dido, Corio-lanus, Queen Elizabeth I, Leicester, Parzifal, Saint Augustine, and above all, Tiresias, the old, blind prophet who confronted Odysseus and Oedipus and who is, in this poem, "throbbing between two lives"—the past and the future, the male and the female, and, most horrifying of all, throbbing between his life and your life.

For many years, and particularly at the time he was working on this poem, Eliot was never without a pocket edition of Dante's *Divine Comedy*, and he uses this poem as a guide to the Inferno of post–World War I Western civilization. He wrote most of the poem in 1921, and it was published in 1922, when he was approaching the age of thirty-five, that of Dante when, in the middle of his journey, he encounters the sins of appetite, violence, and fraud in the year 1300. In 1920 Eliot also en-countered lust without love, violence without meaning, and the fraudulent world of contemporary society.

In 1921, when he was engaged in multiple activities and in a flurry of work on what was to be *The Waste Land*, Eliot suffered a "nervous breakdown" (the term on the records of the bank for which he worked, giving the reason for a six-month leave of absence). He went with his wife, Vivien, to Margate, a seaside resort on the Kent coast, where he wrote sections of Part 3 of his poem. On the advice of friends, he also went to Lausanne for treatment by a well-known pre-Freudian analyst. It was there that he learned to relax, at least long enough for the music of Part 5 ("What the Thunder Said") to flow from him with such perfection that Pound (who edited the entire poem) was to leave it almost untouched.

When he returned to London, Eliot turned over to Pound a poem almost twice the length of the one we now have. It was a jumble of poems: lengthy imitations of Pope in heroic couplets, snatches of verse written as an undergraduate at Harvard, and exercises in mysticism.

Eliot's attitude toward Pound's editorial judgment was one of absolute confidence, an attitude that Pound himself shared. The uncut original manuscript of the poem finally came to light and was published in 1971. We can now see that without Pound the great poem would not have existed: much of it is quite bad. (However, those who love Eliot's poetry cherish even the bad parts and are grateful for the entire manuscript.) Now, Pound was an astute editor and critic, but I doubt if even he suspected the design that was there. Rather, it seems to me that what Pound did was to pull out from the mass of poetry all that was superb—that which had the greatest intensity—and discard the rest. He did not change the order of the sections that remained, but he did make suggestions for rewriting many lines, and actually rewrote some.

I am not contending that Pound co-authored the poem; rather, that he *found* the poem—found the parts that, because they were of Eliot's deepest and most intense concerns, were the best of the poetry. There are lines of feeling and sensitivity connected in a central thrust throughout the poem; these remain, they were not written by Pound, and they are what make the poem a great poem.

However, Joyce's accusation that Eliot failed to acknowledge the poem's indebtedness to *Ulysses* is unwarranted. While he was still working on the poem, Eliot read the manuscript of *Ulysses* in Joyce's apartment in Paris. (He had come bearing from Pound a pair of worn boots for a writer Pound thought of as being destitute; the proud Joyce immediately escorted Eliot out to an expensive restaurant, where he acted as extravagant host.) Eliot said later that he regretted having read the book before he had finished his poem, undoubtedly suggesting his fear of having been overly influenced by it. Eliot would certainly have noted passages such as the description of Bloom's backyard garden toward the end of the Calypso episode—"Want to manure the whole place over, scabby soil. A coat of liver of sulphur. All soil like that without dung. Household slops"—as well as the echoes in Part 3 of *The Waste Land* of Bloom's remark: "The Grand canal, he said. Gasworks," and his reaction to the rat in the cemetery scene in the Hades episode: "Rattle his bones. Over the stones. Only a pauper. Nobody owns."

Within ten lines of Part 3 we find the following: "The rattle of the bones," "A rat crept softly through the vegetation," "While I was fishing in the dull canal/On a winter evening round behind the gashouse," "And bones cast in a little low dry garret,/Rattled by the rat's foot only, year to year." In his *Finnegans Wake* Joyce makes dozens of accusations that Eliot's poem is a plagiarism of *Ulysses*. Joyce is being overly sensitive—he was not the inventor of the first literary wasteland.

The title of the poem and the vegetation-god themes were developed from a book published in 1920, Jessie L. Weston's *From Ritual to Romance*, a literary and anthropological study of the Grail legend. Miss Weston's thesis is that some aspects of Greek and Egyptian myths, Judeo-Christianity, and medieval European ritual and myth—both pagan and Christian—have their roots in a common observance of the death of a vegetation god in the autumn and his resurrection in the spring. Associated with the myth, particularly in medieval times, is a Fisher King who has been wounded (sometimes in the groin) and whose land has consequently become an infertile wasteland; a questing knight who can heal the King, the land, and save himself by asking the proper question; a Castle Perilous, where questing knights must sleep on an altar-bier and be killed and reborn; and a Castle of the Holy Grail, where the knight is shown many marvelous things, including a lance and a cup, a head on a silver platter, and a grail that offers whatever food the questing knight desires.

Miss Weston suggests that the King is a Fisher King because of a long history of religious associations extending back to the captivity of the Jews in Egypt and their meal of fish on the evening before the Sabbath. She notes the Christian adoption of this Friday meal, the early symbolic identification of Christ with a fish, Christ's disciples as "fishers of men," and Celtic myths regarding the mysterious powers to be derived from eating fish, particularly the salmon. The Fisher King is thus associated with the wounded god, with death, deliverance, and rebirth; in other words, with many of Eliot's concerns in his poem.

Miss Weston traces the cup and the lance to drawings on tarot cards that were used in ancient Egypt to forecast the rising of the waters of the Nile, and thus the renewal of fertility in the land. She further suggests that the lance is symbolic of the male sexual organ, and the cup of the female organ.

The Grail itself is the vessel used by the Christ at the Passover supper to offer the wine (His blood) to the disciples. This is merged in medieval times with folk beliefs of the existence of a magic vessel that offers continuous food and drink.

Central to many of the stories is the notion that the wasteland and its King can be healed only if the quester shows compassion for the King's pain, or has the courtesy (and curiosity) to ask the meaning of all the strange things he sees in the Grail Castle. The twentieth-century quester in Eliot's poem does not know how to give, sympathize, or control, and he thus finds only an "empty chapel" at the end of his journey, a chapel where there is no possibility of rebirth, and a Fisher King (perhaps the quester himself) who is willing to settle for something less than salvation.

The poem is divided into five sections, and Eliot and Pound are certainly being influenced here by the five-act structure of Shakespearean plays, a dramatic structure that continued through Racine and Corneille up through nineteenth- and early twentieth-century drama.

Eliot's poem is an epic poem that is at times intensely lyrical; moreover, because of its descriptive settings, dramatic characters, dialogue, and action, it can be considered a dramatic poem by a poet whose long final artistic stage will consist of writing plays in verse.

I do not wish to impose a rigid dramatic structure on the poem, but rather to suggest dramatic *movement* by recalling the six-part psychological structure I presented in the essay on *King Lear*. The hero of the play—in this poem, Tiresias as Modern Everyman—first makes an initial discovery and consequent choice in the exposition section; second, he explores those choices; third, he makes a crucial choice, always a fateful one; fourth, he struggles, but loses in his encounters with the opposition; fifth, he makes his final choice, one that is imposed upon him and is thus unavoidable; and, sixth, there is an evaluation of the life and choices of the hero.

In Part 1 of Eliot's poem the hero's situation is one of death-in-life because of his rejection of love. The two scenes of Part 2 both present characters who question and struggle—at least they do *that*—in their attempt to keep their balance in a society (both upper and lower class) in which lust has overpowered love. In Part 3 the hero explores Elizabethan London, contemporary London, ancient Carthage, and Buddhism (a religion once seriously considered by the young Eliot), finds nothingness to be the crucial choice dictated to him, and that, moreover, he can "connect/Nothing with nothing." In the brief and lyrical falling action of Part 4 the hero is endlessly rising and falling in the underwater currents of the sea, reliving the "stages of his age and youth." Part 5 contains the final choice. Realizing that he cannot say "yes" to the offer of salvation that can only come about if he follows the commands to give, sympathize, and control, the hero decides that if he cannot find salvation, he will at least consider the possibility of setting his land (self) in order. But there can be no evaluation of that choice, as London Bridge comes falling down, and the hero disappears into the black hole of the fragments that conclude the poem.

The epigraph first states the theme of death-in-life: "For I once myself saw with my own eyes the Sibyl at Cumae hanging in a cage, and when the boys said to her, 'Sibyl, what do you want?' she replied, 'I want to die.' "

The idea of a degenerate present is already being suggested here, as this is the Great Sibyl who is the gatekeeper of the underworld, the one who escorts Aeneas into Hades. She had asked Apollo for a life as long as the grains of sand she held in her hand, and it was granted her; unfortunately, she forgot to ask for eternal youth. ("I will show you fear in a handful of dust.") The Great Sibyl thus becomes the embodiment of deterioration and death-in-life, a dread of a meaningless life that Eliot is suggesting is the modern predicament. This suggestion is strengthened when we realize that the lines being quoted are from the *Satyricon* of Petronius, and that the speaker of the lines, the person who has gained superiority over this ancient ritual figure, is Trimalchio, a boastful and ignorant wealthy man.

The title of Part 1, "The Burial of the Dead," comes from the Anglican burial service—and it comes too late, as the inhabitants of the wasteland have been dead since at least the preceding autumn. Spring calls them forth, but—unlike the happy pilgrims of Chaucer's *Canterbury Tales*, to which the opening line is referring—they do not want to go on a pilgrimage but would rather remain buried in a death-in-life where there are no dangerous desires. "First we feel. Then we fall," Anna Livia Plurabelle says in *Finnegans Wake*, and these people have felt and fallen. They do not want to rise again to repeat the painful process.

Eliot brilliantly holds these "free verse" lines together (good verse is never free, Eliot held) through the repetition of participles, a part of speech that reflects the passive state of these dead. (The whole passage, especially the phrase "covering/Earth in forgetful snow," is a powerful reminder of the comparable state of Gabriel at the conclusion of Joyce's short story "The Dead.")

The remainder of this stanza is a remembrance of youth, of a time when there was the possibility of salvation by water, but even then the rootless inhabitants sought shelter from the rain. The suggestion is being made by Eliot that no Grand Tour of the fashionable watering places of Europe is an adequate substitute for the holy place that is the destination of Chaucer's pilgrims.

In the Notes to the poem, Eliot says that "What Tiresias *sees*, in fact, is the substance of the poem," that he is the "spectator," "the most important personage in the poem"—indeed, that "the two sexes meet in Tiresias." In his poem Eliot uses the mythological Tiresias as a commentator on the behavior of his twentieth-century inhabitants of the wasteland, and "shadows" the contemporary characters with such figures from mythology, religion, and literature as Isaiah, Ezekiel, Cleopatra, Dido, Ferdinand, Tereus, Philomela, and many others. It seems to me that Tiresias is both Narrator and Greek Chorus, and that he keeps changing voice and identity, commenting, as does a Greek Chorus, on the actions of the participants, becoming one of them and interacting with them. Indeed, Aeschylus, Sophocles, and particularly Euripides would have been quite comfortable with this twentieth-century version of the *Oresteia, Oedipus the King, Oedipus at Colonus,* and *Bacchae*—a poem about violence and lust without love, about the inexorable power of the past over the present, about the quest for salvation, and about the inviolability of the Dionysian force.

In the second stanza the choral lament of the opening of

the poem changes to a voice from the Hebraic Scriptures, echoing passages from Ezekiel and Ecclesiastes. Indeed, the references to so many previous writings are like ghosts that have returned to haunt this poem. (When the "ghosts" are fully identified in Eliot's Notes, I will not duplicate him, but rather restrict my explanations to those not in the Notes.)

Just as Joyce, in the opening of *Ulysses*, makes reference to the Israelites in captivity in order to relate them to Stephen's position, so Eliot here is using Ezekiel to suggest that modern man is in bondage. In this modern wasteland the world is broken into fragments, there is no water (salvation), and the vegetation is dead. The prophetlike chorus promises to "show you fear in a handful of dust," and this presentation of death-in-life is precisely what constitutes the remainder of the poem.

A voice injected into the first stanza states (in German) that "I am not a Russian woman at all, I come from Lithuania, a true German," and thus insistently announces the misunderstandings and failures of communication that pervade the poem: "What are you thinking of?" and "What you get married for if you don't want children?"

The German lyric in the second stanza is from Wagner's *Tristan und Isolde,* and establishes the note of waiting when the sailor sings of the girl at home he misses: "Fresh blows the wind to the homeland. My Irish child, where are you waiting?"

The "shadow" in this stanza is perhaps death-in-life stalking the inhabitants of the wasteland, and it echoes John Donne's "A Lecture upon the Shadow," as well as specific lines in Beaumont and Fletcher's *Philaster* (III.ii).

In medieval stories the grail-bearer is a woman who directs the questing knight to the castle where the initiation will take place; there she enters bearing love (the grail), and if the quester asks the right questions, she marries him.

Here the grail-bearer offering love is a girl bearing hyacinths, an ancient male sexual symbol and one of the reincarnations of the dead fertility god. The girl's hair is "wet," as she has come from rebirth by water. But the young man's "eyes failed," and he rejects the offer of love because he is neither "Living nor dead," even though he knows he is "Looking into the heart of light, the silence." He is like the neutrals, the uncommitted in the third canto of Dante's *Inferno*, those who never lived and so can never die. The hyacinth-girl stanza concludes with a phrase in German sung by the shepherd in Wagner's opera to the dying Tristan, who waits for the sight of Isolde's ship that will bring both healing and love: "Waste and empty the sea."

I must bring up here an interpretation of *The Waste Land* that was fashionable in the fifties. A number of teachers around the country, claiming either "inside information" or inspired psychological insight (at considerable remove in time and distance), contended that the poem was about the wasteland of either bisexual or homosexual life at the time Eliot was writing.

Given the "bisexual" nature of Tiresias, who had been transformed into a woman for seven years, and the homosexual nature of Mr. Eugenides, this is a defensible interpretation that fails when it is posited as the primary or *only* interpretation of the poem. Further, as the poem condemns the condition of contemporary sexuality, Eliot is possibly just being thorough by including the themes of homosexuality and bisexuality along with heterosexual sterility.

This interpretation is based on Eliot's dedication of his first volume of poetry to Jean Verdenal (a medical student and his best friend when he attended the Sorbonne), on a reading of the hyacinth-girl stanza as Eliot's rejection of Verdenal's offer of love (Hyacinthus was the beautiful youth loved by both Apollo and Zephyrus), and on the interjection of the lines from Shakespeare's *The Tempest*—"Those are pearls that were his eyes"—as the barrier that separates the man from his wife in Part 2. (Jean Verdenal became a medical officer in the French armed forces at the beginning of World War I and was shortly thereafter drowned in the Dardanelles.)

Interesting as this speculative interpretation is, it is dangerous in that it leads to a one-sided reading. It also leads, as

Shakespeareans must by now realize, to valueless speculations about the sexual proclivities of hundreds of thousands of authors who have dedicated their works to members of the same sex. In any case, Eliot told an interviewer, for a story that appeared in the *New York Times* on November 21, 1948, that whatever the poem means to each reader is the meaning of the poem, and that is perhaps where the meaning resides, rather than in psychosexual theories about the life of the poet.

Madame Sosostris, like the goat in "Gerontion," "Had a bad cold"—a marvelous denasal phrase that makes her condition aural. The sources of her name reinforce her phoniness. It is similar to that of a king of Egypt recorded by Herodotus, and to the adopted name of a man impersonating a Gypsy fortune teller in Aldous Huxley's *Crome Yellow*. She thus adds to the sexual ambiguity of the poem.

She is using a tarot deck to tell the fortunes of society people, a degeneration from the original fertility-god forecasting Miss Weston suggests as the original purpose of the cards. The cards, of course, are emblematic of many of the characters we are to meet in the poem: "the drowned Phoenician Sailor" (Phlebas in Part 4), "The lady of situations" (the wife in Part 2), "the one-eyed merchant" (Mr. Eugenides in Part 3), and "the Hanged Man" (the unresurrected fertility god who pervades the poem). She sees the "crowds of people" who inhabit the wasteland, people who are "walking round in a ring" and going nowhere in their endless circling on the "Wheel" of existence.

If the narrator is Tiresias and the prophecy is for this prophet, then Tiresias has certainly lost his ancient powers. In any case, the recipient of the fortune is to tell "dear Mrs. Equitone" that Madame Sosostris will be bringing the horoscope herself, as "One must be so careful these days." One wonders about a world where no one can be trusted to carry a message. But the name of Mrs. Equitone is marvelous—Mrs. Onenote—as are all of Eliot's invented names.

Death by drowning (one of the themes of *Ulysses*) makes its appearance in this stanza, not only with the drowned sailor but with the "pearls" line from *The Tempest* (I.ii.399), and with the admonition to "Fear death by water," an element that is necessary for renewal and rebirth. Madame Sosostris is naturally unable to see what is carried on the back of the one-eyed merchant. The merchant himself, representative of the ancient Phoenicians, who are credited with spreading fertility cults throughout the Aegean and Mediterranean, can no longer be aware of the fertility god. The understated "Thank you," before Madame Sosostris' final request, is a nice touch: the fortune is being told—naturally—for cash.

Unreal city! Unreal because it is not just London but Florence (the echoes from the third and fourth cantos of the *Inferno*), Carthage (Mylae—a reference to the First Punic War in 280 B.C), and anticipates the falling towers of Jerusalem, Athens, Alexandria, and Vienna in Part 5. And two of the darkest and most mysterious writers of all time haunt the stanza with their presence: Baudelaire and Webster.

Stetson (an ordinary name) is questioned about the corpse, obviously a modern-day fertility god he "planted" in his garden last year; the questioner wants to know whether or not it has begun to "sprout." Eliot is being relentless in his presentation of twentieth-century degeneration, as we realize that a London backyard is hardly the place to plant a fertility god and wait for it to "sprout" and "bloom."

The capitalization of "Dog" obviously makes it a symbol (in Webster it's a wolf), but there are not enough clues to what is being symbolized. Perhaps Sirius, the Dog Star, one of the foretellers of the rising of the fertilizing waters of the Nile, but also a star of lust. Perhaps the fertility god himself, denying mankind by digging up his own body, or the Judeo-Christian God (frequently uttered as "Dog" to avoid blasphemy, and used by Joyce in *Ulysses* as "dogsbody") preventing the restoration of ancient religions.

The section ends with a line from Baudelaire as the narrator violently accuses the reader of being a hypocrite, weakens as he recognizes the reader as being like himself, and then collapses in the realization that we are all brothers under the skin, sharing the same condition of helplessness and hopelessness in the wasteland.

In Middleton's play *Women Beware Women*, a woman is engaged in a game of chess in order to keep her attention away from the seduction of her daughter-in-law in a nearby room. The moves on the chessboard reflect the moves of the seduction, and Eliot's choice of "A Game of Chess" for the title of Part 2 is meant to reflect the calculated and mechanical nature of the sexual lives of the twentieth-century characters in this poem. He then provides a contrast of love for love's sake with the echo in the opening lines of Enobarbus' speech in *Antony and Cleopatra*. Some lines later the use of the Latin-derived word "laquearia" is supposed to recall for the reader the description of the paneled ceiling at the banquet in the *Aeneid* that Dido gives for Aeneas at Carthage, another example of committed love. (One wonders how many readers would ever have gotten this without Eliot's Notes.)

The sheer number of objects mentioned in the description of the bedroom is overpowering. The woman's "synthetic perfumes," like the man and woman themselves, are "troubled, confused"; all are drowning in the odors. The characters are synthetic, troubled, confused, and—like the language of the scene itself—neurasthenic. Eliot tells us in the Notes that the phrase "sylvan scene" is from Milton's *Paradise Lost*, but we must go to that poem to discover that this scene is no true Eden, but rather Eden as viewed through Satan's eyes. There are no Adam and Eve in this Eden, but rather the rape of Philomel "by the barbarous king," her brother-in-law, Tereus. Philomel is later transformed into a nightingale, and nothing remains of her except an "inviolable voice." The tense of the line "And still she cried, and still the world pursues" tells us that the world is still pursuing selfish violence. (Eliot is perhaps suggesting a contrast to Keats' "Ode on a Grecian Urn," where that poet also makes use of the present tense, but to sing about a melodist "For ever piping songs for ever new," and of lovers "For ever panting, and for ever young.") The words "Jug Jug" are used in Elizabethan poetry to represent the song of the nightingale, but today the song has become a scatological joke to be heard only by "dirty ears."

The "enclosed" room is suffocating—not only to the man and woman, but to us—and, as in a ghost story, "Footsteps shuffled on the stair." The characters can merely wait for Death's inevitable "knock upon the door."

The dialogue between the man and woman consists of her spoken words and his unspoken responses; in other words, there is no actual communication between the two. They are apparently a far from happy couple, and the scene has been taken as a representation of the married life of Eliot and his wife, Vivien. Those who argue against this call attention to her penciled notations on the manuscript (she made some perceptive suggestions) and her praise for the section.

Eliot tells us in the Notes that the lines about the wind echo Webster; what he does not tell us is that they are specifically from *The Devil's Law Case* and occur in a scene where there is a wounded man in the room.

The word "nothing," which tolls like doom throughout *King Lear*, is used six times; one is reminded also of Ophelia's response to Hamlet: "I think nothing, my lord." Indeed, in this section of "A Game of Chess," *King Lear, Hamlet,* and the other great tragedies have been reduced to a "Shakespeherian Rag." The reference to *The Tempest* ("Those are pearls that were his eyes") implies a reduction: in that play it occurs in a song sung by Ariel as he takes Ferdinand to Miranda, an event that will lead to the rebirth of those stranded on the island. There is no hope for a rebirth of the inhabitants of Eliot's wasteland; the water imagery of *The Tempest* is now only "hot water at ten," to be used for making tea, rather than for lustration, and, if it rains, shelter in a "closed car." They will play their "game of chess"—

the Grail Castle has been reduced to an object on a board—a mechanical and, to them, meaningless act of sex.

They have failed the test presented in the Grail Castle, and they will never know the redemptive power of love. All they can do, while they press their "lidless eyes" (that is *so* Dantesque—without eyelids one would shortly go insane), is wait for Death's knock upon the door. And all we can do is remember the epigraph that Eliot intended for the poem (and that was deleted at Pound's suggestion): mankind's cry in Conrad's *Heart of Darkness*, "The horror! The horror!"

The scene now shifts to a London pub, where two nameless cockney women discuss sex, marriage, and fertility, and we find that the meaningless and mechanistic futility of their lives equals that of the upper-class couple in the elegant bedroom. And here the "knock upon the door" is the voice of the pubkeeper, Death himself, calling out the traditional pub-closing warning: "Hurry up please it's time."

The sacred feast of the Grail Castle has degenerated into a pub-drinking scene where a nameless woman speaking to a nameless listener can only focus on such mechanical aspects of existence as the need for a set of false teeth to make one sexually attractive. She recounts her conversation with Lil, whose husband has been demobilized from the army, a dialogue in which she let Lil know that others would offer the husband a "good time" if Lil didn't. Lil is apparently recoiling from sex, and she claims her recent abortion is the reason she looks older than her age. The fertility god has been aborted, and the sacred meal is to be an ordinary platter of hot pork.

The pub closes with Death's repeated cry that Time has ended, and the final line echoes Ophelia's exit line in the fourth act of *Hamlet*, just after that sweet, mad, barren young woman has sung (uncharacteristically, for her) a bawdy song about sex without love, and just before she goes to her own death by water.

———

Images of fire and water pervade Part 3, "The Fire Sermon," and they have dual and opposing functions, as fire can purge (Arnaut Daniel in the *Purgatorio*) or destroy (Ulysses in the *Inferno*), and water bring rebirth and purification (lustration in religion and mythology) or death by drowning (the Phoenician sailor, Mr. Prufrock, and Hugh Selwyn Mauberley). The hero of *The Waste Land* is in a limbo where he can find neither death nor rebirth.

The river Thames, choked with debris, is contrasted with the more pristine Thames of Spenser's "Prothalamion," a marriage song, and the nymphs of an earlier time have become contemporary women who have sexual encounters with nameless young men—men who leave no addresses lest they be held accountable for unwanted pregnancies.

The narrator weeps by "the waters of Leman" (another name for Lake Geneva—some of the poem was written in Lausanne), just as the Jews wept for their lost Zion by the waters of Babylon, in Psalm 137. And, instead of hearing at his back Marvell's ("To His Coy Mistress") winged chariot, which urges the lovers to consummate their passion, the speaker is aware only of the rattling bones of grinning Death, of "slimy" rats, of naked dead bodies on the ground, of bones in attics, and of the anthropoid Sweeney (of the earlier "Sweeney Erect" and "Sweeney Among the Nightingales") having sex in what is probably a house of prostitution. (The lines are fragments of a World War I song popular with Australian soldiers at the battle of Gallipoli.)

The castle of the Fisher King is always on the bank of a river, but there is no Grail Castle here—only a "gashouse"—and the King has merged with Ferdinand, who in *The Tempest* is bemoaning the death of his father, who he thinks has drowned (I.ii.389–91). Ariel will come to Ferdinand's rescue, but no salvation figure hovers offstage for modern man. The stanza closes with a line from Verlaine's "Parsifal" ("O those children's voices singing in the dome"), reminding us of the young knight who adored the Grail, and who maintained his purity throughout his quest. This is juxtaposed, in the next stanza, with the brief, cacophonous reminder of the rape of Philomel by Tereus.

The remainder of Part 3 consists of a series of three contemporary sexual encounters, and they are all perfunctory and sordid.

Smyrna was one of the centers for the spread of fertility cults, but the modern missionary is the homosexual Mr. Eugenides—another marvelous Eliotic name, as he is far from being eugenic. He is grubby, he carries currants (dried grapes—no longer fertile or symbolizing fertility gods), and he speaks vulgar French. The speaker here is identified as the two-sexed Tiresias, and the invitation is to have lunch and then proceed to the Metropole Hotel in Brighton for a sexual weekend that would obviously not be fertile.

Curiously enough, Tiresias makes his first identifiable entrance at the dead center of *The Waste Land*. In his Notes, Eliot provides lines (in Latin) from Ovid's *Metamorphoses* that help in understanding the role of Tiresias in the poem. In summary, Ovid tells us that Tiresias once struck with his staff two snakes who were copulating in the woods and was turned into a woman. He encountered the same snakes in the eighth year of his transformation; now aware of their power, he struck them again and was changed back into a man. Afterward Zeus and Hera are arguing about who gets the greater pleasure in sexual intercourse, the woman or the man. Hera denies Zeus' contention that it is the woman, and so Tiresias—an obvious authority— is summoned to resolve the question. He reveals that it is woman who receives the greater pleasure. Incensed that Zeus now knows this secret, Hera blinds Tiresias; Zeus lightens the penalty by giving Tiresias the power of prophecy. As we know from the experiences of Tiresias in *Oedipus the King* and of Kassandra in the *Oresteia*, the ability to know the future can be a painful burden. Tiresias not only represents the confused and ambiguous nature of twentieth-century masculine and feminine sexuality in this poem, but must experience, in the past, all the future anguish of the characters of *The Waste Land*—and know that neither he nor they have much hope for success in their quest for rebirth.

The second sexual encounter is described in detail, and both the typist and the pimply young man are as shabby and sordid as Mr. Eugenides. Her room is a mess, breakfast dishes still unwashed, various articles of clothing scattered on the divan, and drying clothes spread out on the windowsill. This last image is perhaps meant to contrast with the "Charm'd magic casements" of Keats' "Ode to a Nightingale," but there is no doubt that Eliot's use of the sonnet form is an intentional echo of Shakespeare's use of that form for the scene in *Romeo and Juliet* when those romantic young lovers first kiss.

There has been no pleasure in the encounter for either of them; the young man "gropes" his way out into an "unlit" world, and the young woman is glad that this undesired act is over. "When lovely woman stoops to folly" echoes Olivia's song in Goldsmith's *The Vicar of Wakefield*. But Olivia concludes that such folly is "to die," whereas the young woman in this poem merely paces in boredom about her room and, with a hand as "automatic" as was her body in the act of sex, she "puts a record on the gramophone"—music that is certainly not that of Ariel, but more probably the "Shakespeherian Rag," a popular piece of music of the time.

The following stanza is the only truly peaceful moment in the poem, and the totality of Ferdinand's speech and the song of Ariel which immediately follows (I.ii.387–402) are useful in considering both the entire poem and this stanza:

> FERDINAND: Where should this music be? I' th' air or th' earth?
> It sounds no more; and, sure it waits upon
> Some god o' th' island. Sitting on a bank,
> Weeping again the King my father's wrack,
> This music crept by me upon the waters,
> Allaying both their fury and my passion
> With its sweet air. Thence I have follow'd it,

Or it hath drawn me rather. but 'tis gone.
No, it begins again.

ARIEL'S SONG.
Full fathom five thy father lies;
   Of his bones are coral made;
Those are pearls that were his eyes;
   Nothing of him that doth fade
But doth suffer a sea-change
Into something rich and strange.
Sea-nymphs hourly ring his knell. . . .

The entire speech of Ferdinand shows his true position in the poem as a version of the Fisher King, suggests the mysterious and elusive nature of the quest for salvation, and demonstrates the power of music—not thought—to bring surcease from pain. For just a few moments the narrator in the wasteland finds pleasure in *remembering* hearing the music of ordinary workers, and in calling up the image of fishermen resting near the church of Magnus Martyr, splendid in its Greek perfection. But the pleasing music, the true rest of workingmen, and the "Inexplicable splendour" of religion are not available to the narrator. (The church, located close to the chief London fish market and across from Fish Street Hill, was known as the fisherman's church; Eliot is finding ready-made symbols in London as easily as Joyce did in Dublin.)

In the opening of *Heart of Darkness,* Conrad compares the Thames and the Congo. In the two incantatory stanzas that follow, Eliot is again contrasting the Thames of Elizabethan times with the river he knows. But one must be careful. Eliot, as well as Pound and Joyce, is not *always* extolling a glorious past over a degenerate present, and certainly the nonproductive "affair" between Elizabeth and Leicester is different from that of the girl in the canoe only in being royal.

The Wagnerian cry at the end of both stanzas is meant to suggest the violation of the three Rhine-daughters, who are bemoaning the theft of the gold (beauty) from the Rhine. The narrator-chorus (Tiresias/Fisher King) mourns the violated beauty of contemporary existence, and then presents the soliloquies of three Londoners, two young women and the narrator himself. The first young woman has been raised in upper-class neighborhoods, but now, knees raised and flat on her back on the bottom of a canoe on the Thames (a truly obscene image), she has been violated by a young man. In a strikingly surrealistic image, the second young woman says that her "feet are at Moorgate" (a slum area of London) and that her heart is "under" her feet—in other words, external to her, or dead and buried, but certainly no longer capable of feeling. Following the sexual intercourse, only an "event" to her, the young man is remorseful; she, however, like the typist in the earlier scene, has felt nothing and consequently resents nothing.

Following Eliot's leave of absence from the bank where he worked, the first stage of his recuperation from his nervous breakdown was a stay at the seaside resort of Margate in Kent. We know that he wrote fifty lines of the poem there, probably this "Wagnerian" section, as he has the narrator telling us that " 'On Margate Sands./I can connect/Nothing with nothing.' " But the narrator here merges with the Fisher King (he is by the water) as he begins to speak about his " 'humble people who expect/Nothing.' " He then becomes the Saint Augustine who writes about his burning with the fires of lust in Carthage —causing one also to think of the Carthaginian Dido, as well as the Stetson of Part 1 who fought with the narrator at Mylae.

Saint Augustine merges into the Buddha of "The Fire Sermon" ("fire is on fire" is a phrase from that sermon), and Eliot tells us in the Notes that this "collocation" of two ascetics is intentional. The calls for the Lord to pluck the sinner out of the fires of lust occur many times in the Hebraic Scriptures, notably in Amos 4–11.

A comparison of the state of sexuality in this Saint Augustine–Buddha section with the earlier sexual incidents in Part 3 shows that, whereas those were mundane and trivial, here the narrator at least has a sense of sin and desires release from lust—if not through love, then at least through the ascetic life.

Although Tiresias appears at the numerical center of the poem, the emotional center is the beautiful brief lyric of Part 4, "Death by Water." I find it significant that Eliot provides no notes for this part, although he certainly could have brought in Adonis' resurrection from water and Lear's "wheel of fire," had he wished. After all, the Notes were written only because the publisher did not want a number of blank pages at the end of the book.

But Eliot leaves the lyric pristine, and I question the rightness of using the appearance of Phlebas in Eliot's earlier French poem, *"Dans le Restaurant,"* as an interpretation of this section, even though Part 4 is mainly a translation of a section of that poem. Phlebas is "new" here, and one does not need to rely upon the earlier poem in order to understand the cleansing that is taking place in this one.

In reading poetry it is important to know when to use the mind to comprehend, and when to use the senses to apprehend; in other words, to know the proper sorts of things to look for. In Eliot, as he himself said, much of the poetry is to be responded to as music.

This lyric and elegiac ode to the death by drowning of a young man is in the great tradition of Milton's "Lycidas," and takes its position in a long line of moving, sad, and tender lyric poems that reach back to the most ancient Greek poetry. His death is the reminder and warning that the "profit and loss" cannot be carried over into an afterlife, that temporal life is in need of the cleansing that death brings, that existence is a continual movement forward toward the future and backward toward the past, a continuing process of death and rebirth (the dead sailor moves from age to youth, not the opposite). The lyric concludes with the theme of mutability, from Dante to Shakespeare, from Shelley to Eliot, one of the most haunting melodies in European poetry.

Eliot wrote all of Part 5, "What the Thunder Said," while he was alone in Lausanne, under treatment for his nervous break-down. Pound made no changes in the preceding part (none were needed), and in Part 5 only suggestions for a few word changes. In concluding his poem Eliot had obviously gained total control, and there is no need here for Pound's directions.

The rhetorical music, the sustained choral tone in the mode of a "two-part" Gregorian chant, and the absolute mastery of rhythmical control reach a sublimity that renders the inability of the hero to find his way out of the wasteland all the more moving and tragic.

The ancient fertility gods offered themselves up for sacrifice to ensure the rebirth of the people of the land, and Christ here merges with them. The opening re-creates the agony and arrest of Christ in the Garden of Gethsemane, followed by His trial and crucifixion. The traditional belief is that Christ spent the three days from Friday to Sunday preaching to the lost souls in Hell; He is thus dead, and no longer available to the inhabitants of the wasteland, and their land has become more barren than at any other time during this poem. The two stanzas that describe the condition of the land make a formal use of image repetition to give an effect of dirgelike chanting. Extracting the images from just the first six lines reveals this tight patterning:

> water rock
>   rock water road
>   road mountains
>   mountains rock water
>   water
>   rock

The opening of the next stanza is puzzling, as Eliot tells us in the Notes that the passage was "stimulated" by an account of Antarctic explorers who told of having a sensation that there was one more member of the expedition walking along with them "than could actually be counted." We will have to take the poet's word that the lines were "stimulated" by that account, but there is little doubt that Eliot is referring to the journey of Christ's disciples to Emmaus (Luke 24:13–27) when they believed that Christ walked with them, even though they could not see Him. Perhaps the soundest interpretation of this passage is that there is a Saviour (Attis, Adonis, Christ), but the condition of the inhabitants of the wasteland prevents them from seeing Him.

With cries that cover the earth, the women lament the deaths of Osiris, Attis, Adonis, Jesus—of all the mutilated "hanged gods" who promise hope of benefits for humanity; but they are helpless before the onslaught of the barbarians who are swarming over the earth. In his Notes, Eliot refers the reader to Hermann Hesse's *A Glimpse into Chaos,* which pictures eastern Europe drunkenly singing as it goes to its own self-destruction, as saints and seers listen to the song with tears. In the poem Eliot presents a chaotic civilization whose cities are cracking, bursting, and whose towers are falling:

> Jerusalem Athens Alexandria
> Vienna London
> Unreal

The next stanza is the Hieronymus Bosch *music* of a world gone mad—a woman drawing her hair out tight and fiddling music on it, "bats with baby faces" crawling "head downward down a blackened wall," towers "upside down," and "voices singing out of empty cisterns and exhausted wells." The stanza screams hysterically at the reader, denying intellectual interpretation, demanding visceral response.

When a questing knight finally reaches the Castle Perilous, he finds it ruined and empty, and passes on in despair. But this has been only an illusion, a test, the most crucial one of all, and he has failed it. The "empty chapel" our quester finds may be an illusion only because he has not the faith required to re-create it; or it may be, as some suggest, the symbol of decayed Western religion. The crowing of the cock, the bird that traditionally drives away the evil spirits of the night, makes both of those readings problematic, for there is a "flash of lightning" and "a damp gust /Bringing rain." The wind *will* bring the rain—it does not arrive in this poem, but there is at least the promise, and the expectant hope of the inhabitants in the following stanza who wait for it.

What the narrator, one of the twentieth-century inhabitants of the wasteland, hears is the voice of the thunder god proclaiming in Sanskrit—one of the most ancient of the Indo-European languages—the way toward salvation: *Datta*, give; *Dayadhvam*, sympathize; *Damyata*, control.

In the Hindu fable to which Eliot refers the reader in his Notes, gods, men, and demons ask their "Father" to speak to them. He answers each of them with "DA," and each interprets the syllable in his own way: *Datta, Dayadhvam, Damyata.*

Through the extensive use of "we" and "our," the poet envelops the reader in the narrator's inability to accept the command. We have given our bodies in lust, rather than our souls in love, and all we will leave behind is an empty body in an empty room; locked in the prison house of our own needs and satisfactions, we have been unable to hear and sympathize with the torments of our fellow prisoners; we want to be controlled by others, rather than exert the control necessitated by free will.

In some versions of the medieval Grail stories, the salvation of the knight depends upon asking the right question, and in others the question brings salvation to the Fisher King and his land. In the following stanza the narrator and the Fisher King are again one. There is no rain, no water, no rebirth, but the Quester-King can "at least set my lands in order"—make an attempt to rearrange the ruined and barren landscape of the individual soul and the collective society. *If* Eliot has the thirty-eighth chapter of Isaiah in mind, then there is some hope in this. In that chapter Isaiah transmits the Lord's word to the dying Hezekiah, that he should "set thine house in order: for thou shalt die, and not live." Hezekiah prays to the Lord, reminding Him that he had walked beside Him in "truth," with a "perfect heart," and done "that which is good." The Lord allows Hezekiah to live.

The rearrangement consists of shoring up the fragmented self with fragments of the past: poetry comes forward out of the past to shore up the present poem; poetry will comfort the poet and his poem.

In his Notes, Eliot offers identifications of the fragments, but not translations. In the first line Arnaut Daniel, the Provençal poet, waits in the refining fire of God's love; in the next, Philomela is waiting for the renewal of spring; and in the third the isolated Prince of Aquitaine waits in the ruined tower for renewed acceptance. In Kyd's *Spanish Tragedy*, Hieronymo will "fit" (make) a play that will result in the death of his son's murderers. Literature becomes action, not thought: the mirror of art transforms reality.

The repeated word "shantih," which Eliot translates as " 'The Peace which passeth understanding,' " can only be read as a prayerful hope for the future rather than as a description of the present condition.

And so, London Bridge falling down all around, the Narrator–Reader–Fertility God–Fisher King remains alone and in pain because *we* have failed to ask ourselves the compassionate question. The land will remain barren until some future quester, a different sort from the "we" of the poem, one who is able to give, sympathize, and control, arrives. More than six decades after it was written, the poem awaits a generation of readers who will find the wasteland, or even the prospect of one, antique and curious, far removed from their own experience of life.

Ulysses

Joyceans occupy opposing camps in defense of their interpretations of *Ulysses*. Those in the camp flying pessimistic black flags think that nothing of import happens to Leopold Bloom on June 16, 1904, that Leopold and Stephen will never find release from their isolation and despair, and that the novel is completely devoid of the qualities of friendship, love, and magnanimity. There are many well-known generals in this camp, including some who have opined that Stephen has a predictable future as just another drunken Dublin character, and that it is not imaginable that he will awake from his nightmare. To these readers, nothing happens in *Ulysses*.

A revised edition of the novel was published in 1984, and the more than five thousand errors occurring in the book have been corrected—errors caused by Joyce's friends, who took many liberties in typing the final manuscript, and by French typesetters who did not understand English. With the publication of the new edition, some Joyceans have announced that they will consider deserting to the opposing camp, the camp flying the joyful multicolored pennants of a novel in which the last word is "Yes." This camp has always believed that Stephen is speaking for Joyce when he argues for the "eternal affirmation of the spirit of man in literature," and that the experiences of Leopold, Stephen, and Molly on that significant re-birth-day will markedly change their lives. To these readers, everything happens.

This is the camp whose trenches were first dug in the 1920s by my Columbia teacher, colleague, and friend, the late William York Tindall, who returned to the United States in that decade with a banned copy of *Ulysses*, purchased from Sylvia Beach at her bookstore, Shakespeare and Company, the original publisher. Tindall taught the first course on Joyce in this country, and the students had to stand in line in the university library for their hour with this outlawed book that Tindall bound in lumber and chained to a reading table.

Let us take an aerial view of both camps.

In the camp where nothing happens, Stephen, who begins the day in the seaside tower he rents from the government, is badgered by his roommate, Buck Mulligan, into turning over the key to the tower. He then teaches his students history and poetry in what is apparently a mediocre school, one that he doesn't intend to teach in after this day. Following this abbreviated schoolday—it is a Thursday—Stephen goes for a walk along the Dublin beach, where he meditates on Irish nationalism, Roman Catholic heretics, his abortive escape to Paris, and the clutching fingers of his family.

The scene then shifts to Leopold Bloom preparing breakfast for his wife, a frowsy woman who has let herself go, but who is preparing for one of her numerous infidelities, which will commence at four o'clock that afternoon. Through suggestive hints she lets the passive, henpecked Bloom know this, and he acquiesces by announcing that he plans to have dinner out and go to the theater.

Following this, Bloom wanders aimlessly about the streets of Dublin, rests in a church, goes to a public bath, attends the funeral of an acquaintance, stops in the newspaper office to check on an advertisement (Bloom's current profession is that of advertising solicitor), and has lunch.

We leave Bloom for a while and return to Stephen, who has also been at the newspaper office and then gone out with some of the writers for drinks. Stephen is now in the National Library talking to the librarian and various literary lights; he is somewhat drunk, and the "literary" conversation has mainly to do with Shakespeare. Following this, in the Wandering Rocks episode, the author gives a kaleidoscopic view of many characters in the book as they wander the streets of Dublin.

We return to Bloom, who has a meal in the Ormond Street

Hotel, where he is subjected to the humiliation of hearing Blazes Boylan in the adjoining bar having a drink before going off to his four-o'clock assignation with Bloom's wife. He next goes to a tavern, where he gets into a verbal and almost physical fight with the anti-Jewish nationalistic Citizen, who chases the weak-willed Bloom out of the bar. He then wanders along the strand, masturbates in his pants while watching a crippled girl, and goes to a maternity hospital to check on the progress of a woman who is really no more than an acquaintance, where he runs into the drunken Stephen. He follows Stephen to the red-light district, rescues him from a fight, takes him to an all-night café to recuperate, and then to the kitchen of his house, from which Stephen departs into the night—neither he nor Bloom any wiser for the day each has spent.

The book concludes with the lascivious Molly pleasurably recalling her afternoon in bed and her anticipated further assignations with Blazes Boylan, as well as her numerous preceding sexual affairs.

Such is the view of the pessimist generals and their followers. Now let us look at the camp where *everything* happens, the one the detractors refer to as the "goody-goody" camp.

The foundation of this camp lies just beneath the surface, and, though sometimes barely visible, it is solidly based; this foundation was laid by Homer and it goes by the name of the *Odyssey*. T. S. Eliot, writing about *Ulysses* a year after the book appeared, called Joyce's invention of a "mythical method" a step "toward making the modern world possible for art," toward "order and form. . . ." The myth of Homer's text *is* the meaning of Joyce's text, and the *Odyssey* is a work about atonement, at-one-ment, of father and son, of husband and wife; it sings of *nóstos*—homecoming and a new beginning. The *Odyssey* gives meaning, as well as "order and form," to *Ulysses*, rather than serving as a lofty contrast to a degraded present (the pessimistic view).

The novel begins with Stephen, the modern-day Telemachos who has been dispossessed not just by his roommate but by the

English, the Irish Catholic Church, and the demands of his family, symbolically handing over the key to his home to Buck Mulligan. The nets of family, religion, and nationalism that he failed to escape in his abortive flight to Paris at the end of *A Portrait of the Artist as a Young Man* are going to be ripped to shreds during the course of this positive and affirmative day. Teaching the school lessons is another reminder to Stephen of what he was and what he will be unless he fights for his freedom as an artist. Determined to give up his ties to Ireland, he walks along the beach, and in the course of his meditation he firmly rejects family, religion, and nationalism as he abandons the temptation to visit relatives, thinks of Catholic heretics, and recalls the futility of the Irish nationalists he met while in Paris. Throughout all of the first three episodes Stephen is oppressed by the guilt he has felt since he refused his mother's dying request that he kneel and pray by her bedside. By the end of this long day that guilt will be exorcised.

The scene now shifts to the generous, kind, and gentle Leopold Bloom, lovingly preparing breakfast for his beautiful and musically gifted wife, Molly. On this day Molly will finally become unfaithful after ten years without sexual intercourse, as Bloom, who guiltily feels responsible for the death of their infant son, Rudy, ten years ago, cannot bear the idea of intercourse and the subsequent creation of fragile life. By the end of this mythical and mystical day Molly is determined to change his mind on this matter and Bloom finds himself considering having another child.

As we follow Bloom around through the remainder of his morning's activities, we find that he is friendly, kind, courteous, and considerate toward everyone he meets, and that he is deeply pained by what he knows Molly and Blazes will be doing at four o'clock that afternoon. But Bloom, like his counterpart and model, Odysseus, has great fortitude, ultimately accepts the reality of experience—even when that reality is mysterious and strange and cruel—and is determined to survive. There are no accidents in either Homer or Joyce—every word serves a purpose. Thus, the word "perhaps" is of utmost importance in Bloom's thoughts in the Sirens episode as he begins to question his guilt and consider fatherhood: "I too. Last my race. Milly young student. Well, my fault *perhaps*. No son. Rudy. Too late now. *Or if not? If not? If still?*" [emphasis mine].

Stephen, in the newspaper office, escapes another trap when he resists the suggestion that he become a journalist—to do so would turn him into Gabriel in Joyce's story from *Dubliners*, "The Dead."

But it is in the scene in the library that Stephen moves toward a complete acceptance of self, a step that does not become final until his atonement with his spiritual father, Leopold Bloom. In the conversation about Shakespeare, Stephen repeatedly emphasizes the importance of the artistic use of his own experiences as the subject matter for his art. Stephen has already progressed a long way since the morning walk on the beach when he wrote that perfectly awful poem about the vampire's kiss, a piece of Irish mystical verse worthy of the worst Irish Celtic-twilight poetical nonsense. "Ten years," Buck Mulligan says, speaking about Stephen in the Wandering Rocks episode. "He is going to write something in ten years." And we know that he will, not only because we observe the observing young artist in the library as he thinks to himself about these Dubliners: "Hold to the now, the here, through which all future plunges to the past," and a few pages later: "Anxiously he glanced in the cone of lamplight where three faces, lighted, shone. *See this. Remember*" [emphasis mine].

The 1984 critical and synoptic edition of *Ulysses* provides the answer to the question Stephen poses to his dead mother in the Circe episode: "Tell me the word, mother, if you know now. The word known to all men." Three crucial and significant sentences Joyce wrote in another part of his manuscript were inadvertently left out of the first edition and consequently all subsequent ones until the edition of 1984. In the scene in the National Library we now find Stephen thinking to himself: "Do you know what you are talking about? Love, yes. Word known to all men."

Before the revised edition many commentators assumed that the implied answer to the question Stephen asks his mother is the word "death." This is puzzling, as many readers since William York Tindall have known that the answer had to be "love." This has always been evident from the Cyclops episode, when Bloom says "everybody knows that it's the very opposite of that that is really life," and Joyce continues with the definition of life: "Love, says Bloom. I mean the opposite of hatred."

These words, when considered along with "Stephen's views on the eternal affirmation of the spirit of man in literature" in the Ithaca episode, and Molly's resounding "Yes" as the final word of the book, make it even more puzzling why some critics had to wait for a 1984 edition to spell it out for them that this is a book of affirmative Love, and not negative Death.

Stephen-Telemachos and Bloom-Odysseus do not actually come together until the Oxen of the Sun episode (in the maternity hospital), but they have been drawing closer and closer to each other as the day progresses. Bloom first sighted Stephen at around eleven o'clock that morning when he saw, from the funeral carriage, Stephen walking on the beach. In the next episode Bloom sees Stephen in the street, and on the front steps of the library Stephen and Buck watch Bloom exiting between them.

After Stephen leaves the library, he visits a bookstall, among other places, in the Wandering Rocks episode. There he makes the most painful rejection of family yet when he encounters his sister, Dilly. The Dedalus family is poverty-stricken, but Dilly must certainly share Stephen's love of books and learning, as she has just bought, for a penny, a French primer. After finding out from Dilly that the family has pawned his books, he responds inwardly with great sympathy for his sister: "She is drowning. Agenbite. Save her. Agenbite." Stephen has a good deal of money in his pocket, as he was paid that morning by Mr. Deasy at the school, but he dare not give money to his sister, as helping her would be allowing the net to entrap him: "She will drown me with her, eyes and hair. Lank coils of seaweed hair around me, my heart, my soul. Saltgreen death." Stephen passes on, his eyes on the life of the artist that lies before him.

In the Sirens episode, which takes place in the Ormond Street Hotel dining room and bar at four o'clock that afternoon, we return to Leopold Bloom. Bloom must reach the bottom before he can rise again, and Joyce takes him there as Bloom is forced to listen to the crass and vulgar Blazes Boylan in the adjoining bar having the drink that will make him late for his visit to Molly Bloom. This is the only episode in the novel where Bloom is truly downcast and sad—as he has every right to be: "Bloom heard a jing, a little sound. He's off. Light sob of breath Bloom sighed on the silent bluehued flowers. Jingling. He's gone. Jingle. Hear." And a few minutes later: "Yes: all is lost."

Bloom has plunged to the bottom; he is Odysseus battered by the storm, clinging to the last remaining log of the destroyed raft. And just as the salt-caked Odysseus will come ashore to be rejuvenated by his Nausicaa, a few hours later Bloom will find Gerty McDowell, his own Nausicaa in the episode of that name, when, instead of treating her like a princess and thus showing his own nobility, as Odysseus does, our dear Poldy will secretly pump his hand in his pocket and masturbate over her. But not so secretly that she isn't fully aware of what he is doing.

Beginning with the scene in the hotel, Bloom becomes more and more assertive; it is only a few minutes after Blazes leaves the bar that Bloom thinks: "Well, my fault perhaps. No son. Rudy. Too late now. Or if not? If not? If still?" And upon exiting from the hotel, Bloom lets out a resounding fart, "Pprrpffrrppffff," directed toward the sentimental Dubliners gathered around the piano singing traditional Irish ballads.

From the hotel Bloom goes to a tavern, where he incurs the enmity of the nameless Citizen. The Citizen primarily attacks Bloom's religion, and in this he is as incorrect as most readers of the book: Bloom is not Jewish, as, although his father was, his mother was Irish Catholic, and Bloom himself has been baptized three times: first in an Episcopal church, second in some kind of fundamentalist sect, and finally in the Catholic church of the Three Patrons. Bloom is a Judeo-Christian Everyman. Joyce makes another spiritual connection between father and son by having Bloom and Stephen baptized in the same Catholic church by the same priest—not, of course, at the same time. To complete the complicated religious affiliations of these characters, it should be noted that Molly is actually Jewish, as her mother was a Spanish Jew and her father an Irish Catholic; Molly's primary religious function, however, seems to be of simultaneous earth mother and Every-woman.

In the argument with the Citizen, Bloom continues his growing assertiveness: the unnamed narrator tells us Bloom was so excited that he "near burnt his fingers with the butt of his old cigar." (This is, of course, the episode called Cyclops: Bloom is Odysseus with the flaming beam of olivewood he used to put out the eye of Polyphemos.) It is here Bloom argues that force, hatred, and living in the past are "not life for men and women . . . everybody knows that it's the very opposite of that that is really life." When Alf asks him what that opposite is, Bloom replies firmly and simply: "Love . . . I mean the opposite of hatred."

Poldy loves Molly, his daughter, Milly, and his dead son, Rudy—note how Joyce connects the family through the name endings, and has Molly include him in the family when she calls him "Jamesy" in her soliloquy—and Stephen loves literature and Ireland. Yes. Stephen/Joyce does love Ireland: at the end of *A Portrait of the Artist as a Young Man* he exiles himself from his country to become the "conscience of his race."

I leave the Nausicaa episode to your own pleasurable reading: it contains the only passages in literature where it is necessary to speak about tumescent and detumescent prose rhythms, as well as orgasmic ejaculatory plosive phonemes. But I strongly contend that Poldy's brazen masturbation is intended by Joyce to be a further indication of Poldy's onward and upward behavior following his descent in the Sirens episode.

At the maternity hospital, where Bloom has gone to inquire after the difficult labor of Mrs. Purefoy, he discovers Stephen drinking in the interns' lounge with some medical students and young doctors. Stephen by this time is quite drunk, and when he leads them out to a pub across the street, Bloom, concerned about the son of his acquaintance, Simon Dedalus, follows him. What Bloom does not consciously realize is that Stephen has become his son, Rudy, for him. The metempsychosis (transmigration of souls)—a word that haunts the book from Molly's first mention of it—has been accomplished.

The Circe episode, which follows, is the longest section of the book, and it was among the last to be written and revised— a necessary step on Joyce's part, as the Circe episode is self-reflective in that it echoes and mirrors the entire novel.

Stephen enters Bella Cohen's house of prostitution singing the introit for the paschal (resurrection) mass: *Vidi aquam egredientem de templo a latere dextro*—I saw a stream of water coming from the temple. Stephen is "flourishing" his walking stick: he has been resurrected himself in his own act of climactic assertion, a climactic scene that has been omitted from the book by Joyce and one that must be resurrected and reconstructed from teasing snatches of comments by Stephen and Bloom in this episode and the next. Apparently, Stephen went to the Westland Row station at ten past eleven to meet Buck Mulligan for the last tram to the tower section (it is in the Oxen of the Sun episode that Buck suggests this). Buck and Haines attempted to elude Stephen—Buck had the key—and Stephen chased after Buck and punched him in the face with his fist. We can deduce this only from Stephen's remark to Bloom later in Circe that he has hurt his hand somehow, and Bloom's reminder to Stephen in Eumaeus that, after what happened at Westland Row station, Stephen won't be able to sleep in the tower that evening. Stephen has assertively and positively broken one of his compelling chains to Ireland: a place to live.

Then, in anticipation and foreshadowing of Stephen's climactic act of freedom from guilt over his mother, Stephen sings triumphantly *Salvi facti sunt*—they are made whole—and "flourishes his ashplant, shivering the lamp image, shattering light over the world." Note that he shatters the *image* of the lamp in his imagination, not the lamp itself: that will not happen until almost the end of the episode.

The reader of the Circe episode is frequently confused about what is reality and what is imagination because the scenes flow seamlessly from the interior world of Bloom and Stephen to the external world of the house of prostitution. Most of the writing about *Ulysses* refers to the interior scenes in Circe as hallucinations; they are no such thing, as they are beyond the reach of Bloom and Stephen, consisting, as many of them do, of information in the book they could not possibly have—ideas that have occurred, for instance, only in the minds of other characters. The character hallucinating in the Circe episode *is the book itself,* and it is having a grand old fantastic time with its own creations as it participates in fantasizing its own hero-validating trip to Hades.

In the essay on the *Odyssey* I suggested that Odysseus' travels through the magic worlds of Circe and Kalypso and the islands of other strange creatures were a journey through the interior landscape of his soul, where he met monsters of wrath and lust with which he had to come to terms in purging himself of the war spirit before he could return to Ithaka. In the Circe episode Joyce presents us with the fantastic purgatorial landscapes of the souls of Bloom and Stephen.

The scenes with Bloom present distorted reflections of his daily life which graphically illustrate his guilty feelings of responsibility for the death of Rudy, his masochism and desire for punishment, the voyeuristic and fetishistic nature of his sexual substitutes for intercourse, his androgyny ("O, I so want to be a mother"), and, oddly enough—for they have been only slightly suggested in his experiences that day—his delusions of grandeur, his conception of himself as Emperor, President, King, Christ, and Moses. If dreams, fantasies, and journeys through the wicked landscape of the spirit serve to purge the mind of harmful garbage, then both Bloom and Odysseus succeed in this fruitful task.

We saw in both Greek epic and Greek tragedy the purging process of so many characters: Achilleus of his wrath, Odysseus of his war spirit, early Greek society of its reliance on blood-vengeance instead of civil justice, and Oedipus of his guilty feeling of responsibility for murder and incest. Homer's Circe turned men into pigs; Joyce's Circe turns Bloom from pig into man when, following his horrendous purging journey into Nighttown, he has the celestial vision of his son, Rudy, as a twelve-year-old schoolboy, unconsciously equates him with Stephen—his spiritual son—and then reaches down with love and compassion to lift Stephen up out of his squalor.

For Stephen, having gone through his own purging experience in Nighttown, is now ready for renewal and dedication to literature instead of to the bottle and the brothel. Stephen's vision of the ghost of his mother is the only true hallucination in the Circe episode: he is drunk, physically weary, and has been without food for almost twenty-four hours—all conditions making him ripe for hallucinations. Stephen's experience is unlike Bloom's: when we are presented with Bloom's violent interior experiences, there is no evidence from other characters that he is behaving in any unusual way; indeed, at times only a split second has passed during the course of one of Bloom's thirty-page interior journeys. But everyone in the room notices Stephen's strange behavior, his conversation with his—to them—invisible mother, and his smashing of the lamp that represents his guilt.

After Bloom has rescued Stephen from the fight with the two English soldiers, he takes him to the cabman's shelter, where there is always food, drink, and alcohol available. Stephen, however, in refusing to eat the hard roll, is rejecting the mass of salvation being offered by Leopold Paula Bloom. (Paula: "light to the gentiles.") The mass cannot be consummated here; it can only take place when the *nóstos*, homecoming, is complete and Bloom and Stephen have reached the Ithaca episode and are at home in Bloom's kitchen with Molly, the spirit of the Holy Ghost, hovering above them in her bedroom.

It is two o'clock in the morning when Bloom and Stephen arrive at Number Seven Eccles Street, and we find that Bloom had forgotten his key that morning, making the two men a "keyless couple." Thus, not only does Bloom have difficulty getting into his own house but, when he later enters the parlor, he bumps into furniture in the dark, as Molly and Blazes have, sometime during that long afternoon and evening, rearranged the living-room furniture. The parallel to the *Odyssey* is amusing: both Odysseus and Bloom return to homes that have been "rearranged" by suitors. But the parallel is also profound, in that Penelope's final test of Odysseus is her lie to him about the moving of the bed. Molly tests and challenges Poldy by "moving" his bed, and he has spent the day coming to terms with this reality.

The word "host," applied to Bloom, sounds again and again in this episode as Bloom, in his role as Christ figure and priest, prepares and offers the mass to Stephen. The wine for this "jocoserious" mass is Epps's cocoa, which is produced in mass quantities and thus is a "massproduct," and Bloom serves the cream in a cup "ordinarily reserved for the breakfast of his wife Marion (Molly)." In other words, Stephen is symbolically offered Molly's milk. Of this offer of cocoa and milk:

Was the guest conscious of and did he acknowledge these marks of hospitality?

His attention was directed to them by his host jocosely, and he accepted them seriously as they drank in jocoserious silence Epps's massproduct, the creature cocoa.

Both the mass and the novel are "jocoserious," and Stephen still has one last temptation to resist before he is home free, and that is the offer by Bloom that Stephen come make his home with Leopold and Molly. Bloom has been more of a father that day than Stephen's own father ever was, and we know later from Molly's soliloquy that she eagerly approves of the idea. But Stephen firmly rejects the offer, as the mass of salvation has taken effect, and he and Bloom go out in the garden, where they simultaneously urinate against the same tree (a male bonding and a comic purifying ritual), and Stephen goes off into the night, accompanied by strains of music from a "jew's harp."

Stephen has made the exit from his own guilt-ridden hell of Dublin, and Bloom has escaped *his* punishing guilt. Joyce firmly tells us this when he quotes a biblical passage about the escape of the Israelites from the bondage of Egypt as Stephen and Bloom leave the kitchen and go out into Bloom's garden. The first "spectacle" the two men witness is "The heaventree of stars hung with humid nightblue fruit." Joyce makes reference here to the exit of Dante and Virgil from the confines of Hell when he echoes the words "Heaven" and "stars" from the final two lines of the *Inferno*. "Stars," which also occurs as the final word in both the *Purgatorio* and the *Paradiso*, is perhaps the most remembered image in the *Divine Comedy*. Joyce seems to be suggesting future realms of existence for his two "heroes."

Stephen and Poldy do not exit from this book into Heaven, but they do exit from their own hells, and both enter a Purgatory where they will refine themselves into new men. The fire that refines in both cases will be woman: for Bloom, Molly, and for Joyce, Nora, a hotel maid who had "sauntered" over to Joyce and, on June 16, 1904, the day of Joyce's salvation memorialized in this novel, "took me in her arms and made me a man."

In the time sequence Joyce outlined for his book, he assigned no specific time to Molly's episode, Penelope, thus suggesting that it takes place outside of time, in eternity, and that it actually has its existence outside the novel altogether. That is the meaning of the small solid black circle that Joyce placed at the end of the Ithaca episode just before Molly's soliloquy: this symbol was the traditional nineteenth-century typesetter's mark indicating the end of a book. Joyce may have had in mind the belief of some ancient commentators that the twenty-fourth book of the *Odyssey* was a later addition, that the poem ended when Odysseus and Penelope went to bed in Book 23. They were puzzled by the events in Book 24, and by the absence of Penelope. Molly, the Penelope of *Ulysses*, is an overwhelming presence in the final episode of this mock-epic.

Molly's stream of consciousness consists of eight unpunctuated sentences: her birthday is September 8. As this is also the traditional birth date celebrated as that of the Virgin Mary, and eight is associated with her—as well as the color blue—then there is no question but that Joyce intends Molly to be not only the bedroom Holy Ghost, earth mother, and Everywoman brooding above Poldy and Stephen in the kitchen below, but the third member of the human trinity of God the Father, Poldy; God the Son, Stephen; and God the Holy Ghost and "jocoserious" Virgin Mary, Molly Bloom.

Molly's section differs markedly from the rest of the book: there is clarity and directness in the writing, and Molly herself outdoes her husband in forthrightness, honesty, and sense of humor. Although the form—eight sentences—symbolizes the Virgin Mary and is at the same time a realistic imitation of Nora Joyce's epistolary style, Molly's musings are not burdened with symbolic content. She is the archetypal realist, and God knows this is necessary as a corrective balance to her fantasy-laden husband, Poldy. Although both Poldy and Stephen can be guilty of phony pseudo-intellectuality as well as philosophical hogwash, Molly is guilty of neither of these things. Why? *Because Molly accepts:* she lives in the world and accepts the world as it is. She does not try to account for what happens, she accepts herself and others without explaining, justifying, rationalizing, or excusing. She feels no guilt or remorse for her infidelity that afternoon: only surprise and relief in the fact that God didn't strike her dead with the lightning bolts He sent across the skies of Dublin as she and Blazes were having their numerous orgasms. God probably didn't, she decides, because of the Hail Mary she was saying at the time. Molly unites the spiritual and the sensual in a marvelous fashion. Joyce is, of course, wittily and ironically referring to the Olympian-sent thunder and lightning that precipitated the sexual union of Dido and Aeneas in the *Aeneid*.

Molly, like Zeus, Aphrodite, Athena, and Demeter—her Greek earth-mother counterpart—is beyond good and evil, even more so than they, because she does not place herself or any other human being in the category of either good or evil. Molly is not only the eternal feminine spirit formulated by Goethe and Jung, she is the undying jocoserious spirit of endless human hope:

> . . . I dont care what anybody says itd be much better for the world to be governed by the women in it you wouldnt see women going and killing one another and slaughtering when do you ever see women rolling around drunk like they do or gambling every penny they have and losing it on horses yes because a woman whatever she does she knows where to stop sure they wouldnt be in the world at all only for us they dont know what it is to be a woman and a mother how could they where would they all of them be if they hadnt all a mother to look after them what I never had . . .

Molly's poetry differs from that of Stephen and Poldy: it is simple and pastoral, especially when she links the world of nature and flowers and roses, her favorite flower, with the world of love and sexuality.

Molly seems not to know the words "if" and "until" and "unless": she dictates no limitations or restrictions to others, but accepts them as they are. She is a living embodiment of the opening of Shakespeare's Sonnet 116:

> Let me not to the marriage of true minds
> Admit impediments; love is not love
> Which alters when it alteration finds,
> Or bends with the remover to remove.

O no, it is an ever-fixed mark,
That looks on tempests and is never shaken . . .

Molly knows everything about Bloom: the "smutty" photo-
graphs in his unlocked desk drawer, the letters from his female
pen pal, his unorthodox sexual substitutions for intercourse,
and his love and devotion to her. She recalls her painful swollen
breasts, full of milk after the death of Rudy:

. . . I had to get him to suck them they were so hard he said it was
sweeter and thicker than cows then he wanted to milk me into the tea
well hes beyond everything I declare somebody ought to put him in
the budget if I only could remember the 1 half of the things and write
a book out of it the works of Master Poldy yes . . .

All of her yeses, including the final ones, are for Poldy.
Within the space of only a few dozen words in thinking about
Blazes, she uses forms of the negative *nine* times; Joyce knows
what he is telling us with that repetition. After her renewed
discovery that afternoon of the pleasures of sexual intercourse,
an activity she has been denied for ten years, Molly is determined
to seduce her husband, and, from the detailed description she
gives of how she is going to go about doing it—she knows Bloom
and how to excite him—there is no question but that she will
succeed, especially since we have heard Bloom earlier in the
day considering it himself.

The defenders of the pessimistic camp are incorrect: June
17 is not going to be a repeat of June 16 for Poldy and Molly
and Stephen. For all three this has been a day of momentous
symbolic rebirth. *Ulysses*, we have seen, is certainly *not* completely
devoid of the qualities of love, friendship, and magnanimity,
virtues some Joyceans find that the novel totally lacks. The love
Molly and Poldy have for each other combines all three of the
Greek roots we looked at in connection with the Greek epic:
those of *érōs*, sexual love, *philía*, friendly love, and *agápē*, spiritual
love; the friendship between Poldy and Stephen, brief though

it is, is warm with the tenderness and care of comradeship,'and the results will last their lifetimes.

Magnanimity, indeed, is the greatest feature of this novel, and the simplest dictionary definition expresses this great quality shared by Molly and Poldy and Stephen: "loftiness of spirit enabling one to bear trouble calmly, to disdain meanness and revenge, and to make sacrifices for worthy ends."

I have made no pretense of being even-handed in this presentation of an aerial view of the opposing camps of Joycean criticism, as I have provided a far more complete inspection and verification of the matériel in the optimistic camp than I have of that in the pessimistic camp. But then, the pessimists have tended never to go into much textual detail in revealing the exact nature of their offensive system. What it comes down to is that the doomsday Bloomsday readers are giving the book a realistic reading, whereas Tindall and his followers are giving it both a realistic and a symbolic one.

Joyce's book demands that it be read as a dynamically charged presentation of redemption and salvation; the very title itself, *UlYssES*, emblazes the word *YES*, and the presence of the subtext of the *Odyssey* further encourages this interpretation. The structure of the text announces its mystical nature: the three episodes (trinity) of the first section, the Telemachy; the twelve episodes (apostles) of the Wanderings; and the final three episodes (again, the trinity) of the *Nóstos*.

The very first sentence contains the word "cross," as well as lather—soap for cleansing. Stephen himself has not had a bath for nine months, the period of gestation, and he is going to be reborn in this work. Bloom carries around a bar of lemon soap in his pocket the entire day, as well as the potato symbolizing Ireland that his Irish Catholic mother gave him years ago. The sweatband inside his hat reads "Plasto's High Grade Ha" as the T—the cross—has been worn away by Poldy/Christ's sweat: he is badly in need of resurrection from the life in which he is crucifying himself. Stephen and Poldy and Joyce are inscribing upon their own bodies in blood the novel *Ulysses*, the text that becomes the working out of their own salvation.

In reading the book, we are overwhelmed (Middle English: turn over, drown—oh, do not ask the "overwhelming question," Prufrock advises; and he drowns) by the images of water and drowning: the book opens with Stephen's view of the sea and it closes with Molly's remembrance of the sea. In between, there are numerous jokes about urinating as well as actual urinations, particularly the final symbolic ones of Poldy and Stephen together and Molly alone on her chamber pot with the sleeping Bloom above her on the bed.

Though Joyce has chosen to leave lambs out of the book— he only uses what would be widely available in the streets of Dublin—his other major New Testament image is that of Christ as water or bread. The bread images begin to gather together in force as Joyce approaches the symbolic mass. The following is from the opening pages of the Eumaeus episode:

. . . the smell of James Rourke's city bakery, situated quite close to where they were, the very palatable odour indeed of our daily bread, of all commodities of the public the primary and most indispensable. Bread, the staff of life, earn your bread, O tell me where is fancy bread, at Rourke's the baker's it is said.

Some of the most subtle uses of connected symbolic imagery are in that episode and in the Proteus episode. At the conclusion of Proteus, Stephen looks over his shoulder and sees a three-masted schooner: his vision would thus be (t T t), nothing less than the scene of the crucifixion itself, with Christ on the central cross flanked by the two thieves. In the Eumaeus episode, when Bloom is urging Stephen to eat a piece of bread, and the red-haired skipper of the three-masted schooner is in the room, Bloom says that the rolls are as hard as the skipper's bricks— the cargo inside the three-masted schooner, which has thus brought to Stephen the primary symbol of redemption.

In *Finnegans Wake* Joyce refers to that book as a "crossmess parzel," a crossword puzzle, a cross and a mess and a mass and a parcel of land and a Christmas present. What the Christmas present of *Ulysses* contains is the modernist's displacement of illusion with at-one-ment through the acceptance and affirmation of what Joyce saw as the "lovely nothingness" of everyday life. In "Sweeney Agonistes," Eliot's Mr. Sweeney finds that life is no more than "birth, copulation, and death." *Ulysses* is an *exultation* of the commonplace, what Joyce, writing in Italian to his son in America, calls *"un bellissimo niente."*

Continuing a tradition that we have seen in all the writers examined in these essays, Joyce celebrates the creativity of the family, the joys and sorrows of life, the at-one-ment of author and reader through the shared imaginative re-creation afforded by great literature, and the courage and dignity of which the human spirit is capable.

BIBLIOGRAPHY

HOMER

TEXTS

The Iliad of Homer. Trans. by Richmond Lattimore. Chicago: University of Chicago Press, 1974.
The Odyssey of Homer. Trans. by Richmond Lattimore. New York: Harper and Row, 1967.

SUGGESTED READING

Auerbach, Erich. *Mimesis.* Princeton: Princeton University Press, 1953.
Austin, Norman. *Archery at the Dark of the Moon: Poetic Problems in Homer's Odyssey.* Berkeley: University of California Press, 1975.
Beye, Charles R. *The Iliad, the Odyssey, and the Epic Tradition.* Garden City, N.Y.: Doubleday, 1966.
Bowra, C. M. *Tradition and Design in the Iliad.* Oxford: Clarendon Press, 1930.
Carpenter, Rhys. *Folk Tale, Fiction and Saga in the Homeric Epics.* Berkeley: University of California Press, 1946.
Chadwick, John. *The Mycenaean World.* Cambridge: Cambridge University Press, 1976.
Finley, John H., Jr. *Four Stages of Greek Thought.* Stanford: Stanford University Press, 1966.
———. *Homer's Odyssey.* Cambridge, Mass.: Harvard University Press, 1978.
Finley, M. I. *Homer and the Oral Tradition.* Cambridge: Cambridge University Press, 1977.
———. *The World of Odysseus.* Rev. ed. New York: Penguin, 1979.
Griffin, Jasper. *Homer on Life and Death.* Oxford: Clarendon Press, 1980.
Hopper, R. J. *The Early Greeks.* New York: Harper and Row (Barnes and Noble Import Division), 1976.
Jaeger, Werner. *Paideia: The Ideals of Greek Culture.* 3 vols. Trans. by Gilbert Highet. New York: Oxford University Press, 1945.

Murray, Gilbert. *The Rise of the Greek Epic*. 4th ed. Oxford: Clarendon Press, 1946.

Nagy, Gregory. *The Best of the Achaeans: Concepts of the Hero in Archaic Greek Poetry*. Baltimore: The Johns Hopkins University Press, 1979.

Porter, Howard. Introduction, *Homer· The Odyssey*. New York: Bantam Books, 1962.

Redfield, James M. *Nature and Culture in the Iliad: The Tragedy of Hector*. Chicago: University of Chicago Press, 1975.

Schein, Seth L. *The Mortal Hero: An Introduction to Homer's Iliad*. Berkeley: University of California Press, 1984.

Slatkin, Laura. "Thetis, Achilles, and the *Iliad*." Ph.D. diss., Harvard University, 1979.

Steiner, George, and Robert Fagles, eds. *Homer: A Collection of Critical Essays*. Englewood Cliffs, N.J.: Prentice-Hall, 1962.

Wace, A. J. B., and F. H. Stubbings, eds. *A Companion to Homer*. London: Macmillan, 1962.

Weil, Simone. *The Iliad, or the Poem of Force*. Trans. by Mary McCarthy. Wallingford, Pa.: Pendle Hill, 1956.

Whitman, Cedric H. *Homer and the Heroic Tradition*. New York: Norton, 1965.

AESCHYLUS

TEXT

Aeschylus I. Trans. by Richmond Lattimore. Chicago: University of Chicago Press, 1953.

SUGGESTED READING

Baldry, H. C. *The Greek Tragic Theatre*. New York: Norton, 1973.

Else, Gerald. *The Origin and Early Form of Greek Tragedy*. Cambridge, Mass.: Harvard University Press, 1965.

Herodotus. *The Histories*. Trans. by Aubrey de Sélincourt. Baltimore: Penguin, 1954.

Kitto, H. D. F. *Greek Tragedy: A Literary Study*. 3rd rev. ed. New York: Methuen, 1966.

Kott, Jan. *The Eating of the Gods: An Interpretation of Greek Tragedy*. New York: Random House, 1973.

Kuhns, Richard F. *The House, the City and the Judge: The Growth of Moral Awareness in the Oresteia.* Indianapolis: Bobbs-Merrill, 1962.

Rosenmeyer, Thomas G. *The Art of Aeschylus.* Berkeley: University of California Press, 1982.

SOPHOCLES

TEXT

Sophocles I. Trans. by William Arrowsmith et al. Chicago: University of Chicago Press, 1954.

SUGGESTED READING

Aristotle. *On Poetry and Style.* Trans. by G. M. A. Grube. Indianapolis: The Library of Liberal Arts, 1958.

Bowra, C. M. *Sophoclean Tragedy.* Oxford: Clarendon Press, 1944.

Dodds, E. R. *The Greeks and the Irrational.* Berkeley: University of California Press, 1959.

Herodotus. *The Histories.* Trans. by Aubrey de Sélincourt. Baltimore: Penguin, 1954.

Kirkwood, G. M. *A Study of Sophoclean Drama.* Ithaca, N.Y.: Cornell University Press, 1958.

Knox, Bernard. *The Heroic Temper: Studies in Sophoclean Tragedy.* Berkeley: University of California Press, 1964.

———. *Oedipus at Thebes.* New Haven: Yale University Press, 1957.

O'Brien, Michael J., ed. *Oedipus the King: A Collection of Critical Essays.* Englewood Cliffs, N.J.: Prentice-Hall, 1968.

Thucydides. *The Peloponnesian War.* Trans. by Rex Warner. Baltimore: Penguin, 1954.

Woodward, Thomas, ed. *Sophocles: A Collection of Critical Essays.* Englewood Cliffs, N.J.: Prentice-Hall, 1966.

EURIPIDES

TEXT

Euripides V. Trans. by William Arrowsmith et al. Chicago: The University of Chicago Press, 1959.

SUGGESTED READING

Aristotle. *On Poetry and Style*. Trans. by G. M. A. Grube. Indianapolis: The Library of Liberal Arts, 1958.

Conacher, D. J. *Euripidean Drama: Myth, Theme and Structure*. Toronto: University of Toronto Press, 1967.

Dodds, E. R. *Euripides: Bacchae*. 2nd ed. Oxford: Oxford University Press, 1960.

———. *The Greeks and the Irrational*. Berkeley: University of California Press, 1959.

Grube, G. M. A. *The Drama of Euripides*. London: Methuen, 1941.

Harrison, Jane Ellen, ed. *Themis: A Study of the Social Origins of Greek Religion*. Boston: Carrier Pigeon, 1963.

Huxley, Aldous. *Ends and Means*. New York and London: Harper and Brothers, 1937.

Murray, Gilbert. *Euripides and His Age*. 2nd ed. London: Oxford University Press, 1965.

Norwood, G., ed. *Essays on Euripidean Drama*. Berkeley: University of California Press, 1954.

Otto, Walter F. *Dionysus: Myth and Cult*. Dallas: Spring Publications, 1981.

Segal, Erich, ed. *Greek Tragedy: Modern Essays in Criticism*. New York: Harper and Row, 1983.

Webster, T. B. L. *The Tragedies of Euripides*. London: Methuen, 1967.

ARISTOPHANES

TEXT

The Wasps, The Poet and the Women, The Frogs. Trans. by David Barrett. New York: Penguin, 1964.

SUGGESTED READING

Aristotle. *On Poetry and Style*. Trans. by G. M. A. Grube. Indianapolis: The Library of Liberal Arts, 1958.

Arnott, P. D. *Greek Scenic Conventions in the Fifth Century B.C.* Oxford: Clarendon Press, 1962.

Dover, K. J. *Aristophanic Comedy*. Berkeley: University of California Press, 1972.

———. *Greek Homosexuality*. Cambridge, Mass.: Harvard University Press, 1978.

Droiset, M. *Aristophanes and the Political Parties at Athens*. Trans. by James Loeb. London: Macmillan, 1909.

Ehrenberg, V. *The People of Aristophanes*. New York: Barnes and Noble, 1974.

Frye, Northrop. *Anatomy of Criticism*. New York: Atheneum, 1966.

Lever, Katherine. *The Art of Greek Comedy*. London: Methuen, 1956.

Lord, Louis E. *Aristophanes: His Plays and Influence*. London: Harrap, 1925.

Murray, Gilbert. *Aristophanes*. Oxford: Clarendon Press, 1965.

Norwood, G. *Greek Comedy*. New York: Hill and Wang, 1963.

Pickard-Cambridge, A. W. *Dithyramb, Tragedy, and Comedy*. 2nd ed., rev. by T. B. L. Webster. Oxford: Clarendon Press, 1962.

Sifakis, G. M. *Parabasis and Animal Choruses*. London: Athlone Press, 1971.

Thucydides. *The Peloponnesian War*. Trans. by Rex Warner. Baltimore: Penguin, 1954.

VIRGIL

TEXT

The Aeneid. Trans. by Robert Fitzgerald. New York: Vintage Books (Random House), 1984.

SUGGESTED READING

Commager, Steele, ed. *Virgil: A Collection of Critical Essays*. Englewood Cliffs, N.J.: Prentice-Hall, 1966.

Dudley, Donald R., ed. *Virgil*. New York: Basic Books, 1969.

Johnson, W. R. *Darkness Visible: A Study of Vergil's Aeneid*. Berkeley: University of California Press, 1976.

Knight, W. F. Jackson. *Roman Vergil*. London: Faber, 1944; rev. ed., Harmondsworth: Penguin, 1966.

Otis, Brooks. *Virgil: A Study in Civilized Poetry*. Oxford: Oxford University Press, 1963.

Putnam, Michael C. J. *Essays on Latin Lyric, Elegy, and Epic*. Princeton: Princeton University Press, 1982.

————. *The Poetry of the Aeneid*. Cambridge, Mass.: Harvard University Press, 1966.

GOTTFRIED

TEXT

Tristan, trans. by A. T. Hatto. New York: Penguin, 1960.

SUGGESTED READING

Darrah, John. *The Real Camelot: Paganism and the Arthurian Romances*. London: Thames and Hudson, 1981.
Ferrante, Joan M. "Tristan: A Comparative Study of Five Medieval Works." Ph.D. diss., Columbia University, 1963.
Herodotus. *The Histories*. Trans. by Aubrey de Sélincourt. Baltimore: Penguin, 1954.
Jackson, W. T. H. *The Anatomy of Love: The Tristan of Gottfried von Strassburg*. New York: Columbia University Press, 1971.
Jaeger, C. Stephen. *Medieval Humanism in Gottfried von Strassburg's Tristan and Isolde*. Heidelberg: Carl Winter, 1977.
Loomis, Gertrude Schoepperle. *Tristan and Isolt: A Study of the Sources of the Romance*. 2 vols. Ed. by Roger S. Loomis. New York: Burt Franklin, 1963.
Loomis, Roger S., ed. *Arthurian Literature in the Middle Ages*. Oxford: Oxford University Press, 1959.
————. *The Grail: From Celtic Myth to Christian Symbol*. New York: Columbia University Press, 1964.

DANTE

TEXT

Dante's Inferno. Trans. and comment. by John D. Sinclair. New York: Oxford University Press, 1961.

SUGGESTED READING

Auerbach, Erich. *Dante: Poet of the Secular World*. Chicago: University of Chicago Press, 1961.
Barbi, Michele. *Life of Dante*. Trans. and ed. by Paul G. Ruggiers. Berkeley: University of California Press, 1954.

Brandeis, Irma, ed. *Discussions of the Divine Comedy*. Boston: Heath, 1961.

————. *The Ladder of Vision*. London: Chatto and Windus, 1960.

Cosmo, Umberto. *A Handbook to Dante Studies*. Oxford: Blackwell, 1950.

Eliot, T. S. "Dante." *Selected Essays: 1917–1932*. New York: Harcourt, Brace, 1932.

Fergusson, Francis. *Dante*. New York: Macmillan, 1966.

Freccero, John, ed. *Dante: A Collection of Critical Essays*. Englewood Cliffs, N.J.: Prentice-Hall, 1965.

Hollander, Robert. *Allegory in Dante's Commedia*. Princeton: Princeton University Press, 1969.

Mazzeo, Joseph. *Varieties of Interpretation*. Notre Dame: University of Notre Dame Press, 1978.

Reade, W. H. *The Moral System of Dante's Inferno*. 1909. Reprint. Port Washington, N.Y.: Kennikat, 1969.

Santayana, George. *Three Philosophical Poets: Lucretius, Dante, and Goethe*. Cambridge, Mass.: Harvard University Press, 1922.

Toynbee, Paget J. *Dictionary of Proper Names and Notable Matters in the Works of Dante*. 2nd ed., revised by Charles S. Singleton. Oxford: Clarendon Press, 1968.

Vernon, William W. *Readings on the Inferno of Dante*. 2nd ed. London: Methuen, 1906.

MONTAIGNE

TEXT

The Complete Essays of Montaigne. Trans. by Donald M. Frame. Stanford: Stanford University Press, 1965.

SUGGESTED READING

Auerbach, Erich. *Mimesis*. Princeton: Princeton University Press, 1953.

Buffum, Imbrie. *Studies in the Baroque from Montaigne to Rotrou*. New Haven: Yale University Press, 1957.

Frame, Donald M. *Montaigne: A Biography*. San Francisco: North Point Press, 1984.

————. *Montaigne's Discovery of Man: The Humanization of a Humanist*. New York: Columbia University Press, 1955.

Poulet, Georges. "Montaigne." *Studies in Human Time*. Trans. by Elliot Coleman. Baltimore: Johns Hopkins University Press, 1956.

SHAKESPEARE

TEXT

The Tragedy of King Lear. Baltimore: Penguin, 1970.

SUGGESTED READING

Bradley, A. C. *Shakespearean Tragedy*. 2nd ed. London: Macmillan, 1926.
Charlton, H. B. *Shakespearian Tragedy*. Cambridge: Cambridge University Press, 1952.
Freud, Sigmund. "The Theme of the Three Caskets." *Character and Culture*. New York: Macmillan, 1963.
Freytag, Gustav. *Technique of the Drama*. 1894. Reprint. New York: Johnson Reprint Co., 1968.
Frye, Northrop. *Fools of Time*. Toronto: University of Toronto Press, 1967.
Granville-Barker, H. *Prefaces to Shakespeare*. Vol. I. Princeton: Princeton University Press, 1946.
Kermode, Frank, ed. *Four Centuries of Shakespearian Criticism*. New York: Avon, 1974.
Knight, G. Wilson. *The Wheel of Fire*. New York: Methuen, 1949.
Van Doren, Mark. *Shakespeare*. 1939. Reprint. Westport, Conn.: Greenwood, 1982.
Wilson, H. S. *On the Design of Shakespearian Tragedy*. Toronto: University of Toronto Press, 1957.

CERVANTES

TEXT

Don Quixote. Trans. by Walter Starkie. New York: New American Library, 1964.

SUGGESTED READING

Auerbach, Erich. *Mimesis*. Princeton: Princeton University Press, 1953.
Borges, Jorge Luis. *Labyrinths*. New York: New Directions, 1969.

Nabokov, Vladimir. *Lectures on Don Quixote*. Ed. by Fredson Bowers. New York: Harcourt Brace Jovanovich, 1983.

Nelson, Lowry, ed. *Cervantes: A Collection of Critical Essays*. Englewood Cliffs, N.J.: Prentice-Hall, 1969.

Ortega y Gasset, José. *Meditations on Quixote*. New York: Norton, 1963.

Predmore, Richard. *The World of Don Quixote*. Cambridge, Mass.: Harvard University Press, 1967.

Unamuno, Miguel de. *Our Lord Don Quixote*. Princeton: Princeton University Press, 1968.

SWIFT

TEXT

Gulliver's Travels. Ed. by Robert A. Greenberg. 2nd ed. New York: Norton, 1970.

SUGGESTED READING

Carnochan, W. G. *Lemuel Gulliver's Mirror for Man*. Berkeley: University of California Press, 1968.

Ehrenpreis, Irvin. *Swift: The Man, His Works, and the Age*. 3 vols. Cambridge, Mass.: Harvard University Press, 1962–83.

Murry, J. Middleton. *Jonathan Swift*. New York: Noonday Press, 1955.

Plato. *The Republic*. Trans. by Desmond Lee. Baltimore: Penguin, 1955.

Rosenheim, Edward W. *Swift and the Satirist's Art*. Chicago: University of Chicago Press, 1963.

Watkins, W. B. C. *The Tragic Genius of Swift, Johnson, and Sterne*. Princeton: Princeton University Press, 1939.

Williams, Kathleen. *Jonathan Swift and the Age of Compromise*. Lawrence: University of Kansas Press, 1958.

DOSTOEVSKY

TEXT

The Brothers Karamazov. Trans. by Constance Garnett, rev. by Ralph E. Matlaw. New York: Norton, 1976.

SUGGESTED READING

Belknap, Robert. *The Structure of The Brothers Karamazov*. The Hague: Mouton, 1967.

Frank, Joseph. *Dostoevsky: The Seeds of Revolt, 1821–1849*. Princeton: Princeton University Press, 1976.

———. *Dostoevsky: The Years of Ordeal, 1850–1860*. Princeton: Princeton University Press, 1983.

Gibson, Boyce A. *The Religion of Dostoevsky*. London: SCM Press, 1973.

Grossman, Leonid. *Dostoevsky: His Life and Work*. New York: Bobbs-Merrill, 1975.

Jackson, Robert L. *The Art of Dostoevsky: Deliriums and Nocturnes*. Princeton: Princeton University Press, 1981.

Kabat, Geoffrey C. *Ideology and Imagination: The Image of Society in Dostoevsky*. New York: Columbia University Press, 1978.

Matlaw, Ralph E. *The Brothers Karamazov: Novelistic Technique*. The Hague: Mouton, 1957.

Mochulsky, Konstantin. *Dostoevsky, His Life and Work*. Trans. by Michael A. Minihan. Princeton: Princeton University Press, 1967.

Wasiolek, Edward. *Dostoevsky: The Major Fiction*. Cambridge, Mass.: M.I.T. Press, 1964.

Wellek, Rene. *Dostoevsky: A Collection of Critical Essays*. Englewood Cliffs, N.J.: Prentice-Hall, 1962.

ELIOT

TEXT

Selected Poems. New York: Harcourt Brace Jovanovich, 1964.

SUGGESTED READING

Ackroyd, Peter. *T.S. Eliot: A Life*. New York: Simon & Schuster, 1984.

Bergonzi, Bernard. *T. S. Eliot*. New York: Macmillan, 1972.

Bradbrook, M. C. *T. S. Eliot*. London: Longmans, Green, 1965.

Braybrooke, Neville, ed. *T. S. Eliot: A Symposium*. New York: Farrar, Straus, 1958.

Cattaui, Georges. *T. S. Eliot*. New York: Funk & Wagnalls, 1966.

Drew, Elizabeth. *T. S. Eliot: The Design of His Poetry*. New York: Scribner, 1961.

Eliot, T. S. *Selected Prose of T. S. Eliot*. Ed. with an Intro. by Frank Kermode. London: Faber, 1975.

———. *The Waste Land: A Facsimile and Transcript of the Original Drafts*. Ed. by Valerie Eliot. New York: Harcourt Brace Jovanovich, 1971.

Frye, Northrop. *T. S. Eliot*. Chicago: University of Chicago Press, 1981.

Gallup, Donald C. *T. S. Eliot: A Bibliography*. London: Hart-Davis, 1969.

Gardner, Helen. *The Art of T. S. Eliot*. New York: Dutton, 1950.

Kenner, Hugh. *The Invisible Poet: T. S. Eliot*. New York: McDowell, Obolensky, 1959.

———, ed. *T. S. Eliot: A Collection of Critical Essays*. Englewood Cliffs, N.J.: Prentice-Hall, 1962.

Knoll, Robert, ed. *Storm over The Waste Land*. Chicago: Scott, Foresman, 1964.

Litz, A. Walton, ed. *Eliot in His Time*. Princeton: Princeton University Press, 1973.

Matthiessen, F. O. *The Achievement of T. S. Eliot*. New York: Oxford University Press, 1958.

Pound, Ezra. *The ABC of Reading*. New York: New Directions, 1960.

Smith, Grover. *T. S. Eliot's Poetry and Plays*. Chicago: University of Chicago Press, 1974.

Southam, B. C. *A Guide to the Selected Poems of T. S. Eliot*. New York: Harcourt, Brace & World, 1968.

Tate, Allen, ed. *T. S. Eliot: The Man and His Work*. New York: Delacorte Press, 1966.

Traversi, Derek. *T. S. Eliot: The Longer Poems*. New York: Harcourt Brace Jovanovich, 1976.

Weston, Jessie L. *From Ritual to Romance*. Cambridge: Cambridge University Press, 1920.

Williamson, George. *A Reader's Guide to T. S. Eliot*. New York: Farrar, Straus & Cudahy, 1953.

JOYCE

TEXT

Ulysses. New York: Vintage Books (Random House), 1961.

SUGGESTED READING

Budgen, Frank. *James Joyce and the Making of Ulysses*. Bloomington: Indiana University Press, rev. ed., 1960.

Eliot, T. S. "*Ulysses*, Order, and Myth." *James Joyce: Two Decades of Criticism*. Ed. Seon Givens. New York: Vanguard Press, 1948.

Ellmann, Richard. *James Joyce*. New York: Oxford University Press, 1959. Rev. ed. 1983.

————. *Ulysses on the Liffey*. New York: Oxford University Press, 1973.

Gifford, Don, with Robert Seidman. *Notes for Joyce: An Annotation of James Joyce's Ulysses*. New York: Dutton, 1974.

Gilbert, Stuart. *James Joyce's Ulysses*. New York: Knopf, 1930. Rev. ed. New York: Random House, 1955.

Goldberg, S. L. *The Classic Temper: A Study of James Joyce's Ulysses*. London: Chatto and Windus, 1961.

Hart, Clive, and David Hayman, eds. *James Joyce's Ulysses: Critical Essays*. Berkeley: University of California Press, 1974.

Joyce, James. *Letters of James Joyce*. Vol. 1, ed. by Stuart Gilbert. New York: Viking, 1957. Vols. 2 and 3, ed. by Richard Ellmann. New York: Viking, 1966.

————. *Selected Letters of James Joyce*. Ed. by Richard Ellmann. New York: Viking, 1975.

————. *Ulysses*. A Critical and Synoptic Edition. 3 vols. Prepared by Hans Walter Gabler et al. New York: Garland Publishing, 1984.

Kenner, Hugh. *Dublin's Joyce*. Bloomington: Indiana University Press, 1956.

————. *Joyce's Voices*. Berkeley: University of California Press, 1978.

————. *Ulysses*. London: Allen & Unwin, 1980.

Levin, Harry. *James Joyce*. Norfolk, Conn.: New Directions, 1941.

Litz, A. Walton. *James Joyce*. Boston: Twayne, 1966. Rev. ed. 1972.

Seidel, Michael. *Epic Geography: James Joyce's Ulysses*. Princeton: Princeton University Press, 1976.

Tindall, William York. *A Reader's Guide to James Joyce*. New York: Noonday Press, 1959.

INDEX

257